Dragons
Chinese Teaching Specialists

AQA GCSE Chinese

Textbook 1

AQA GCSE Chinese – Textbook 1 has been approved by AQA for the new GCSE specification. The book is the first part of a new two-part series and is aimed at students with some prior knowledge of Chinese: in order to begin this book, students should have a knowledge of about 200 words and should be able to write 50-100 characters.

This course is aligned to the new specification of Mandarin Chinese GCSE and is written with the requirements of non-heritage learners in mind. The course covers all four skills and is designed to increase the confidence of learners. Aiming to provide everything students need to master the language, it is complete with interactive activities, cultural insight, study tips and detailed grammar explanations. Topics are revisited throughout the book, providing students with many opportunities to consolidate their learning. Wherever possible, activities are grounded in real-life situations which students are likely to encounter when they interact with other Chinese speakers.

A workbook and online portal accompany the textbook, giving opportunity for extra practice and enabling teachers to track students' progress.

Contents

Xi'an: Units 4 - 5

Taipei: Units 6 - 8

Contents (continued)

How to use this book

The activities in Textbook 1 (of the 2 book series) are set with three **cities** as a backdrop: Shanghai (units 1-3), Xi'an (units 4-5) and Taipei (units 6-8). The aim is to help the learner get to know different parts of the Chinese-speaking world.

Structure

Each unit is divided into **three sections**. The first two sections each introduce two vocabulary tables, two new grammar structures, and one list of **core characters** to write. These sections all progress from easier activities to more advanced activities.

Putting it together
The final section, **Putting it together**, provides more challenging material for you to combine new material with language you already know.

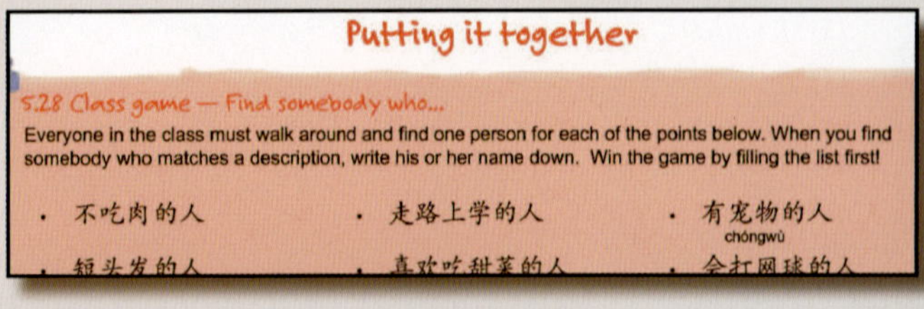
Putting it together

5.28 Class game — Find somebody who...

Everyone in the class must walk around and find one person for each of the points below. When you find somebody who matches a description, write his or her name down. Win the game by filling the list first!

- 不吃肉的人
- 走路上学的人
- 有宠物的人 (chǒngwù)

Reading challenge
Putting it together is followed by a **Reading Challenge**, which presents you with a longer piece of writing, including extra words you have not yet met.

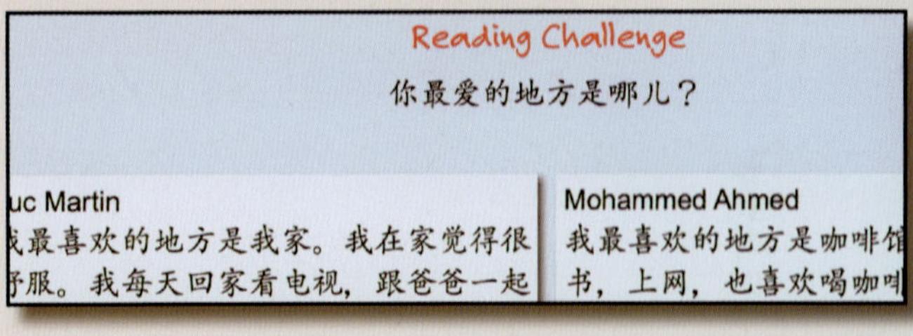
Reading Challenge

你最爱的地方是哪儿？

uc Martin	Mohammed Ahmed
戈最喜欢的地方是我家。我在家觉得很予服。我每天回家看电视，跟爸爸一起	我最喜欢的地方是咖啡馆书，上网，也喜欢喝咖啡

Now you can...
Each unit ends with a "**Now you can...**" section that summarises the content of the chapter, including all the core characters in the unit. This section is particularly useful for revising what you learnt earlier in the course.

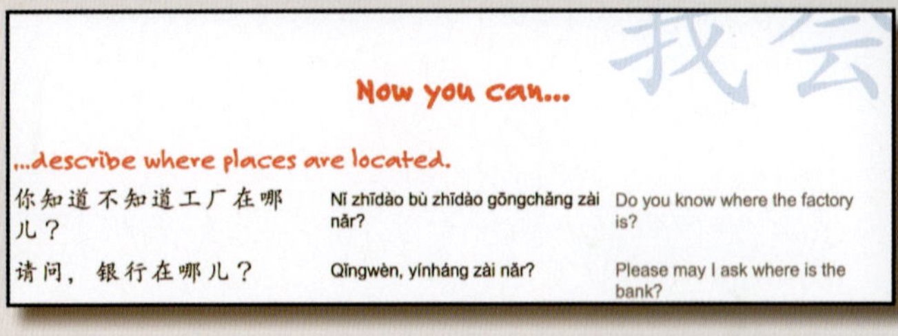
Now you can...

...describe where places are located.

你知道不知道工厂在哪儿？	Nǐ zhīdào bù zhīdào gōngchǎng zài nǎr?	Do you know where the factory is?
请问，银行在哪儿？	Qǐngwèn, yínháng zài nǎr?	Please may I ask where is the bank?

Unique features of this series

Pinyin support is written underneath some characters to aid the student with pronunciation. Pinyin is gradually removed as the student's knowledge of the vocabulary increases. This ensures that the student is supported at all stages and is encouraged to focus on characters when reading. For rarer characters, such as names, pinyin is always supplied.

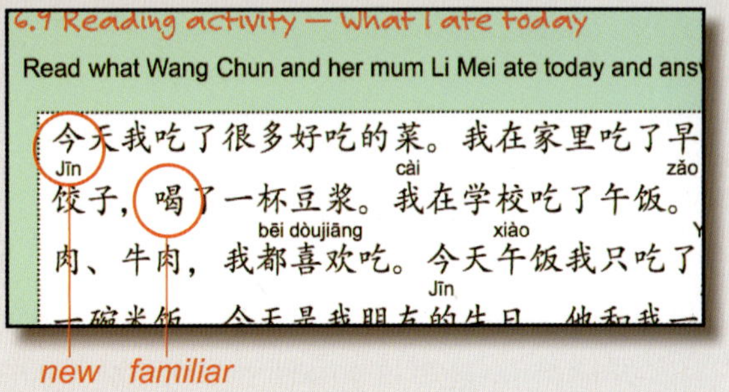
6.9 Reading activity — What I ate today

Read what Wang Chun and her mum Li Mei ate today and ans

今天我吃了很多好吃的菜。我在家里吃了早饺子，喝了一杯豆浆。我在学校吃了午饭。肉、牛肉，我都喜欢吃。今天午饭我只吃了

Types of activity are indicated with the following icons:

 Listening activity

 Pair activity

 Group activity

 Reading and/or writing activity

Activity levels are indicated with the following icons to help the teacher differentiate the class activities:

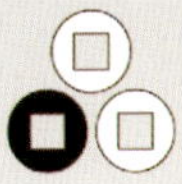 Introduces a topic or new structure

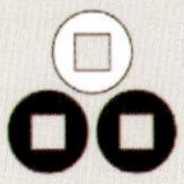 Helps provide greater familiarity or fluency

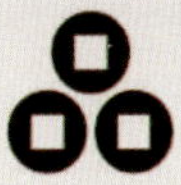 Exercises creative or analytical skills

How to use this book (continued)

Features of each Unit

About the language

…contains the most important new grammar structures introduced in the unit. This section includes explanations and example sentences.

About the language: 还是，adj + 的，list + 都 (dōu)

还是

还是 means 'or'; it is used when asking 'A or B?' questions. Note you do not say 吗 in these questions.

你要喝茶还是咖啡？	Do you want to drink tea or coffee?
我们打网球还是乒乓球？	Shall we play tennis or ping pong?
图书馆在左边还是在右边？ (tú)	Is the library on the left or the right?
他喜欢大狗还是小狗？	Does he like big dogs or small dogs?

Language in action

…introduces colloquial phrases which you will encounter in everyday life in China.

Language in action — Compliments

Modesty is important in Chinese culture, especially when receiving praise. In English, we might respond to a compliment by saying 'thank you', but in Chinese culture this could seem impolite. It is more common to deny the compliment and either to put oneself down or praise the other person more highly. Here are a couple of examples:

A: 你中文说得很好！ (de)	You speak Chinese well!
B: 不是！我的中文很不好。	No I don't! My Chinese is very bad.

Study skills

…helps the student learn Chinese more effectively and efficiently.

Study skills — Improving your tones

Speaking with correct tones is very important for communication in Chinese. If you change the tones when you speak, you could change the meaning quite drastically. For example:

Mā yào shuìjiào = Mum wants to sleep
Mǎ yào shuǐjiǎo = The horse wants dumplings

As you can see, little mistakes could lead to big misunderstandings. Here are a few tips for improving your tones:

- Slow down. It is easier to say the tones one by one than all together. When you're practising a sentence, start very slowly, making sure each tone is correct, before speeding up.

Character focus

…looks at the details of Chinese characters, with the aim of helping the student memorise characters more easily and accurately.

1.27 Character focus — Unit 1 Review

Here are some characters you have learnt this chapter, together with similar characters from before. Can you spot the elements in common?

Review	Meaning	Pinyin	New	Meaning	Pinyin
元	currency of China	yuán	玩		
很			跟		
男			动		
欢			戏		

Did you know

…contains cultural information about the Chinese-speaking world, often relating to the city in which the unit is based.

Did you know?

Beijing Opera is one of the many famous performing arts traditional to Chinese culture. Colourful and dramatic, operas mix music, dance, acrobatics, poetry and mime, and they look and sound quite different to our…

Please log on to **www.secondaryschoolchinese.com*** for detailed schemes of work to help you make the most of all the activities provided in the book.

*Other resources are beyond the scope of the AQA approval process and have not been entered for approval.

GCSE Themes Finder

Use this page to find which units in the series of books covers the themes set out by the AQA GCSE exam specification.

The number to the left of the decimal is the book number and the number to the right is the unit number. So:

GCSE 1

1.2 refers to Unit Two in the *AQA GCSE Chinese Textbook 1* (this book)

GCSE 2

2.13 refers to Unit Thirteen in the *AQA GCSE Chinese Textbook 2*

Theme 1: Identity and culture

Topic 1: Me, my family and friends:	1.5	2.16	2.18	2.19
Relationships with family and friends:	1.1	1.3	2.16	2.18
Marriage / partnership:	1.3	2.16	2.18	
Topic 2: Technology in every day life:	2.14	2.18	2.19	
Social Media:	2.14	2.18		
Mobile technology:	2.14	2.19		
Topic 3: Free-time activities:	1.1	2.10	2.18	2.19
Music:	1.1	2.19		
Cinema and TV:	2.18	2.19		
Food and eating out:	1.6	2.18		
Sport:	1.1	2.10	2.19	
Topic 4: Customs and festivals in Chinese-speaking countries/communities:	1.3	2.13		

Theme 2: Local, national, international & global areas of interest

Topic 1: Home, town, neighbourhood and region:	1.2	2.12	2.16	2.17
Topic 2: Social issues:	1.7	2.15	2.17	2.18
Charity / voluntary work:	2.15			
Healthy / unhealthy living:	1.1	1.7	2.10	
Topic 3: Global issues:	2.12	2.17		
Music:	1.1	2.19		
The environment:	2.17			
Poverty / homelessness:	2.12	2.17		
Topic 4: Travel and tourism:	1.8	2.9		

Theme 3: Current and future study and employment

Topic 1: My studies:	1.7	2.11		
Topic 2: Life at school / college:	1.7	2.11		
Topic 3: Education post-16:	2.11	2.15		
Topic 4: Jobs, career choices & ambitions:	1.3	2.11	2.15	2.19

欢迎来上海!

Welcome to Shànghǎi!

Main languages:
Mandarin, Shanghai dialect

The Bund 外滩 (Wàitān)

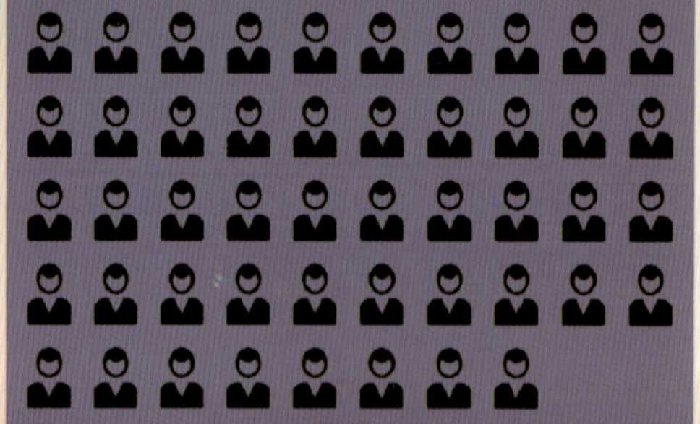

人口 24 000 000

Steamed Crab 大闸蟹 (dà zhá xiè)

The Shanghai Museum 上海博物馆 (Shànghǎi bówùguǎn)

More people live in Shanghai than the whole of Australia!

我的爱好

Unit Objectives

...how to talk about your interests and hobbies.
...how to arrange to meet up with friends.
...how to ask permission.
...about music in China.

Part 1 Interests

VOCAB

表演	biǎoyǎn	to perform, a performance
唱歌	chàng gē	to sing
打电话	dǎ diànhuà	to make a phone call
画画	huà huà	to draw, to paint
拍照片	pāi zhàopiàn	to take a photo
上网	shàng wǎng	to go online
弹钢琴	tán gāngqín	to play the piano
弹吉他	tán jítā	to play the guitar
跳舞	tiào wǔ	to dance
听音乐	tīng yīnyuè	to listen to music
玩儿游戏	wánr yóuxì	to play a game

1.1 Shared interests

Find one classmate and ask what he or she likes to do. Try to find five interests you have in common.

Tiào wǔ and chàng gē

跳舞 tiào wǔ and 唱歌 chàng gē are both two words, not one. By itself, □□□ means *jump* and wǔ means *a dance*, so □□□□ wǔ is literally *to jump a dance*. Similarly, chàng means *to sing* and gē means *song* so chàng gē is literally *to sing a song*.

1.2 What do they like doing?

Listen to the recording. In your notebook, write down what the speakers like and don't like doing.

e.g.	likes	dancing
	doesn't like	making phone calls
1)	likes	
	doesn't like	
2)	likes	
	doesn't like	
3)	likes	
	doesn't like	
4)	likes	
	doesn't like	

Use what you know!

You already know how to say the following activities:

玩儿电脑 (wán ... nǎo)	to play on the computer
看电视 (shì)	to watch TV
看电影 (yǐng)	to watch a film
看书	to read a book
看报纸 (bàozhǐ)	to read a newspaper
玩儿手机 (wán ... shǒujī)	to play on the phone

vocab

姓	xìng	to be called (surname)
艺术	yìshù	art
跟	gēn	together with
天天	tiāntiān	every day
都	dōu	all; in every case
好玩儿	hǎo wánr	fun, funny
爱好	àihào	hobby; to be interested in

姓 (xìng)

姓 (xìng) means either 'surname' or 'to be called' when talking about surnames. To ask someone's surname, you say 你姓什么 (nǐ xìng shénme?), or more formally, 您贵姓 (nín guì xìng?), which literally means 'your honourable surname?' and is an implied question.

爱好 (àihào)

In the word 爱好 (àihào), you will notice that 好 changes tone and becomes 4th tone instead of 3rd.

1.3 Listening activity — All about me

Listen to 陈洪 (Chén Hóng) introduce himself. Then, in your notebook, write the answers to fill the blanks below.

1) Chén Hóng studies ....

2) He attends class with ....

3) He likes to .... and does it every day.

4) He also thinks it's fun to ....

1.4 Pair activity — Where are you going?

With a friend, practise the dialogue below, substituting other places and activities.

A: 你去哪儿？

B: 我去公园。
gōngyuán

A: 你跟谁一起去？
gēn qǐ

B: 我跟我朋友一起去。
gēn qǐ

A: 你去公园做什么？
gōngyuán zuò

B: 我去公园画画。
gōngyuán huà huà

	去哪儿？	做什么？ (zuò)
1)	图书馆 (tú guǎn)	看书
2)	朋友家	看电视 (shì)
3)	超市 (chāoshì)	买面包 (mǎi bāo)
4)	动物园 (dòngwùyuán)	玩儿 (wán)
5)	伦敦 (Lúndūn)	拍照片 (pāi zhàopiàn)
6)	学校 (xiào)	上艺术课 (yìshù kè)

1.5 Group activity – Do you feel the same way?

Ask other classmates what their interests are. Make note of who likes what.

你有什么爱好？
ài
What hobbies do you have?

我喜欢看书。我天天都看书。
dōu
I like reading books. I read books every day.

Either: 我也喜欢看书。很有意思！
yìsi
I also like reading books. It's fun!

or: 看书不好玩儿。我喜欢画画。
wán huà huà
Reading books is not fun. I like painting.

Language information: 跟/和 …… 一起 ……
gēn hé qǐ

When two or more people do an activity together, you can use the word 跟 (gēn).
Use the word order:

(A) 跟 (B) 一起 (verb).

So, for example:

我跟妈妈一起画画。 gēn qǐ huà huà	I paint with my mother.
她跟我朋友一起跳舞。 gēn qǐ tiào wǔ	She dances with my friend.
你跟我一起玩儿游戏吧。 gēn qǐ wán yóuxì ba	Play a game with me.

Notice that this order is different to English. In Chinese you say 'I with you together sing'.

Also, 跟 (gēn) can be replaced with 和 (hé). These are alternatives to the example sentences above:

我和妈妈一起画画。 / 她和我朋友一起跳舞。 / 你和我一起玩儿游戏吧。
hé qǐ huà huà / hé qǐ tiào wǔ / hé qǐ wán yóuxì ba

Going somewhere to do something

When you want to describe going to a place to do an activity, in Chinese you simply say 'go place do activity'.

我去公园踢足球。 gōngyuán tī zúqiú	I go to the park to play football.
妹妹去图书馆看书。 mèimei tú guǎn	Little sister goes to the library to read.
他去学校弹吉他。 xiào tán jí	He goes to school to play the guitar.

The only exception is when going home to do something – you must say 回家 (huí jiā) and not 去家 (qù jiā).

我回家上网。 huí wǎng	I go home and use the internet.

1.6 Writing activity — Word order practice

Translate the following sentences into Chinese, referring to the grammar notes above. Use characters wherever you can; otherwise, use pinyin. Be careful to use the correct word order!

1) She plays games with her older sister.
2) He goes to work in France.
3) My mother works in the hospital.
4) He eats rice with his friend.
5) She goes to the zoo to read.
6) Her friend goes home to watch TV.

Writing Characters

你好！

我姓陈，我叫洪。我住在上海。
xìng Chén　jiào Hóng　zhù　hǎi

我天天都跟我哥哥一起去上学。
dōu gēn　gēge　qǐ

我喜欢学习英文，因为老师很好玩
xí　yīnwèi　wán

儿。哥哥喜欢学习艺术和音乐。
Gēge　xí　yìshù　hé　yīnyuè

他会弹钢琴，也喜欢唱歌。我们五
tán gāngqín　chàng gē

点钟下课，回家做作业。我们也
kè　huí　zuò　yè

喜欢去公园玩儿。我们有很多爱
gōngyuán wán　ài

好。你的爱好是什么？
ài

This is the first letter you receive from a Chinese pen-pal. Check your comprehension by noting whether each statement below is true or false. Write the answers in your notebook.

	✓ 正	✗ 误
1) His surname is Hóng.	○	○
2) He lives in Shanghai.	○	○
3) He goes to school with his younger brother.	○	○
4) His English teacher is boring.	○	○
5) His brother likes to study maths and music.	○	○
6) His brother plays the piano and sings.	○	○
7) They finish class at 5pm.	○	○
8) After doing their homework, they play on the computer.	○	○
9) They have many hobbies.	○	○

1.8 Pair activity — Chatting online

Instead of writing a reply to the letter (activity 1.7), arrange to chat online. Find a classmate and act out the call; then reverse roles for more practice.

Tell your pen-pal:

Your hobbies — 我的爱好是……。(ài)

Who is in your family — 我家有……口人。我有一个哥哥。(gēge)

Your friend's names — 我的朋友姓……。他/她叫……。(xìng　jiào)

Your pen-pal should ask you:

Where you live — 你住在哪儿？(zhù)

What you like to eat — 你喜欢吃什么？

What games you like to play — 你喜欢玩儿什么游戏？(wán　yóuxì)

You should finish the chat by saying you must go:

Sorry, I have to go! — 对不起，我要走了！(Duì　qǐ　zǒu le)

Goodbye! — 再见！拜拜！(Zài jiàn　Bàibai)

Language in action — Taking a photo

Taking photos is very popular in Chinese culture, especially when doing things together with friends. Here are a few useful expressions you can use when taking photos:

我们照个相吧。(zhào xiàng ba) Let's take a photo.

一、二、三！ One, two, three!

茄子！(qié) Say cheese! (literally, 'eggplant')

再来一张！(zài zhāng) Let's take another one!

好了！(le) OK, got it! (when there is no need for more)

1.9 Creative writing activity — My interests

Write a paragraph about what you like to do. You can use the prompts below to help you. Write in characters whenever you can; otherwise, use pinyin.

我姓(xìng) [surname]，我的名字(míngzi)是 [first name]。我家在 [place]。我是 [nationality]。我 [age] 岁。我很喜欢 [activity] 和(hé) [activity]。我天天都跟(dōu gēn) [person] 一起(qǐ) [activity]。我们一起(qǐ)去 [place] [activity]。我不喜欢 [activity]。明(míng)天我想去 [place] [activity]。

Did you know?

Shanghai attracts and trains some of the best acrobats in the world. If you visit Shanghai, you must see the famous Shanghai Acrobatic Troupe — plate spinning, chair balancing, hoop diving… the acrobatics show is a performance not to be missed!

1.10 Reading activity — Meeting up

You and a Chinese classmate have exchanged several texts. Read the following exchange and answer the questions in your notebook.

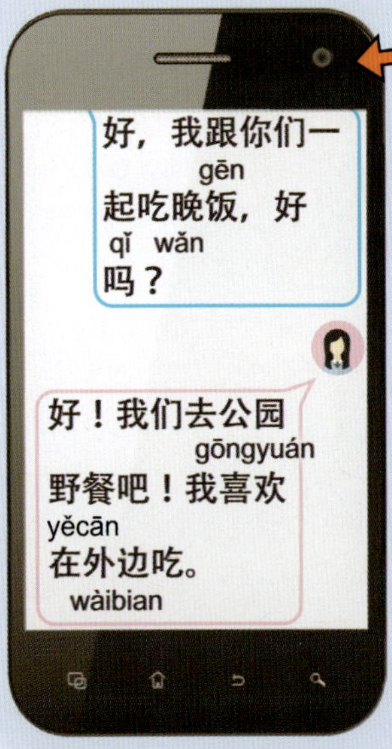

Glossary

野餐 yěcān = picnic

Check your comprehension! Complete the following sentences:

1) Your classmate invites you to ...
2) You say you won't go because ...
3) Your classmate tells you that the class finishes at ...
4) You propose to ...
5) Your classmate suggests a meeting place of ...

1.11 Writing activity — Composing a message

After having dinner together, you decide to invite your friend for a few activities this weekend. Here's a draft of your message. Write it out in your notebook, filling in the missing characters to make it complete.

___ ___！明 ___ 是 ___ ___ 六。你想 ___ 什么？你 ___ 我一起 ___
Nǐ hǎo Míng tiān xīngqī zuò gēn qǐ chī

午饭好不好？我也 ___ 去公园 ___ 篮球。___ ___ 日，我的朋友 ___
xiǎng gōngyuán dǎ lánqiú Xīngqī zài

图 ___ 馆弹吉他、唱歌。我们去听吧！你喜欢 ___ 什么 ___ ___？
tú shū guǎn tán jí chàng gē tīng ba tīng yīnyuè

Study skills — A useful technique for memorisation

Learning Chinese requires memorising a large number of characters, so it is important to work on some useful techniques for memorisation. Here is a method to help you make sure you really know what you are learning.

一 Think of 15 words you want to memorise. Write these words in pinyin down the right hand side of a piece of paper. This will be your memorisation quiz. Then put your books to one side!

二 Draw columns across the rest of the page – these will mark off each attempt at memorisation.

三 Try to remember how to write each of the words using characters and write them down in the first column. Don't worry if you make mistakes, just write anything you remember.

四 Using another colour pen, look at the answers (check your book), correct, complete and score yourself.

五 On a piece of scrap paper, write the characters you got wrong over and over again for a couple of minutes, until you can write them fluently.

六 Now fold the paper over the first column so that your first attempt is hidden (but the pinyin column still shows). Take a break! You worked hard and your brain needs some time to process all the information.

七 After your break, return to step 3 and have another attempt in the next column. You should find that your score improves each time. Keep repeating steps 3-6 until you get a perfect score. When you get a perfect score, you can stop – you have completely memorised those words!

Section 2: Sports

VOCAB

打羽毛球	dǎ yǔmáoqiú	to play badminton
打网球	dǎ wǎngqiú	to play tennis
打乒乓球	dǎ pīngpāngqiú	to play table tennis
游泳	yóuyǒng	to swim
活动	huódòng	activity
运动	yùndòng	sport

Language note

The word 'play' in Chinese changes depending on the activity. Here are the main words to remember:

打 dǎ	~篮球 lánqiú, ~羽毛球 yǔmáoqiú, ~网球 wǎngqiú
踢 tī	~足球 zúqiú
弹 tán	~钢琴 gāngqín, ~吉他 jí
玩儿 wán	~游戏 yóuxì, ~电脑 nǎo, ~手机 shǒujī

1.12 Listening activity — Which sports?

Listen to the recording and match the pictures together, writing the answers in your notebook.

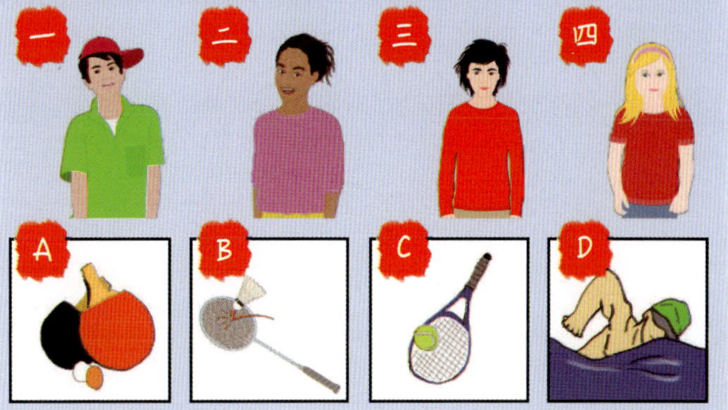

1.13 Pair activity — What can they do?

The table below shows which sports these four people can do. Find a classmate and take turns asking about the table using the dialogue below. Then ask which sports your partner can do.

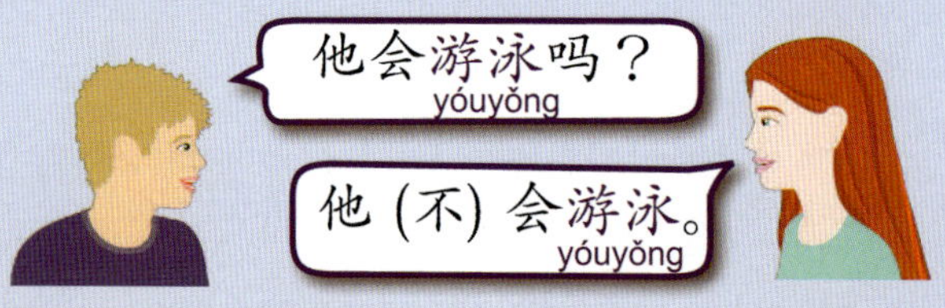

	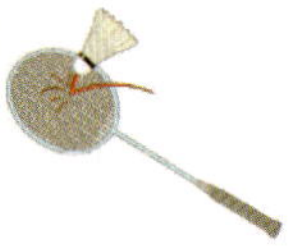	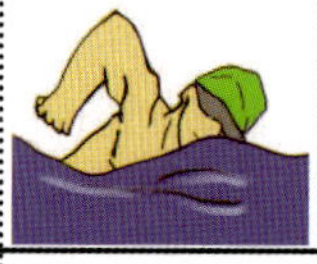				
林林 Línlín			✓	✓	✓	✓
Samantha	✓					
小张 Xiǎo Zhāng		✓			✓	✓
Seb	✓		✓			

vocab

能	néng	can (possibly)
还	hái	also; still
还没（有）	hái méi (yǒu)	still haven't; not yet
可以	kěyǐ	can; may
没关系	méi guānxi	it doesn't matter (for forgiving)

1.14 Listening activity — Making plans

Listen as people make plans. Take note of the activity proposed, as well as the alternative day proposed. Write your answers in your notebook.

e.g.	proposed activity	going to play in the park
	alternative day	tomorrow
1)	proposed activity	
	alternative day	
2)	proposed activity	
	alternative day	
3)	proposed activity	
	alternative day	

With a partner, practise proposing activities. The first person should suggest an activity, then the other can give an enthusiastic response.

我们一起去学校弹吉他，好吗？
qǐ xiào tán jí

Shall we go to school to play the guitar?

好！我们可以弹吉他，还可以唱歌。
kěyǐ tán jí hái kěyǐ chàng gē

Yes! We can play the guitar and sing as well.

做什么？	还可以 hái kěyǐ
去公园打篮球 gōngyuán dǎ lánqiú	打网球 dǎ wǎngqiú
回家吃饭 huí	喝中国茶 chá
去公园踢足球 gōngyuán tī zúqiú	打羽毛球 dǎ yǔmáoqiú
去图书馆上网 tú guǎn wǎng	看报纸 bàozhǐ
去学校做作业 xiào zuò yè	玩儿电脑 wán nǎo

1.16 Pair activity — Not free today!

Practise proposing activities with your partner. This time, the other person should decline the invitation, suggesting an alternative day. Use the prompts below or make up your own.

我们一起去学校弹吉他，好吗？
qǐ xiào tán jí

Shall we go to school to play the guitar?

对不起！我今天不能去。明天去吧！
Duì qǐ jīn néng Míng ba

Sorry! I can't today. Let's go tomorrow.

做什么？	哪天？
去公园打篮球 gōngyuán dǎ lánqiú	星期二
回家吃饭 huí	星期三晚上 wǎn
去公园踢足球 gōngyuán tī zúqiú	星期五
去图书馆上网 tú guǎn wǎng	星期六上午
去学校做作业	星期天

Language information: 会 / 可以 / 能
kěyǐ néng

There are three ways to say 'can' in Chinese. Here is how they are different:

会 (huì) means you 'can' do something you have learnt how to do. For example, play the guitar, swim or speak Chinese.

我会弹吉他。 tán jí	I can play the guitar.
他会游泳。 yóuyǒng	He can swim.
爸爸会说中文。	Dad can speak Chinese.

可以 (kěyǐ) means it's okay to do something, or there is the option to do something. It is used when asking for permission or talking about options and alternatives.

我可以上网吗？ kěyǐ wǎng	Can I go online?
你不可以玩儿手机。 kěyǐ wán shǒujī	You can't play with the mobile phone.
我们可以吃饭。 kěyǐ	We can eat. (We have the option of eating now.)

能 (néng) is used when talking about whether something is possible or impossible. For example, if the road is blocked, it is not possible to drive through. Or, if I'm ill in bed, it is impossible to go to school.

我不能来学校。 néng xiào	I can't come to school.
他不能喝牛奶。 néng nǎi	He can't drink milk.
我的电脑不能上网。 nǎo néng wǎng	My computer can't get online.

Let's review the differences between 会, 可以 and 能 by comparing three ways to say 'I can (or can't) drive' in Chinese:

我会开车。 kāichē	I can drive. (I have learnt how.)
我不会开车。 kāichē	I can't drive. (I have never learnt.)
我可以开车。 kěyǐ kāichē	I can drive. (I am allowed to drive. / It is an option for me to drive.)
我不可以开车。 kěyǐ kāichē	I may not drive. (I am not allowed to drive.)
我能开车。 néng kāichē	I can drive. (I am capable of driving.)
我不能开车。 néng kāichē	I can't drive. (I am incapable of driving.)

Language information: 还 hái

还 has a range of meanings. Its basic meaning is 'still' or 'yet'.

我还不知道她的名字。 I still don't know her name.
hái zhīdào míngzì

我还没有去。 I have not gone yet.
hái

Another meaning of 还 is 'also', but it can only be used in some cases. It is generally used when the subject of the sentence does multiple activities of the same type. Here are some examples:

一 我很喜欢运动。我喜欢打网球，还喜欢打篮球。
yùndòng dǎ wǎngqiú hái dǎ lánqiú
I really like sports. I like playing tennis and also like playing basketball.

二 我今天有很多作业。我有中文作业，还有英文作业。
jīn yè yè hái yè
I have a lot of homework today. I have Chinese homework and also English homework.

三 他的中文很好。他会说中文，还会唱中国歌。
hái chàng gē
His Chinese is very good. He can speak Chinese and can also sing Chinese songs.

四 我的手机很好，能打电话，还能上网。
shǒujī néng dǎ huà hái néng wǎng
My mobile phone is very good. It can make calls and also go online.

五 我们今天能去，明天还能去。
jīn néng míng hái néng
We can go today; we can also go tomorrow.

1.17 Reading activity — Translation match

Match the following with the correct translation. Write the answers in your notebook.

1) 他不能跑步。
néng pǎobù
○ He can't run.
○ He is not allowed to run.

2) 她可以踢足球。
kěyǐ tī zúqiú
○ She has learnt to play football.
○ It is okay for her to play football.

3) 妈妈不会跳舞。
tiào wǔ
○ Mum can't dance (well).
○ Mum can't dance. (Perhaps she is ill.)

4) 我妹妹不可以开车。
mèimei kěyǐ kāichē
○ My younger sister doesn't know how to drive.
○ My younger sister is not allowed to drive.

5) 老师会说法文。
fǎ
○ The teacher knows how to speak French.
○ The teacher may speak French.

字 Writing Characters

Did you know?

Beijing opera is one of the many famous performing arts traditional to Chinese culture. Colourful and dramatic, operas mix music, dance, acrobatics, poetry and mime, and they look and sound quite different from our Western operas. Movement is key.

1.18 Writing activity — Translation match

Translate the following sentences into Chinese. Don't translate the parts in brackets – these are for further information. Use characters wherever you can; otherwise, use pinyin.

1) She cannot swim. (She hasn't learnt how.)
2) He cannot go to school. (Because the road is blocked.)
3) They can take photos. (It is allowed.)
4) You may not see the teacher! (Not allowed.)
5) My friend cannot eat beef. (She is allergic.)

1.19 Writing activity — Expand your vocabulary!

Using a dictionary, look up how to write the following words and write each in Chinese characters. We'll practise using them later:

- hǎochī (delicious)
- hǎohē (nice to drink)
- hǎotīng (nice to listen to)
- hǎokàn (beautiful)
- hǎoxué (easy to learn)
- hǎohàn (hero)

Did you know?

杭州 (Hángzhōu) is a beautiful city in East China famous for its tea and its scenery, including a pagoda overlooking West Lake. The pagoda is linked to the Legend of the White Snake, which is a very famous Chinese story. You can visit Hángzhōu in a day trip from Shànghǎi on the train.

Vocab

打太极拳	dǎ tàijíquán	to do Tai Ch'i
放风筝	fàng fēngzheng	to fly a kite
练书法	liàn shūfǎ	to practise calligraphy
下中国象棋	xià Zhōngguó xiàngqí	to play Chinese chess

Language in action — Playing a match

China's most popular sports are basketball, table tennis and badminton. If you get invited to play sports with your Chinese friends, here are some useful phrases you might need while playing.

该你了。 (gāi ... le)	It's your turn.
几比几？ (bǐ)	What's the score?
三比四。 (bǐ)	It's 3:4.
三平。 (píng)	It's 3 all.

1.20 Reading activity — People and their hobbies

Copy and fill the table below according to what the following three people say about their hobbies.

我很喜欢练书法。我天天跟我朋友一起练。我去他家练。我不喜欢画画。
liàn fǎ gēn qǐ liàn liàn huà huà

我不喜欢运动。我不会打羽毛球，也不会打乒乓球。我喜欢玩儿游戏！
yùndòng dǎ yǔmáoqiú dǎ pīngpāngqiú wán yóuxì

我跟我哥哥一起下中国象棋。我们在家里玩儿。
gēn gēge qǐ xiàngqí lǐ wán

我很喜欢看书。我看英文书，还看中文书。我天天去图书馆看书。我跟
hái tú guǎn gēn

马钟一起去。我们不喜欢放风筝。
Mǎ Zhōng qǐ fàng fēngzheng

	I like to...	I do it (where?)	I do it with (whom?)	I don't enjoy...

1.21 Writing activity — Playing a match

1) In pairs, create a sketch in which you talk about activities you like, including where you go and with whom you do them. Write in your notebook.

A: 你喜欢__________吗？

B: 喜欢/不喜欢。

A: 你去哪儿__________？

B: 我去__________。

A: 你跟谁__________？
gēn

B: 我跟__________一起__________。
gēn qǐ

2) Arrange a time to play a sport together.

A: 我们一起打__________球，好吗？
qǐ dǎ qiú

B: 好！几点？

A: __________点。

3) Now try to re-enact the whole sketch from memory!

1.22 Reading activity — Which sports?

Read the following, look at the options to complete the statements below and write the answers in your notebook.

我做很多运动。我喜欢游泳、打网球和跑步。我还喜欢打篮球。我不会打乒乓球。
zuò yùndòng yóuyǒng dǎ wǎngqiú hé pǎobù hái dǎ lánqiú dǎ pīngpāngqiú
我的中文老师是中国人，他会打乒乓球。他说乒乓球很好玩儿，我可以学。我妹妹
dǎ pīngpāngqiú pīngpāngqiú wán kěyǐ mèimei
不喜欢运动。她喜欢看书、看电影，还喜欢跟朋友一起喝咖啡。我天天跟妹妹一起
yùndòng yǐng hái gēn qǐ kāfēi gēn mèimei qǐ
去学校图书馆做作业。图书馆很大，书很多。
xiào tú guǎn zuò yè Tú guǎn

1) The narrator likes to: swim / play tennis / play football / sing / play ping pong

2) The narrator's teacher is: English / Chinese / interesting / old

3) The narrator's teacher says ping pong is: fun / not interesting / easy to learn

4) The narrator's sister likes to: perform / read / watch TV / watch films / drink coffee with friends

5) Who goes with the narrator to the library? his friend / his older sister / his younger sister

6) The narrator says that the library is: small / old / big / fun

1.23 Writing activity — Activity lists

Look at the activities in the reading above and sort them based on what you like and don't like. Make two lists, entitled '我喜欢' and '我不喜欢.'

1.24 Writing activity — Activities around Shanghai

Look at the pictures below and write a paragraph about what people from Shanghai like to do in their free time.

Section 3: Putting it together

1.25 Reading activity — Summer camp

Read the following advertisement for a summer camp and answer the questions in your notebook:

1) Where is the summer camp being held?
2) What sport activities are on offer?
3) Where do participants live?
4) Can participants access the internet?
5) What kind of food is provided?
6) How long does the camp last?
7) On what date does the camp finish?
8) How much does the camp cost?

你想去中国上海吗？
hǎi

来跟我们一起玩儿吧！
gēn qǐ wán ba

七月十五日到八月五日，你可以和中国家
dào kěyǐ hé
庭一起住三个星期。家里都能上网，也有
tíng qǐ zhù lǐ dōu néng wǎng
很多中文书。天天可以喝中国茶，吃中国
kěyǐ
菜，还有很多中国传统活动。一起来吧！
hái chuántǒng huódòng qǐ ba

七月十五日 —— 八月五日（三个星期）。

1200美元
měi

电话：130-378-888-78
huà

你可以：
kěyǐ

- 学中文
- 玩儿游戏 (wán yóuxì)
- 游泳 (yóuyǒng)
- 打网球 (dǎ wǎngqiú)
- 听中国音乐 (tīng yīnyuè)
- 做中国菜 (zuò cài)

Glossary

家庭	jiātíng	= family
传统	chuántǒng	= traditional

1.26 Group activity — At the summer camp

Imagine you have arrived at the camp advertised above. Introduce yourself to the other participants (your classmates) and talk about what activities you'd like to do. You can use the profiles below.

孙朋
Sūn
- 中国人
- 住在北京 (zhù)
- 喜欢篮球 (lánqiú)
- 不喜欢看书

James Smith
- 英国人
- 住在伦敦 (zhù Lúndūn)
- 喜欢游泳 (yóuyǒng)
- 不喜欢玩儿电脑 (wán nǎo)

Tracy Fields
- 美国人
- 住在纽约 (zhù Niǔyuē)
- 喜欢弹吉他 (tán jí)
- 不喜欢跳舞 (tiào wǔ)

You could finish the conversation by proposing: 我们一起去吃冰淇淋吧！
qǐ bīngqílín ba

Character focus — Unit 1 Review

Here are some characters you have learnt this chapter, together with similar characters from before. Can you spot the elements in common? Copy the table in your notebook and fill in the blanks.

Review	Meaning	Pinyin	New	Meaning	Pinyin
元	currency of China	yuán	玩		
很			跟		
男			动		
欢			戏		
友			爱		

1.27 Writing activity — My schedule

Write a schedule of your typical Monday, giving the times and activities in a list. Include as many items as you can and write in characters whenever possible. See to the right for an example.

九点：跟我朋友一起去学校
gēn qǐ xiào

十点：上法文课
fǎ kè

十一点：弹钢琴
tán gāngqín

三点：上中文课
kè

四点：打网球
dǎ wǎngqiú

五点：看电视
shì

Traditional Chinese instruments

Chinese traditional music gets its distinctive sound from a wide range of beautiful musical instruments. Here are some of the most common instruments you might see in China.

笛子
dízi

二胡
hú

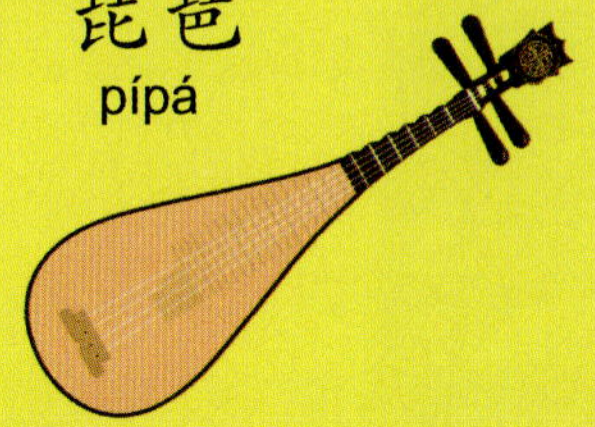

琵琶
pípá

唢呐
suǒnà

大鼓
gǔ

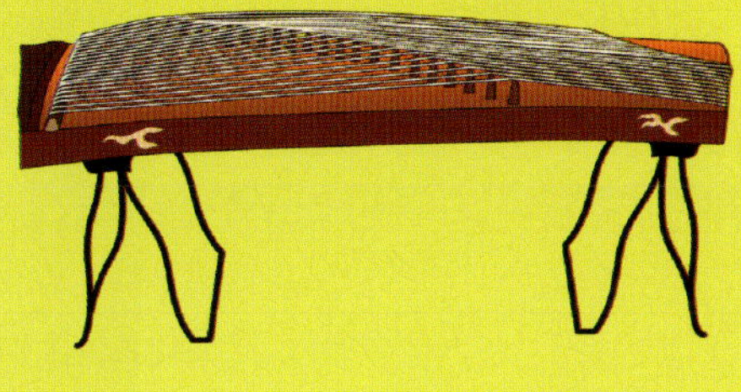

古筝
gǔzhēng

Chinese Chess

As chess spread around the world, it evolved in different ways. Chinese chess has some similarities with chess as played in the West. However, the pieces came to reflect traditional Chinese warfare. Here is a rundown of the pieces and how they can move. The pieces are usually black and red instead of black and white. They are placed on the intersections of the chessboard lines, not on the squares. Notice that the pieces on opposing sides have different Chinese characters, as when the game developed, they were often not distinguished by colour.

Black	Red	English Name	Movement and powers
將	帥	General	Similar to the king in chess, the general moves inside the palace area. A general also may not move directly in front of the other general if there are no pieces in between.
士	仕	Advisor	The advisors also may not leave the palace. They can only move along the diagonal lines.
象	相	Elephant	Elephants move two places diagonally, but may not cross the river. They cannot jump over any pieces.
馬	傌	Horse	A horse is similar to a knight in chess, but its movements may be blocked by a piece that stands directly next to it.
車	俥	Chariot	The chariot behaves exactly like the rook (also known as castle) in chess.
砲	炮	Cannon	Definitely the coolest piece in the game, the cannon can move like a rook, but it can only take by jumping over exactly one piece.
卒	兵	Soldier	Like the pawn in chess, the soldier moves forwards one space. However, after crossing the river it can also move sideways. It never moves back, and nothing happens when it reaches the end of the board.

Reading Challenge

我的爱好

你好，我叫李冬。我有很多爱好。我喜欢画画、滑雪、篮球和戏剧。

画画很有意思，每个星期三下午5点钟我和我朋友一起上美术课。美术老师很好。我朋友的画很好看。他明天有展览，我要和我家人一起去看。

滑雪也很有意思。我会滑雪，可是我妹妹不会。冬天我和我哥哥一起去法国的雪山滑雪，因为英国没有很多山。夏天法国的山上没有雪，所以我们不去法国。暑假，我和我的中国朋友一起打篮球。

很多英国人不喜欢篮球，因为没有意思。可是，我很喜欢打篮球。我想做篮球运动员，因为运动员天天可以打篮球。我和我的中国朋友每天坐公共汽车去学校，我们在那里打篮球。

我也喜欢戏剧。我不上戏剧课，可是我常常去看表演。今年3月我和我妈妈一起坐火车去市中心看戏剧表演。演员演得很好。

Glossary

戏剧	xìjù	= drama
展览	zhǎnlǎn	= exhibition
暑假	shǔjià	= summer holidays
滑雪	huáxuě	= to ski
冬天	dōngtiān	= winter
夏天	xiàtiān	= summer

对不对? True or false?

1) 李冬星期三上午上美术课。
2) 李冬和他家人去看展览。
3) 李冬的哥哥不喜欢滑雪。
4) 李冬的妹妹去法国。
5) 李冬不在家打篮球。

Answer the questions in English

1) Who will have an exhibition?
2) Who can't ski?
3) Why don't they go to France in the summer?
4) What job does Li Dong want to do in the future and why?
5) When does Li Dong play basketball?
6) How does Li Dong get to school?
7) Does Li Dong study drama?
8) What did Li Dong do with his mother?

我会

Now you can...

...talk about your interests and hobbies

我喜欢运动和音乐。	Wǒ xǐhuan yùndòng hé yīnyuè.	I like sport and music.
我的爱好是弹吉他。	Wǒ de àihào shì tán jítā.	My hobby is playing guitar.
我喜欢艺术，还会画画。	Wǒ xǐhuan yìshù, hái huì huà huà.	I like art, and I can paint.
我天天都练书法。	Wǒ tiāntiān dōu liàn shūfǎ.	I practise calligraphy every day.
表演很好玩儿。	Biǎoyǎn hěn hǎo wánr.	Performing is really fun.

...talk about sports

我哥哥会打乒乓球。	Wǒ gēge huì dǎ pīngpāng qiú.	My big brother can play pingpong.
妹妹去学校游泳。	Mèimei qù xuéxiào yóuyǒng.	Little sister is going to school to swim.

...arrange to meet with your friends

我们一起去外公园风筝吧。	Wǒmen yìqǐ qù gōngyuán fàng fēngzheng ba.	Let's go together to the park and fly a kite.
你想跟我一起打网球吗？	Nǐ xiǎng gēn wǒ yìqǐ dǎ wǎngqiú ma?	Would you like to play tennis with me?

...ask permission to do things

我可以跟朋友一起看电影吗？	Wǒ kěyǐ gēn péngyǒu yìqǐ kàn diànyǐng ma?	Can I watch a film with my friend?
我哥哥不可以上网。	Wǒ gēge bù kěyǐ shàngwǎng.	My big brother is not allowed to go online.
王春明天不能去。	Wáng Chūn míngtiān bù néng qù.	Wang Chun can't go tomorrow.

...write the following characters:

做 打 跟 和 起 玩 听 爱 音 乐 海 可 以
能 运 动 游 戏 泳 网 球 意 思

怎么去？ Getting Around

Objectives

In this unit, you will learn…

…how to describe where places are located.
…how to arrange a time and place to meet.
…all about Shanghai.

Section 1: Around Town

Vocab

这儿/这里	zhèr/zhèlǐ	here
那儿/那里	nàr/nàlǐ	there
哪儿/哪里	nǎr/nǎlǐ	where
公司	gōngsī	company
饭店	fàndiàn	hotel
(超级)市场	(chāojí) shìchǎng	(super) market
邮局	yóujú	post office
银行	yínháng	bank
饭馆	fànguǎn	restaurant
商店	shāngdiàn	shop
中心	zhōngxīn	centre
市中心	shìzhōngxīn	city centre
工厂	gōngchǎng	factory

这 (zhè), 那 (nà) and 哪 (nǎ)

Look closely at the words for 'here', 'there', 'where', 'this', 'that' and 'which'. To remember the difference, it's useful to know that the words that have an 'r' in the English also have 儿 (er) in the Chinese.

这 this	那 that	哪 which?
这儿/这里 here	那儿/那里 there	哪儿/哪里 where?

超市 (chāoshì)

The word for supermarket was directly translated from English into Chinese: 超级 (chāojí) means 'super' and 市场 (shìchǎng) means 'market'. Most people use the shortened word, 超市 (chāoshì).

2.1 Listening activity — Where are you going?

Listen to the recording and match the question number with the correct image. Write the answers in your notebook. You should repeat each question and answer aloud as you hear it.

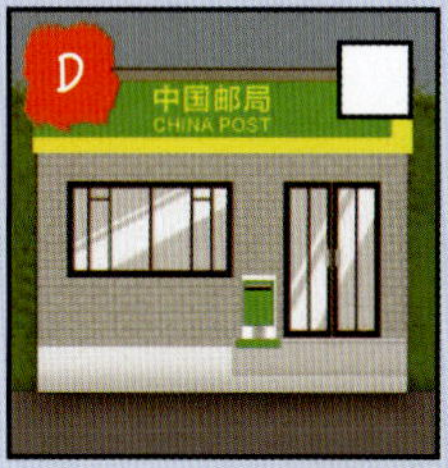

With a partner, use the prompts below to practise asking where people are and where they are going. Use either 去 or 在, and make sure the questions and answers match!

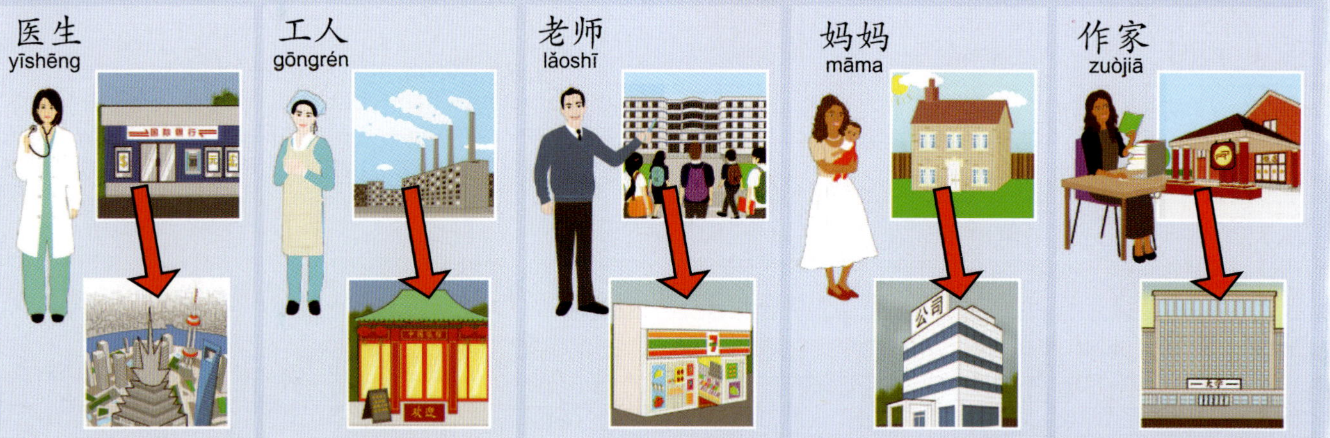

Directions

VOCAB

请问	qǐng wèn	May I ask...
左边	zuǒbian	left side
右边	yòubian	right side
前边	qiánbian	in front
后边	hòubian	behind
对面	duìmian	opposite
路口	lùkǒu	intersection

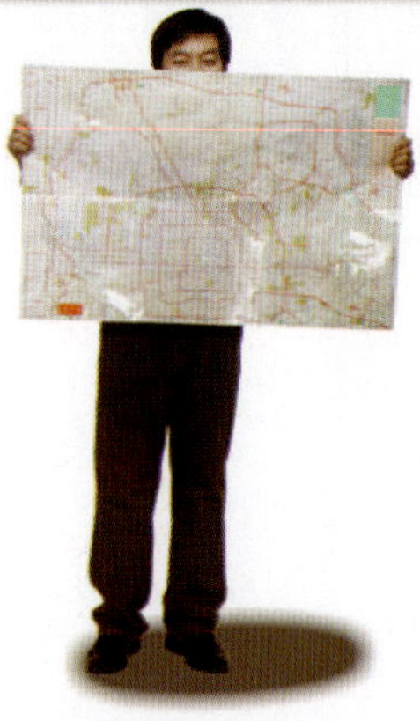

2.3 Listening activity — Giving the location

Listen to the following exchanges and write down in your notebook where each place is located. Before you start the exercise, you may want to revise some of the places you've already learnt:

医院 图书馆 我的家

公园 动物园 学校
xiào

1) The bank is supermarket
2) The post office is in front of the
3) The is the park
4) The factory is to the right of the
5) The hotel is
6) The library is the zoo
7) Where is there a restaurant?

2.4 Pair activity — Looking at a map

Look at the map of Yuyuan Garden below. With a partner, practise asking and giving the locations for various places.

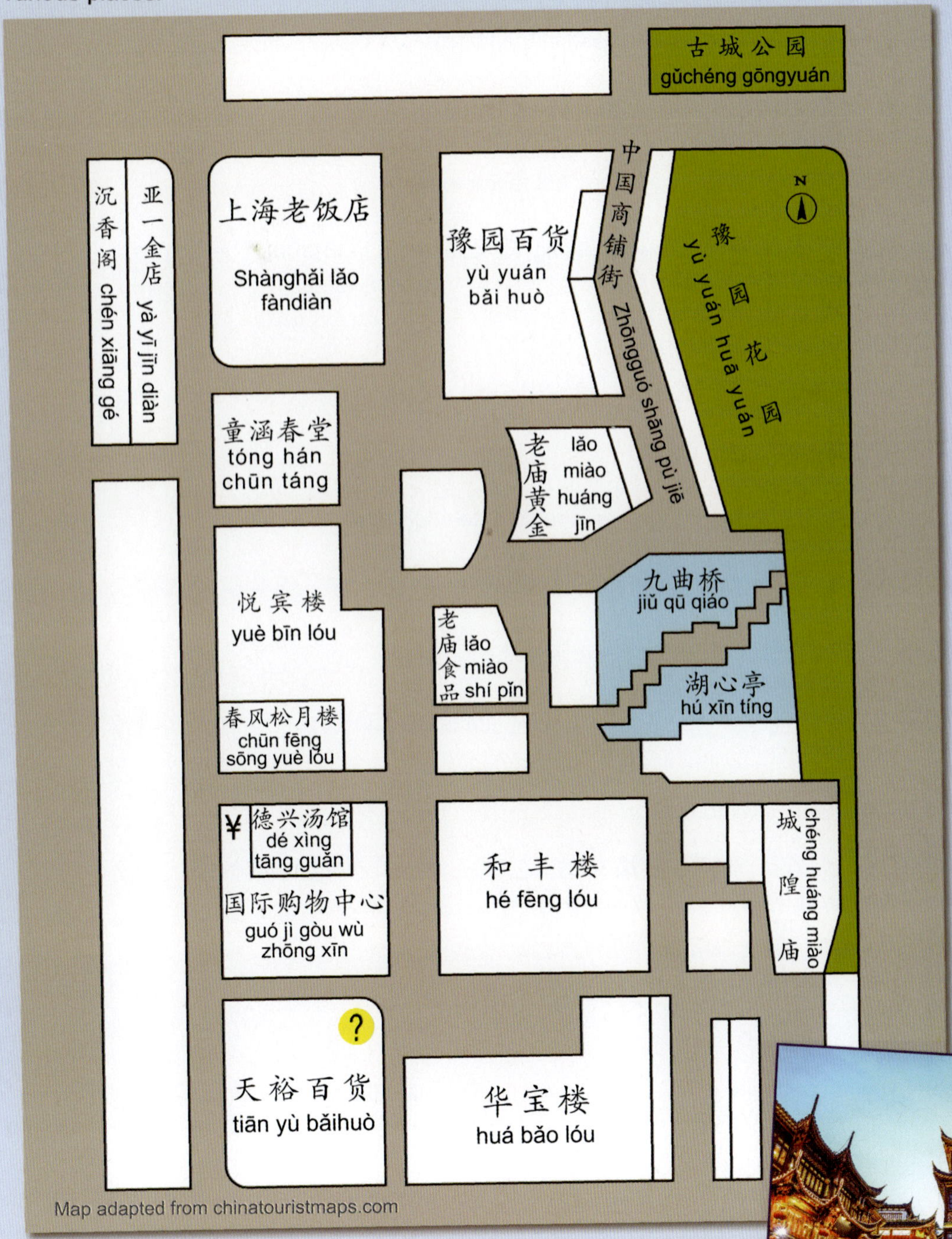

Yuyuan Gardens Shopping Area

请问。(A) 在哪儿？
Qǐng wèn

Excuse me, where is (A)?

(A) 在 (B) 对面。

(A) is opposite (B).

谢谢！再见！
Xièxie

Thanks! Bye!

About the language: 在 for location

Remember that the word 在 describes where something takes place. For example:

我在图书馆看书。	I read in the library.
爸爸在商店工作。 shāngdiàn	Dad works in a shop.
他们在饭馆吃饭。	They eat in the restaurant.

Similar to sentences with 跟, the word order when using 在 is different in English. The Chinese order is 'I in the library read'.

(A) 在 (B) 的 (position)

在 can also be used to describe where things are in relation to each other:

我家在商店的后边。 shāngdiàn hòubian	My home is behind the shop.
你家在银行的左边。 yínháng zuǒbian	Your home is to the left of the bank.
他家在超市的对面。	His home is opposite the supermarket.

You can also say these sentences without 的:

我家在商店后边。 (shāngdiàn hòubian) 你家在银行左边。 (yínháng zuǒbiān) 他家在超市对面。

一 Look at the map of Yuyuan opposite to help you fill in the blanks for the following sentences. Write the answers in your notebook.

1) 沉香阁在亚一金店的________。
Chén xiāng gé yà diàn

2) 老庙食品在悦宾楼的________。
miào shí pǐn yuè bīn lóu

3) 华宝楼在天裕百货的________。
Huá bǎo lóu yù bǎihuò

4) 九曲桥在湖心亭的________。
qū qiáo hú xīn tíng

5) ________在豫园百货的左边。
yù bǎi huò zuǒbian

二 Translate the following into Chinese. Use characters where you can; otherwise use pinyin.

1) My house is to the right of the supermarket.
2) The hospital is to the left of the hotel.
3) The factory is across from the bank.
4) The company is to the left of the intersection.

Writing Characters

请问 qǐng wèn

前边 qián bian

后边 hòu bian

左边 zuǒ bian

右边 yòu bian

对面 duì miàn

饭店 fàn diàn

饭馆 fàn guǎn

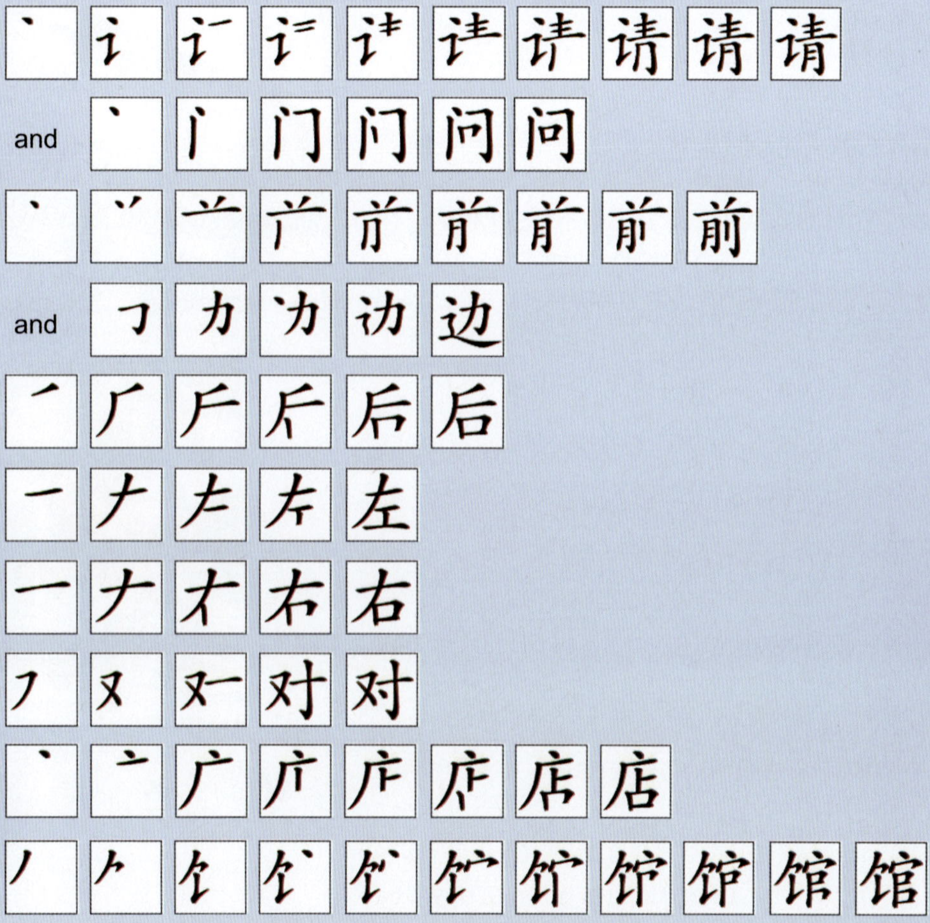

Did you know?

Familiar with HSBC? This awesome neo-classical building housed the headquarters of the Shanghai branch of HSBC from 1923 to 1955. It is now the Shanghai Pudong Development Bank. If you go to the Bund in Shanghai (see Around Shanghai on page 46) you will see many amazing buildings like this one.

2.6 Reading activity — Where is the shop?

陈洪：老师好！
Chén Hóng

老师：陈洪，你好！你去哪儿？
Chén Hóng

陈洪：我去商店买笔。你呢？
shāngdiàn bǐ ne

老师：我去银行。你去哪家商店？商店在哪儿？
yínháng shāngdiàn shāngdiàn

陈洪：商店在邮局的对面。
Shāngdiàn yóujú

老师：邮局在哪儿？
Yóujú

陈洪：邮局在工厂左边。你知道不知道工厂在哪儿？
Yóujú chǎng zuǒbiān zhīdào zhīdào chǎng

老师：我不知道！
zhīdào

陈洪：工厂在银行的左边，我们一起走吧！
chǎng yínháng zuǒbiān

老师：好，走吧！

Read the above dialogue and write in your notebook whether each statement is true or false.

	✓ 正	✗ 误
1) Chen Hong is talking to his teacher.	○	○
2) Chen Hong is going to buy a bag.	○	○
3) The shop is behind the post office.	○	○
4) The post office is to the left of the company.	○	○
5) The factory is to the left of the bank.	○	○
6) Chen Hong and the other person will go in the same direction.	○	○

2.7 Pair Activity — Excuse me, where is the hotel?

In pairs, devise a short sketch in which one person is completely unfamiliar with the town and trying to find the hotel, and the second person keeps giving directions relative to other places. Model your dialogue on the reading above, 'Where is the shop?'. Open with 请问 (qǐng wèn) since you are acting as strangers.

Did you know?

Shanghai boasts an interesting mix of architectural design: space-aged sky scrapers, classical buildings and Chinese traditional-style architecture like that in Yuyuan Garden.

Lujiazui high-rise district

Language in action — When is good for you?

It's useful to be able to accept and decline invitations politely. A gracious phrase to use when turning someone down is 我有事儿 (wǒ yǒu shìr); literally, 'I have a matter to attend to'. It is fine to be vague in this way, not specifying why you cannot accept.

Another common way to accept or decline is to say 行 (xíng, 'fine') or 不行 (bù xíng, 'not fine').

星期一行吗？ xíng	How about Monday?
我（那天）有事儿。 shì	I've got something I need to do (on that day).
可以改天吗？ gǎi	Can we do a different day?
行/不行 xíng xíng	OK / Not OK
都可以。	Either way is fine.

2.8 Listening activity — Arranging to meet up

Listen to the following three dialogues and fill a table similar to the one below with the correct information.

几点见？	在哪儿见？

Language note: 见

再见 (zàijiàn), which is a way of saying goodbye, literally means 'again see'. On its own, 见 (jiàn) means 'to see', but it is also used to mean 'meet' as in the English 'meet you later'. So you can say 我们在学校见 (wǒmen zài xuéxiào jiàn) to mean 'We'll see (meet) at school' and 我们三点见 (wǒmen sāndiǎn jiàn) to mean 'We'll see (meet) at 3 o'clock.'

2.9 Pair activity — Meeting up

With a partner, practise suggesting times and places to meet. Use the table for prompts. **Remember always to say the time first!**

几点见？	在哪儿见？
四点	邮局 yóujú
两点 liǎng	豫园 Yù
晚上七点 wǎn	饭馆前边 qiánbian
上午八点	东方明珠塔 Dōngfāng zhū tǎ
下午一点	动物园
上午十一点	银行后边 yínháng hòubian

2.10 Reading activity — Text exchange

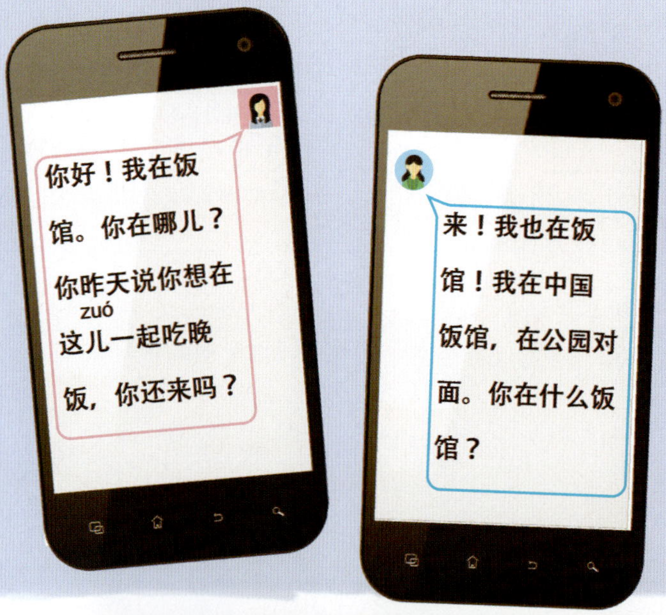

Read this text message exchange you had with your friend and answer the questions. (You show up in pink, your friend in blue.)

1) Where are you?
2) What did your friend say yesterday?
3) What do you ask your friend?
4) Where is your friend now?
5) Where is your friend in relation to the park?
6) What does your friend ask you?

Those who want to escape the city can head to the peaceful water village of 周庄 (Zhōuzhuāng), a popular destination situated just outside of Shanghai city limits.

2.11 Writing activity — The text exchange continues...

Below is the text message conversation continued from the reading activity above. In your notebook, copy and complete the exchange by filling in the missing characters.

☐ 在 法 ☐ ☐ ☐，在 ☐ ☐ ☐ ☐ ☐。
Wǒ fǎ guó fàn guǎn fàn diàn de zuǒ bian

公园 ☐ ☐ ☐ ？
Gōngyuán zài nǎ -r

公园在 ☐ 校的 ☐ ☐。
Gōngyuán zài xué xiào qián bian

☐，我 ☐ ☐！
Hǎo huì lái

2.12 Writing activity — Describing location

On the map below, each box represents a different building in the neighbourhood. Look at the map (or create your own) and write seven sentences describing where one place is in relation to another.

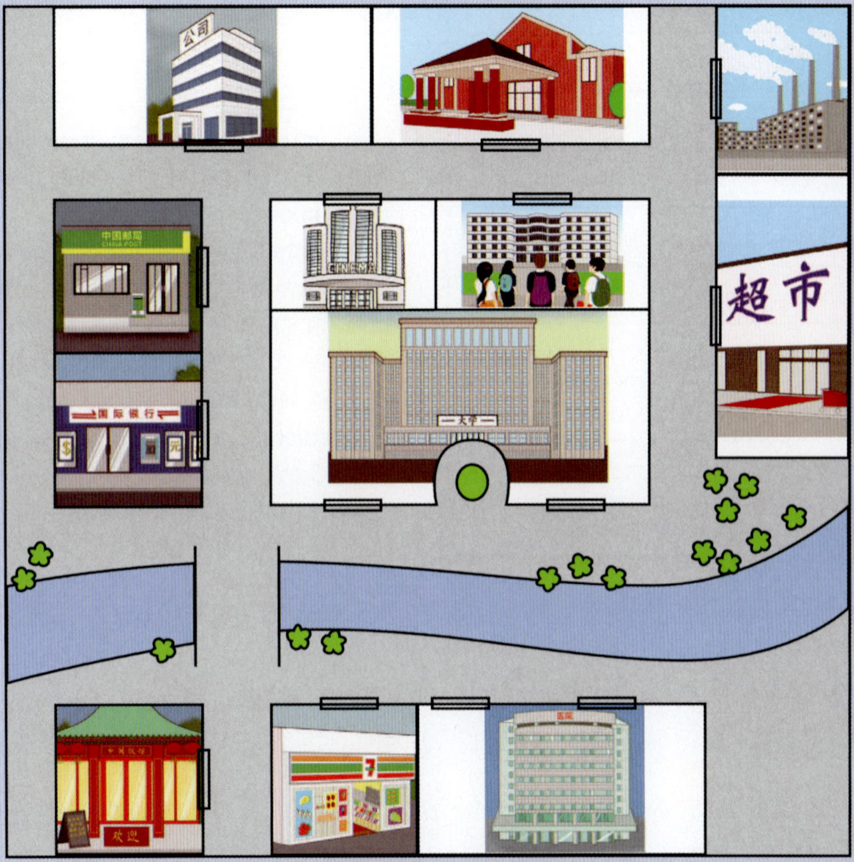

Study skills — Improving your tones

Speaking with correct tones is very important for communication in Chinese. If you change the tones when you speak, you could change the meaning quite drastically. For example:

Mā yào shuìjiào = Mum wants to sleep
Mǎ yào shuǐjiǎo = The horse wants dumplings

As you can see, little mistakes could lead to big misunderstandings. Here are a few tips for improving your tones:

一 Slow down. It is easier to say the tones one by one than all together. When you're practising a sentence, start very slowly, making sure each tone is correct, before speeding up.

二 Exaggerate the tones. When you hear Chinese people speak, they often speak so fast that you don't realize they are using the tones; in fact, the tones are there, but they are quite subtle. Don't try to copy them just yet; in the earlier stages of learning, you should exaggerate your tones. When you have mastered them, you can make them more subtle.

三 Beware of your native intonation. When you speak Chinese, by habit you will use the same patterns of intonation for your own language unless you concentrate on over-riding this habit. For example, English speakers tend to raise their voices at the end of questions. If you do this in Chinese, it can change the tones (and meaning) of the sentence!

Section 2: Modes of transport

vocab

骑	qí	to ride
坐	zuò	by (+transport)
汽车	qìchē	car
出租车	chūzūchē	taxi
公共汽车	gōnggòng qìchē	public bus
火车	huǒchē	train
自行车	zìxíngchē	bicycle
船	chuán	boat
地铁	dìtiě	underground
走路	zǒulù	to walk

车 (chē)

- The word 车 (chē) can refer to any type of wheeled transport. If the type is not specified, you are left to deduce what type is meant from context. Alone, 车 (chē) usually means 'car', 'taxi', or 'bus'.
- Note that 'to take a taxi' can be 坐出租车 (zuò chūzūchē) or 打车, using the same 打as in 打网球 and 打电话 (diànhuà).
- 公交车 (gōngjiāochē) and 巴士 (bāshì) are other common words meaning 'bus'. 的士 (díshì) is a word for 'taxi' that derives from Cantonese, and 计程车 (jìchéngchē) is the word for 'taxi' in Taiwan.

2.13 Listening activity — I'm taking the boat!

Listen to the recording. In your notebook, match the question number to the corresponding picture.

2.14 Pair activity – Saying how you travel

1) Work with a partner. Pick one of the pairs below and say the mode of transport; then your partner should tell you the corresponding place you are going.

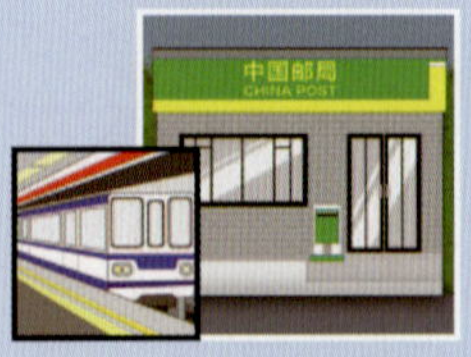

2) Now discuss with your partner what mode of transport you would use for each of the journeys below. You may need to research online to find a good answer.

- Your house to your school
- Your house to the nearest shops
- The Bund to People's Park
- Lujiazui to Shanghai Pudong International Airport
- The Forbidden City to the Temple of Heaven

Vocab

怎么	zěnme	how?
上车	shàng chē	to get on a vehicle
下车	xià chē	to get off a vehicle
站	zhàn	station; stop

站 (zhàn)
One meaning of 站 (zhàn) is 'station'. It is found in the words 火车站 (huǒchē zhàn) and 公共汽车站 (gōnggòng qìchē zhàn).

2.15 Listening activity – Where to?

Listen to the recording, which will be played **twice**. The second time, try to repeat what you hear after each line. Then answer the following questions in your notebook:

1) Where is the woman going?
2) Where is she getting on the bus?
3) Where is she getting off the bus?
4) Where is the bank in relation to the factory?

2.16 Pair activity – Getting on and off the bus

With a partner, practise the dialogue below until you've memorised it. Swap roles so you both can say every line. (Note: a good way to memorise lines is to break them down and say one line over and over until you can say it perfectly; then go on.)

A: 你去哪儿？

B: 我去图书馆。

A: 你怎么去？
zěn

B: 我坐公共汽车去。
zuò gòngqìchē

A: 你在哪儿上车？
chē

B: 我在医院上车。车站在医院对面。
chē Chēzhàn

A: 你在哪儿下车？
chē

B: 我在饭店下车。图书馆在饭店的左边。
diàn chē diàn zuǒbian

Shanghai City Centre

About the language: 很多 and 坐 (zuò)

很多

There are two ways to say 'a lot of...' in Chinese; both use the words 很多.

上海有很多商店。 (shāngdiàn)
上海的商店很多。 (shāngdiàn)
Shanghai has many shops.

图书馆有很多书。
图书馆的书很多。
The library has many books.

她有很多朋友。
她的朋友很多。
She has many friends.

To say 'not many' you can say 没有很多 or 不多. Here are some examples:

纽约没有很多自行车。 (zìxíngchē)
纽约的自行车不多。 (zìxíngchē)
New York doesn't have many bicycles.

这里没有很多人。
这里的人不多。
There aren't many people here.

奶奶没有很多钱。 (Nǎinai, qián)
奶奶的钱不多。 (Nǎinai, qián)
Grandmother doesn't have much money.

坐 (zuò)

To say 'go by bus', 'go by train,' etc. in Chinese, you use the word 坐 (zuò) which literally means 'sit'.

她坐公共汽车去商店。 (zuò, gòng qìchē, shāngdiàn) — She goes by bus to the shop.

我坐火车去北京。 (zuò, chē) — I go by train to Beijing.

妹妹坐出租车去饭馆。 (zuò, chūzūchē) — Younger sister goes by taxi to the restaurant.

The exceptions to this are modes of transport that you ride (as opposed to 'take'). For these, use 骑 (qí).

我骑自行车去银行。 (qí, zìxíngchē, yínháng) — I ride my bycycle to the bank.

她骑马回家。 (qí) — She rides the horse home.

弟弟骑摩托车去市中心。 (qí, mótuōchē, xīn) — Younger brother rides the motorbike to the city centre.

Bicycles are a popular form of transportation in China, seen here in a traditional alleyway.

2.17 Writing activity — Transport

Look at the grammar notes above, copy the Chinese sentences below into your notebook and fill in the blanks.

1) 他 [go by] 自行车去学校。 (zìxíngchē, xiào)
2) 她 [go by] 出租车去饭店。 (chūzūchē, diàn)
3) 爸爸 [go by train] 去公园打篮球。
4) 弟弟坐 [bus] 去市中心买书。 (zuò, xīn)
5) 妹妹骑 [motorbike] 去饭馆吃饭。 (qí)
6) 我坐船去 [bank] 。 (zuò chuán)

People in China often use scooters to get around.

Writing Characters

坐 zuò
车 chē
走 zǒu
路 lù
车站 chē zhàn
里 lǐ
汽车 qì chē
市场 shì chǎng
怎么 zěn me
心 xīn

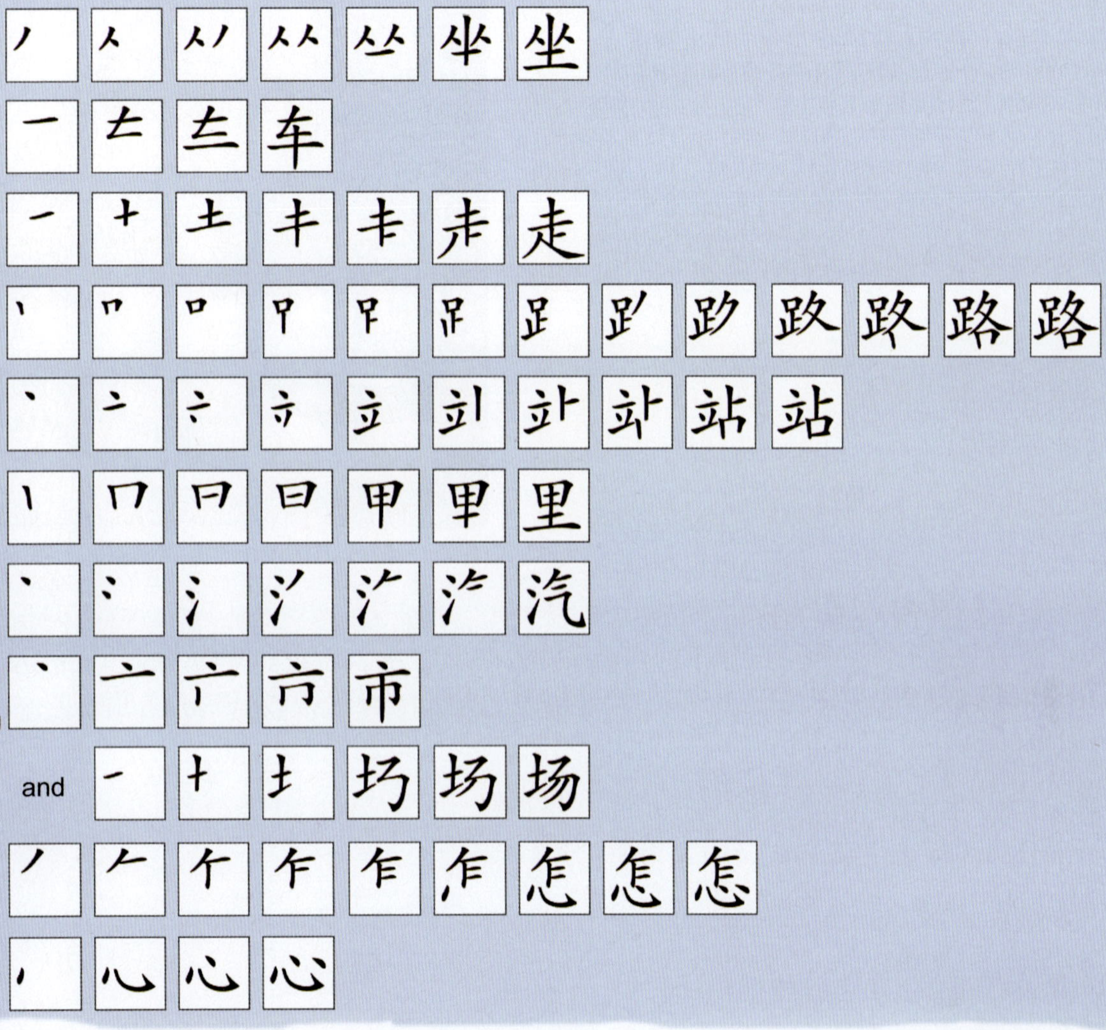

2.18 Reading activity — Commuting

Read about how each person normally goes to work or school and answer the questions in your notebook.

我是医生，天天都去医院工作。我坐火车去医院。
(zuò zuò chē)

我是学生。我跟我朋友一起走路去学校。我们九点钟上学。
(lù xiào)

我是作家。我在图书馆里工作。我坐地铁去市中心工作。
(lǐ zuò dìtiě xīn)

我是服务员，在饭馆工作。我坐公共汽车去工作。车站在饭馆对面。
(fúwùyuán zuò gòng qìchē Chēzhàn)

1) How does the doctor get to work?
2) How does the student get to school? Who goes with him? What time does school start?
3) Who works in the restaurant? How does he get to work?
4) Where does the writer work? How does she get to the city centre?

Language in action — Taxis

Communicating with taxi drivers is an important survival skill! In general, taking taxis is easy: a taxi that is available for hire has a lighted sign 空车 (kōng chē, 'empty car') in the front window, so it's very clear which taxis you can flag. When you get in, the taxi driver will pull down the sign to start the meter.

到哪儿？ Dào	Where do you want to go?
到火车站。 Dào chēzhàn	To the station.
在这儿下车。 chē	Please let me out here. / You can get out here.

2.19 Sketch — Taking a taxi

In pairs, create a sketch in which one of you is a taxi driver and the other needs a lift to work. Prompts are given below, but feel free to chat about other things during the ride! Chinese taxi drivers are very friendly.

The driver should:

- Ask where the passenger is going. (到哪儿？) Dào
- Ask what the passenger does for work. (你做什么工作？)
- (At the end of the ride) tell the passenger when to get out. (你在这儿下车!) chē

The passenger should:

- Say how he/she normally goes to work. (我天天都……去工作 。)
- Say that today he/she is unable to use that mode of transport (我今天不能……)
- (At the end of the ride) ask what the taxi fare is (多少钱？) qián

哥哥：上午好！
今天我跟我朋友一起
去豫园玩。我在路口
Yù lù
上车，在银行下车。
chē yínháng chē
我五点回家。
妹妹

2.20 Reading activity — A note from your sister

Your sister has gone out and left you a note (see left). Read it, then complete the multiple choice questions below.

1) Your sister has written the note...
   in the morning / in the afternoon / in the evening
2) She is going to meet her friend at the...
   park / zoo / Yuyuan Garden / Great Wall
3) They will...
   perform / play computer games / have dinner / have fun
4) She will get on the bus at...
   the intersection / school / the bank / opposite the bank
5) At five o'clock she will...
   get off the bus / arrive at her friend's house / return home / have dinner

2.21 Writing activity — A note for your sister

Before your sister returns home, you go out to the shops. In your notebook, write out the note below that lets her know where you are. Replace the pinyin with characters.

妹妹：

我 [qù] 商(shāng) [diàn] 买 [mǐfàn hé niúròu] 了。我 [zǒu lù qù]。商(Shāng) [diàn] 在 [fànguǎn de hòubian]。今 [tiān] 豫(Yù)园 [hǎo wánr ma]？我 [liù diǎn zhōng] 回 [jiā]。

哥哥

2.22 Writing activity — A big journey

Plan a journey from one place to another, listing the steps you need to take to get there. Make the journey as complicated as you can for extra practice. You can also mention what time each part of the journey happens. Use the model to the right to help you.

我在 (place)。我想去 (place)。

我 (mode of transport) 去 (1st stop)。

我 (mode of transport) 去 (2nd stop)。

我在 (station name) 上车(chē)。

我在 (station name) 下车(chē)。

Character focus

Here are three important characters you may see in public places. In your notebook, make a column for each and then list (in English) examples of places that use each character; this should help you get a sense of each character's meaning.

店 (diàn) ...is used for types of shops

场 (chǎng) ...is used for open spaces

馆 (guǎn) ...is used for special buildings

商场 mall

市场 market

饭馆 restaurant

飞机场 airport

剧场 theatre

博物馆 museum

理发店 hairdresser

大使馆 embassy

书店 bookshop

花店 florist

图书馆 library

茶馆 tea house

咖啡店 coffee shop

药店 pharmacy

广场 square

便利店 convenience shop

停车场 car park

体育馆 gym

运动场 stadium

服装店 clothes shop

Putting it together

2.23 Pair activity — Sightseeing in Shanghai

You and your classmates are on an exchange in Shanghai and have just returned from a fun day out sightseeing. You've all done different things – now compare notes! Work in pairs or small groups and use the following ideas to help you get started.

Talk about:

- Where you went (你去哪儿了？)
  我去(外滩/豫园/南京东路)了。
  Yù Nán Dōnglù
- What time you went to each place (你几点去？)
  我(九点)去。
- How you got there (你怎么去？)
  zěn
  我(坐地铁/走路/骑自行车)去。
  zuò dìtiě lù qí zìxíngchē
- Who went with you? (你跟谁一起去？)
  我跟(我朋友/老师/我的中国妈妈)去。
- What you did (你做了什么活动？)
  我(打网球/做运动/拍照片)。

Imagine you are on holiday in Shanghai with your family. Write a postcard home to your Chinese teacher about what you have been doing. You can use the following prompts to help you, but of course you can add more and make it your own!

老师好！我在上海！我 [month] 月 [date] 日来到了上海，[month] 月 [date] 日要回英国。

我跟 [person] 一起来上海。我看了 [place 1] 和 [place 2]。我们 [means of transport] 去。我吃了 [food 1] 和 [food 2]。我喝了 [drink]。我在这儿 [activity]。很有意思！
si

上海很好玩！

再见！

2.24 Reading activity — Taxi

After reviewing the taxi language on page 43, read the following dialogue between a taxi driver and his passenger and answer the questions in English in your notebook.

A: 你好！到哪儿？
Dào

B: 到'披萨大王'。
Dào Pīsà Wáng

A: 那是不是饭馆？

B: 是。在南京东路。我在那儿工作。
Nán Dōnglù

A: '披萨大王'，我知道。那是不是美国公司？
Pīsà Wáng zhīdao sī

B: 是。美国有很多'披萨大王'，英国也有。
Pīsà Wáng

A: 中国也有！这儿的'披萨大王'很多，也很贵。
Pīsà Wáng

B: 在英国，'披萨大王'不贵。
Pīsà Wáng

A: 好，饭馆在这儿，在银行的后边。
yínháng hòubian
可以下车了！十八块。
chē kuài

B: 好，谢谢！
xièxie

1) Why is the passenger going to Pizza King?
2) Where is Pizza King found around the world?
3) What does the driver say about Pizza King in China?
4) Where is this particular Pizza King?
5) How much is the taxi fare?

Around Shanghai

Shanghai is China's largest and most international city. It has a population of over 24 million people – that's more than the population of Australia! Getting oriented in such a large city can seem daunting, but it is not hard to get around when you know a few basics.

Shanghai sits on the Huángpǔ River 黄浦江 (Huángpǔ Jiāng), which runs south-north and feeds into the enormous estuary of China's longest river, the Yangtze 长江 (Chángjiāng). The western shore of the Huangpu is the older part of the city and is called 浦西 (pǔ xī), meaning 'west of the Huangpu'. The eastern shore is the newer part of Shanghai and is called 浦东 (pǔ dōng), meaning 'east of the Huangpu'.

Although Shanghai measures over 30 miles across, all of its main attractions are conveniently located close together. Some main sights to know are:

People's Park and People's Square 人民公园，人民广场

These two large areas are right next to each other and make up the heart of central Shanghai. Here you can relax in the park away from the noise of the city, and you can also see the Shanghai Museum with its incredible collection of ancient Chinese art.

Nanjing Road East 南京东路

Linking People's Park with the river, Nanjing Road East is Shanghai's busiest shopping street. There are many enormous department stores and places to eat and drink. It is usually bustling with activity.

The Bund 外滩

The waterfront on the west bank of the Huangpu River is called 'the Bund'. It is home to some impressive buildings that show off Shanghai's international history. It is a popular place to go for a walk and admire Shanghai's city scenery.

Yuyuan Garden 豫园

Yuyuan is a famous garden and old shopping area in Shanghai. It is known for its Soup Dumplings 小笼包 (xiǎolóngbāo) and its bendy bridge with 9 corners. As a traditional Chinese garden, it combines water, rocks, walls and plants in a beautiful way.

Lujiazui 陆家嘴

Across the river from the Bund is Lujiazui, which is Shanghai's main business district. This area is home to Shanghai's most famous skyscrapers, including the Oriental Pearl Tower 东方明珠塔 (dōngfāng míngzhū tǎ), the Jin Mao building and the Shanghai World Financial Center.

Cultural activity: Jiànzi 毽子

Kicking the 毽子 (jiànzi) is an ancient Chinese game in which players kick a shuttlecock in the air, trying to keep it from touching the ground.

The shuttlecock was traditionally made using four feathers attached to a few Chinese coins. You can easily make your own using some metal washers, feathers, some string and some tape.

Reading Challenge

你最爱的地方是哪儿？

Luc Martin
我最喜欢的地方是我家。我在家觉得很舒服。我每天回家看电视，跟爸爸一起吃晚饭，聊天。我家不大，也不漂亮，可是有花园。花园里有很多花。

Mohammed Ahmed
我最喜欢的地方是咖啡馆。我很喜欢看书，上网，也喜欢喝咖啡！我是埃及人，我们的咖啡没有牛奶，也没有糖。我们的咖啡杯很小。

Rosie James
我最喜欢的地方是电影院，因为我喜欢看电影。我最喜欢的电影是《Toy Story》的三部电影。我最喜欢的演员是Tom Hanks。他很聪明，也很有意思。

李光
我住在首尔。我最喜欢的地方是商场。首尔的商场很大，很漂亮。星期六我去商场买东西。我喜欢买衣服和书。买东西以后，我回家休息。

山本光子
我最喜欢的地方是森林。我在森林跑步，看花。城市里有很多车，很多人。我喜欢安静的地方。日本有很多森林，也有很多山。

高萍萍
我最喜欢的地方是动物园。我最喜欢的动物是猴子，因为我属猴。动物园也有很多鱼。我最喜欢红色的鱼。我不喜欢鲨鱼，鲨鱼太可怕了。

丁一文
我最喜欢的地方是运动场。我很爱运动。网球、篮球、羽毛球，我都爱玩。我也喜欢看运动比赛。我跟我妹妹一起打篮球。她打得很好。

Find the person who...

1) Likes walking in nature.
2) Loves to watch sports.
3) Likes shopping.
4) Likes drinking coffee.
5) Is interested in animals.

Writing

Write about your favourite place in Chinese in at least 50 characters. Make sure you mention the activity you do there, and why you like being there.

Glossary

部	bù	= measure word for films
安静	ānjìng	= quiet
埃及人	Āijí rén	= Egyptian person
糖	táng	= sugar
首尔	Shǒu'ěr	= Seoul
猴子	hóuzi	= monkey
属	shǔ	= be born in the year of
鲨鱼	shāyú	= shark
可怕	kěpà	= scary

我会

Now you can...

...describe where places are located.

你知道不知道工厂在哪儿？	Nǐ zhīdào bù zhīdào gōngchǎng zài nǎr?	Do you know where the factory is?
请问，银行在哪儿？	Qǐngwèn, yínháng zài nǎr?	Please may I ask where is the bank?
银行在超市后边。	Yínháng zài chāoshì hòubian.	The bank is behind the supermarket.

...say where you do things and how you get there.

爸爸在商店工作。	Bàba zài shāngdiàn gōngzuò.	Dad works at a shop.
老师骑自行车。	Lǎoshī qí zìxíngchē.	The teacher rides a bicycle.
你怎么去？	Nǐ zěnme qù?	How do you go there?
我坐火车去北京。	Wǒ zuò huǒchē qù Běijīng.	I take the train to Beijing.
你坐公共汽车去。	Nǐ zuò gōnggòng qìchē qù.	You take the bus to go there.
你在哪儿上车？	Nǐ zài nǎr shàng chē?	Where do you get on? (Used for buses and trains.)
在学校上车。	Zài xuéxiào shàng chē.	Get on at the school.

...arrange a time and place to meet.

几点见？	Jǐ diǎn jiàn?	What time shall we meet?
我们十点在饭店见！	Wǒmen shí diǎn zài fàndiàn jiàn!	We'll meet at 10 o'clock at the hotel.
走吧！	Zǒu ba!	Let's go!

...say if there are many or few of something.

上海有很多商店。	Shànghǎi yǒu hěn duō shāngdiàn.	Shanghai has a lot of shops.
上海的商店很多。	Shànghǎi de shāngdiàn hěn duō.	Shops in Shanghai are many.
这里的人不多。	Zhèlǐ de rén bù duō.	There are not many people here.

...write the following characters:

请 问 前 后 左 右 边 对 店 馆 坐 走 路 站
里 汽 车 市 场 怎

我家 My Family

Objectives

In this unit, you will learn…

…how to introduce yourself and others.
…how to talk about family and pets.
…how to say what jobs people do.
…about Chinese family structures.

Section 1: Meet the family

Vocab

老公	lǎogōng	husband (informal)
老婆	lǎopó	wife (informal)
父母	fùmǔ	parents
爷爷	yéye	paternal grandfather
奶奶	nǎinai	paternal grandmother
阿姨	āyí	'aunt' (see note on page 55)
叔叔	shūshu	'uncle' (see note on page 55)
女士	nǚshì	Ms
鸟	niǎo	bird
鱼	yú	fish

Use what you know!

You already know how to say the following words:

先生	Mr; husband (formal)
太太	Mrs; wife (formal)

父母 (fùmǔ)

父母 means the same as 爸爸妈妈 but is more formal. 父 (fù) is short for 父亲(fùqīn, 'father') and 母 (mǔ) is short for 母亲(mǔqīn, 'mother').

爷爷 (yéye) and 奶奶 (nǎinai)

爷爷 (yéye) and 奶奶 (nǎinai) refer to your father's parents. To say your mother's parents, use 外公 (wàigōng) and 外婆 (wàipó).

太太 (tàitai)

太太 (tàitai) is similar to 'Mrs' and is mostly used for older or married women. 女士 (nǚshì) can be used more generally and is similar to 'Ms'. The word order is Surname + Title, for example: 'Ms Bai' is 白女士 (Bái nǚshì), and 'Mr Wang' is 王先生 (Wáng xiānsheng).

In China, women do not usually change their surnames when they get married. So, if Mr Wáng Hǎi marries Ms Lǐ Hóng, she will still be Lǐ Hóng. However, she could also be called 王太太 (Mrs Wang), even though her name does not officially change.

3.1 Listening activity — Family

Listen to the recording; in your notebook, number each picture according to the introduction you hear.

Fish

Aunty

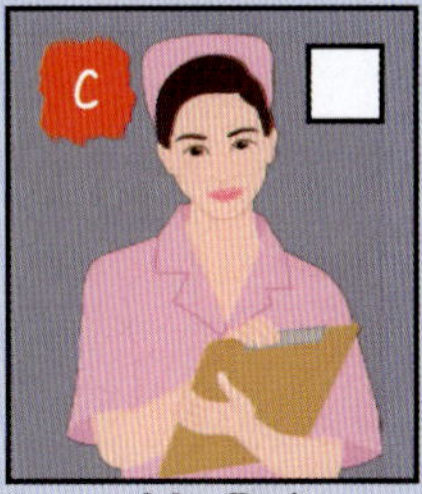

Ms Bai

Grandad

Parents

Husband

Bird

Mr Chen

Mrs Wang

Uncle

Grandmother

3.2 Pair activity — Who is that?

Chen Hong's family tree is given below. Working with a partner, point to members of the family and ask who each person is. Give as many alternative answers as possible to describe each person's place in the family.

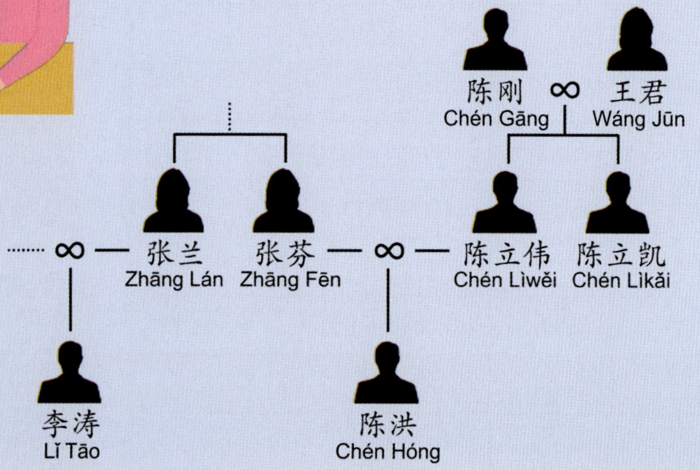

Unit 3 | 第三单元

Vocab

介绍	jièshào	to introduce; talk about
自己	zìjǐ	oneself; myself; yourself
生日	shēngrì	birthday
年	nián	year
宠物	chǒngwù	pet
张	zhāng	measure word for 'flat' things
条	tiáo	measure word for 'strips' of things
它	tā	it
常常	chángcháng	often

In Chinese, dates are given in this format: year-month-day. For example, 14th August 2017 would be

2017年8月14日
nián

The word 它 (tā) is not used as often in Chinese as the English equivalent, 'it'. In most cases, 'it' is simply dropped. For example:

很大。	It is very big.
我喜欢。	I like it.
你买了吗？	Did you buy it?

You usually use 它 (tā) when you need to state 'it' as the subject of a verb. For example:

它想去外边。 Tā	(said of a dog) It wants to go out.
它在中国东部。 Tā bù	(said of a city) It is in eastern China.

3.3 Listening activity — Short introductions

Listen to the recording and match the people with their birthdays. Write the answers in your notebook.

一	二	三	四	五	六
陈洪 Chén Hóng	小红 Hóng	Tanya	Jason	小梅 Méi	张明 Zhāng

A 2000年8月19日

B 2006年5月23日

C 2005年7月12日

D 2003年8月5日

E 1996年4月28日

F 2005年12月7日

3.4 Class challenge — Birthdays

As a class, arrange yourselves standing in a line in age order. Use the following dialogue to help you work out each person's birth date. See if you can complete the task in under a minute!

3.5 Listening activity — Do you have any pets?

Create a table similar to the one below. Then listen to the recording and complete the table according to what you hear.

Type of pet	How many	Comment
1)		
2)		
3)		

3.6 Class survey — Pets

Go around surveying your classmates about what pets they have. Take care to use the right measure words!

About the language: Measure words and frequency words

More about measure words

When counting things in Chinese, you need measure words. So far you have learnt four: 个 for counting people and things in general, 口 (kǒu) for counting people in a family, 本 (běn) for counting books and 只 (zhī) for counting animals like cats and dogs. Many other objects also take their own special measure words. This unit introduces 张 (zhāng) for flat things, such as 照片 (zhàopiàn)， 纸 (zhǐ) and 桌子 (zhuōzi), and 条 (tiáo) for 'strips' of things, such as 鱼 (yú).

At the back of this book there is a list of all the nouns you have met, accompanied by their measure words. Don't worry about learning them all now; just refer to this list when you need to. If in doubt, use 个 as the measure word and you will be understood.

Frequency

As we saw with 天天, when you want to say how often you do something, you say the frequency word before the verb.
For example:

我天天都上网。	I + every day + go online.
他常常听音乐。 chángcháng	He + often + listens to music.

You will learn other words for frequency later in this book.

A Chinese abacus

Unit 3 | 第三单元

In China, many old people like to keep pet birds. They often take them out in the street to show off and listen to the birds singing with their friends.

3.7 Writing activity — Pet survey

Chen Hong did a class survey of pets; here are the results.

In your notebook, summarise the number of people who have each type of animal. The measure word for each animal is 只 (zhī) except for fish, which uses 条 (tiáo).

Write in characters whenever you can; otherwise use pinyin.

For example:

- 三个人有一只猫。 (zhī māo) (3 people have a cat.)
- 没有人有兔子。 (tù) (No one has a rabbit.)

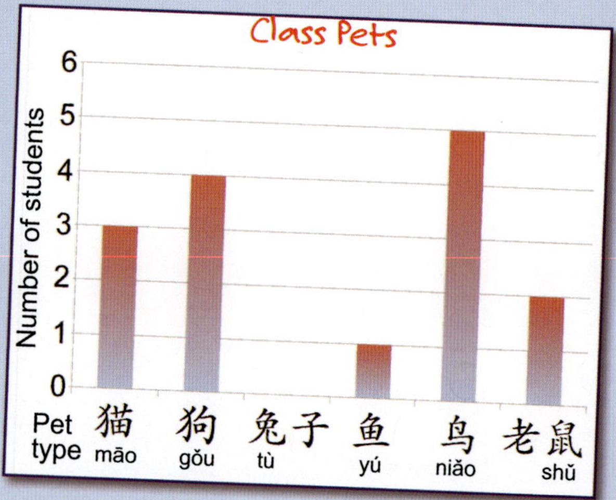

Writing Characters

只	zhī
叫	jiào
姓	xìng
名字	míng zi
知道	zhī dào
还	hái
先生	xiān sheng
年	nián

Frog counting song

Here is a Chinese song that uses different measure words. See how long you can count frogs without making a mistake!

一只蛤蟆一张嘴	zhī háma zhāng zuǐ	One frog, one mouth
两只眼睛四条腿	zhī yǎnjing tiáo tuǐ	Two eyes, four legs
乒乒乓乓跳下水呀	ya	Plip plop, it jumps into the water
蛤蟆不吃水，太平年	Háma píngnián	The frogs don't drink, it is a prosperous year.
两只蛤蟆两张嘴	zhī háma zhāng zuǐ	Two frogs, two mouths
四只眼睛八条腿	zhī yǎnjing tuǐ	Four eyes, eight legs
乒乒乓乓跳下水呀	ya	Plip plop, they jump into the water
蛤蟆不吃水，太平年	Háma píngnián	The frogs don't drink, it is a prosperous year.
三只蛤蟆三张嘴	zhī háma zhāng zuǐ	Three frogs, three mouths
六只眼睛……	zhī yǎnjing	Six eyes, etc...

A frog shadow puppet

3.8 Reading activity — Introducing yourself

Read the following four profiles. In your notebook, mark each statement below as true or false.

一

你好！我姓 Tanaka (田中)，
Tián
叫 Yuki (雪)。我是医生。我
Xuě
的生日是一九七七年四月九
nián
日。我跟我老公一起住在日
本。我们有两只猫。
zhī māo

二

你好，我姓 Raymond，名字叫
Chris。我是美国人。我的生日是
二零零四年十一月一日。我跟
líng líng nián
我的父母一起住在纽约。我有
fùmǔ
弟弟和妹妹。我家有四条鱼。
tiáo yú

三

你好！我姓王，叫王宾。
Wáng Wáng Bīn
我是中国人。爷爷奶奶、
Yéye
我父母和我一起住在上
fùmǔ
海。我没有宠物。我喜
chǒng
欢去动物园看鸟。我常常
niǎo chángcháng
跟我叔叔一起去那里。
shūshu

四

你好，我的名字是 Audrey。
我是法国人。我的生日是一
九五六年二月三日。我住在
nián
巴黎的市中心。我有一只兔
lí zhī tù
子。它喜欢吃菜。
Tā cài

	✔ 正	✘ 误
1) Yuki has one cat.	○	○
2) Yuki was born in 1977.	○	○
3) Chris lives with his grandparents.	○	○
4) Chris has no siblings.	○	○
5) Chris has four fish.	○	○
6) Wang Bin lives with his uncle.	○	○
7) Wang Bin has a bird.	○	○
8) Wang Bin often goes to the park.	○	○
9) Audrey was born in 1968.	○	○
10) Her rabbit likes to eat vegetables.	○	○

Forms of address

For talking to people a generation older than you, say Shūshu 叔叔 (Uncle) for men and say Āyí 阿姨 (Aunty) for women. This doesn't mean you consider them your family; it is just a polite and friendly way to address them. Similarly, you can address elderly men as Yéye 爷爷 (Grandad) and women as Nǎinai 奶奶 (Granny).

3.9 Pair activity — Family photos

Show a classmate photos of a family (yours or another family of your choice -- even one from your favourite TV programme) and talk about each person. You can include:

- Each person's relationship (这是我的……)
- Their names (他姓……, 他的名字是……)
- Whether they have pets (他有……)
- Their birthdays (他的生日是……)
- Their hobbies (他的爱好是……)

3.10 Reading activity — An email from your pen-pal

Your Chinese pen-pal wrote an email introducing his family, but he forgot to attach the photo! Read the email and sketch (and label) a picture of his family based on his description.

你好！

这是一张照片。是我家人。照片有我、我的父母、我的阿姨，还有我的爷爷
zhāng fùmǔ āyí yéye

奶奶。我在左边。阿姨和妈妈在右边。她们跟小狗一起玩儿。爸爸在她们后
Āyí gǒu

边。爷爷奶奶在爸爸左边。我还有哥哥和叔叔，他们不在照片上。
Yéye shūshu

我也想看你家人。你有照片吗？

陈洪 2016年09月16日
Chén Hóng nián

3.11 Writing activity — Your response

Write an email to Chen Hong introducing your family. Copy the note below, fill in the missing characters and then complete the email with your own sentences. Give as many details about your family members as you can.

__ __ !
Nǐ hǎo!

__ __ __ ， __ __ __ __ __ __ 照片， __ __ __ __ __ __ __ 。
Duì bù qǐ wǒ bù néng kàn nǐ de zhàopiàn wǒ hěn xiǎng kàn nǐ jiārén

我来介绍 __ __ __ 。
jièshào wǒ de jiā

请 __ __ __ __ __ 照片。照片上有……
nǐ kàn wǒ jiā de zhàopiàn Zhàopiàn

3.12 Writing activity – Kittens for sale!

Your pet just gave birth! Copy and complete this advert about the baby animals so you can find them homes.

我有 [number] [measure word] 小 [animal] 。它们的名字是 [name] 。它们喜欢吃 [food] ，喜欢喝 [drink] 。它们不贵，一 [measure word] [animal] / [number] 元。

喜欢吗？请打电话：13030031091

(Tā written above 它)

Study skills – Stroke order and direction

There are several benefits to mastering the correct stroke order and direction when writing characters. Firstly, your handwriting will improve; secondly, you will be able to read Chinese people's handwriting more easily; and thirdly, if you write each character in the same way every time, you will develop 'muscle memory' – that is, you won't have to think while you are writing, and the character will come out correct on its own. This makes character memorisation a lot easier!

Here are three tricky characters for stroke order – see if you write them correctly.

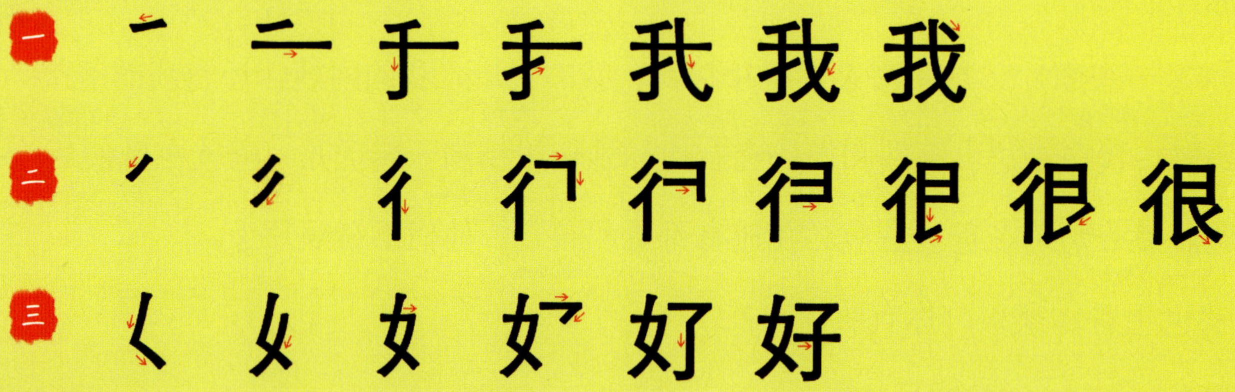

Section 2: Professions

Vocab

演员	yǎnyuán	actor, actress
画家	huàjiā	painter
运动员	yùndòngyuán	athlete
商人	shāngrén	businessperson
护士	hùshi	nurse
工程师	gōngchéngshī	engineer
经理	jīnglǐ	manager

Don't forget!

Don't forget the profession words you've already learnt! Can you still remember these words?

老师　工人　服务员

医生　作家　学生

Language note

You have learnt the character 家 to mean 'home' (and, you may have noticed, as a measure word for some places around town), but it has another meaning: 'expert' or 'specialist'. So 画家 literally means 'expert in painting' and 作家 means 'expert in making (writing)'. Following this pattern, can you guess what the Chinese words for 'musician', 'banker', 'scholar' and 'artist' are?

3.13 Listening activity – What work do they do?

In your notebook, write the numbers 1-7. Then listen to the recording and match the person with his or her profession.

A

B

C

D

E

F

G

3.14 Pair activity – What work does he do?

With a partner, practise these two short dialogues; use the prompts below.

一

二

三

四

五

3.14 Pair activity — Continued from page 58

Vincent Van Gogh

Chanel

Liú Xiáng

Beyoncé

Vocab

将来	jiānglái	future
当	dāng	to do (a job)
得	de	(particle indicating degree)
非常	fēicháng	very; extremely
有一点儿	yǒu yìdiǎnr	a little bit
不太	bú tài	not so
好听	hǎotīng	good to listen to
好看	hǎokàn	pretty; good-looking

Language note

You can use 将来 (jiānglái) to talk about the future. It must always come before the verb or at the beginning of a sentence. For example, 我将来要去上海 means 'I will go to Shanghai in the future.'

3.15 Listening activity — What do you want to be?

Four people tell us what they want to be and why. Listen and write down (in English) the reasons they give for each profession. Write the answers in your notebook.

She wants to be an actress because...

He wants to be an athlete because...

He wants to be an artist because...

She wants to be an English teacher because...

3.16 Group activity — What do you want to be?

Working in groups or as a class, find out what your classmates want to be and why. Make two columns, one for the jobs and one for the reasons. Which jobs are most popular?

Job	Reason

3.17 Listening activity — How well can you...?

Listen to people describing how well they do certain things and note their answers in your notebook.

	非常好 fēicháng	还好	不太好
1)	○	○	○
2)	○	○	○
3)	○	○	○
4)	○	○	○
5)	○	○	○
6)	○	○	○
7)	○	○	○
8)	○	○	○

3.18 Pair activity — How well can you...?

In pairs, discuss how well you can do each of the following. Use 非常好， 还好 and 不太好.

1) 我打羽毛球打得……
de
2) 我唱歌唱得……
de
3) 我跳舞跳得……
de
4) 我打乒乓球打得……
de
5) 我说英文说得……
de
6) 我游泳游得……
de
7) 我骑自行车骑得……
de
8) 我画画得……
de

Unit 3 | 第三单元

About the language: Complement of degree and substitutes for 很

Complement of degree

Chinese has grammar structures called 'verbal complements' that tell you more information about the action taking place. The most important one is called the 'complement of degree'; it tells you how something is done (for example, slowly, quickly, well or badly).

她说得(de)很好。 She speaks well. 他说得(de)不好。 He speaks badly.

The word order is:

Subject + Verb + 得 + Adverb

In this structure, the verb must go directly before 得. But what happens if there is an object in the sentence? (For example, 他说中文 'He speaks Chinese'.) When there is an object, the verb must be repeated. For example:

她说英文说得(de)很好。 She speaks English well. 他说中文说得(de)不好。 He speaks Chinese badly.

Dropping the first verb

The first verb can often be left out, so we have an alternative:

她英文说得(de)很好。 She speaks English well. 他中文说得(de)不好。 He speaks Chinese badly.

The word order is:

Subject + Object + Verb + 得 + Adverb

When the first verb is omitted, it makes it look like the order of the verb and object has been swapped around, since now the object is first. For example:

吃饭吃 becomes 饭吃 ➔ 爸爸饭吃得(de)很快(kuài)。 / 唱歌唱 becomes 歌唱 ➔ 姐姐歌唱得很好听。

看书看 becomes 书看 ➔ 妹妹书看得(de)很多。 / 跳舞跳 becomes 舞跳 ➔ 我的朋友舞跳得(de)很好看。

Substitutes for 很

A good way to express yourself in Chinese is to replace 很 with another word. We have learnt three possibilities this chapter:

这本书很贵。 This book is expensive. / 这本书非常(fēicháng)贵。 This book is extremely expensive.

这本书有一点贵。 This book is a bit expensive. / 这本书不太贵。 This book is not too expensive.

As you saw in the pair activity 'How well can you...?' opposite, you can also combine these words with the complement of degree to more accurately describe how well someone does something:

他歌唱得非常(fēicháng)好。 He sings extremely well. / 我中文说得(de)不太好。 I don't speak Chinese that well.

Writing Characters

非常 fēi cháng — 非 and 常

不太好 — 太

当 dāng — 当

商人 shāng rén — 商

画家 huà jiā — 画

运动员 yùn dòng yuán — 员

得 de — 得

鱼 yú — 鱼

鸟 niǎo — 鸟

条 tiáo — 条

With the new characters, you can also now write:

常常	chángcháng	often
商店	shāngdiàn	shop
画家	huàjiā	artist
太太	tàitai	wife, Mrs
面条	miàntiáo	noodles

3.19 Writing activity — practice with 得

A: Copy and complete the sentences by replacing the English with the appropriate Chinese characters:

1) 他 [eats food] 得(de)很多。

2) 她 [plays tennis] 得(de)很好。

3) 她 [plays games] 得(de)不太好 。

B: Translate the following into Chinese. Use characters wherever you can:

1) She runs well.
2) He sings extremely well.
3) English class is extremely interesting.
4) The horse is a bit big.
5) The teacher is not too busy.

3.20 Reading activity – Pingping's family

Read the text about Pingping's family and complete the statements below, writing the answers in your notebook.

这是我爸爸。他是商人。他在公
司工作。他天天都坐地铁去公
司。我的学校在他公司的对面。
我常常跟他一起坐地铁去学校。
chángcháng

这是我奶奶。奶奶跟我和爸爸
一起住。她有一只鸟。她是画
zhī niǎo
家，画画得非常好。我常常看
de fēicháng chángcháng
她画画。我将来也想当画家。
jiāng dāng

这是我叔叔，他是我爸爸的弟弟。他
shūshu
的名字是张建，他非常有意思。他有
Zhāng Jiàn fēicháng si
很多爱好。他会打网球、游泳，还会
唱歌。他是音乐家，歌唱得很好听。
de
因为他住在美国，我不常去看他。
cháng

1) Pingping lives with...
2) Her father is a...
3) Pingping often goes to school by way of...
4) Pingping's grandmother has a...
5) In the future, Pingping would like to work as...
6) Zhang Jian is Pingping's...
7) Zhang Jian is a...
8) Pingping doesn't often see Zhang Jian because...

Language in action – Compliments

Modesty is important in Chinese culture, especially when receiving praise. In English, we might respond to a compliment by saying 'thank you', but in Chinese culture this could seem impolite. It is more common to deny the compliment and either to put oneself down or praise the other person more highly. Here are a couple of examples:

A: 你中文说得很好！ de	You speak Chinese well!
B: 不是！我的中文很不好。	No I don't! My Chinese is very bad.
A: 你篮球打得很好。 lán de	You play basketball well.
B: 不好，不好。你打得非常好。 de fēicháng	(It's) very bad. You play extremely well.

In the past, the normal response to a compliment was '哪里，哪里' but this has become old-fashioned. Now people say 没有 or 不是.

3.21 Sketch — I'm not that great!

In pairs, act as new acquaintences and create a sketch in which one person compliments the other.

Comment on the other person's...

...bag. （你的包很好看。）

...Chinese. （你说中文说得很好。）
de

...basketball ability. （你篮球打得很好。）
de

...car. （你的车很大、很贵。）

...singing. （你歌唱得很好听。）
de

...dancing. （你舞跳得很好看。）
de

Character focus — Dots

If you look closely, you'll see that the dots in a character sometimes go to the left and sometimes to the right.

This is a detail that is worth paying attention to in order to make your handwriting look beautiful. Here are some examples:

常
The dots at the top all point into the middle

学
The dots at the top go right, right, left

鸟
The top dot goes left, the middle dot goes right

点
The first dot goes left and the others go right

字
The top dot goes right

Putting it together

3.22 Reading activity — Eva Huang

This is an article about a famous Shanghai filmstar. Read it and answer the questions in your notebook.

这是黄圣依(Huáng Shèngyī)。英文名字是 Eva Huang。她是上海的女演员。她的生日是1983年(nián)2月11日。她父母(fùmǔ)都住在上海，爸爸是大学老师，妈妈在报社(shè)工作。

1998-2001年(nián)，黄圣依(Huáng Shèngyī)在北京电影学院(xuéyuàn)上学。2004年(nián)，周星驰(Zhōu Chí)要拍(pāi)电影。这部(bù)电影叫《功夫》(Gōngfu)。黄圣依(Huáng Shèngyī)是《功夫》(Gōngfu)的演员。很多人喜欢《功夫》(Gōngfu)，也喜欢黄圣依(Huáng Shèngyī)。黄圣依(Huáng Shèngyī)有很多工作。她是电影演员，也是电视演员，还会唱歌。她常常(cháng cháng)开(kāi)演唱会。她有自己(jǐ)的音乐公司。

黄圣依(Huáng Shèngyī)喜欢游泳和跑步。她喜欢吃巧克力(qiǎokè lì)，喝奶茶。

Glossary

学院	xuéyuàn	= college
部	bù	= measure word for films
功夫	gōngfu	= Kung Fu
开演唱会	kāi yǎnchàng huì	= to hold concerts
巧克力	qiǎokèlì	= chocolate
报社	bàoshè	= newspaper office

1) What does Huang Shengyi's father do?
2) In addition to being a film star, what does Huang Shengyi do professionally?
3) What are Huang Shengyi's hobbies?
4) What does she like to eat?

3.23 Writing activity — Interview

Imagine you are Eva Huang and you have accepted a request for an interview. Using the information in the article above, write a transcript of the interview, including the reporter's questions and your responses. Here are some sample questions to get you started.

你叫什么？

你是哪里人？

你爸爸做什么工作？

你的生日是几月几日？

你在哪儿上学？

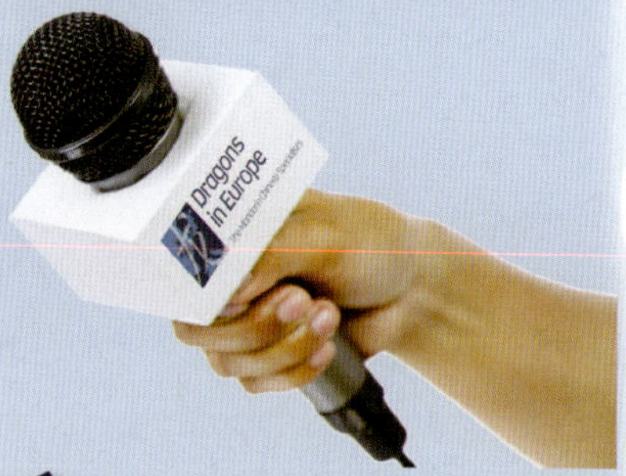

3.24 Writing activity — Short biography

Write a simple biography of a famous person. He or she can be from any country and be dead or alive, as long as you have enough information. Include:

Name (他姓……，名字是……)

Birthday (他的生日是……)

Residence* (他住在……)

Don't forget to put the country before the city!

Family (他家有……)

Nationality (他是……人)

(他当……)
dāng

Pets (他喜欢宠物，有……)
chǒng

3.25 Speaking activity — What job might suit?

Below are profiles of six young students. With a partner, discuss what profession might be most suitable for each person and why. If you don't know how to say the profession, you can say the workplace instead.

For example:

他将来可以在图书馆工作。/ 他将来可以当医生，因为他喜欢科学。
jiāng jiāng dāng kē

When you have finished, compare your ideas with others in the class.

一 我非常喜欢宠物：狗、猫、鱼、鸟、兔子、马。我也喜欢看书。我不喜欢数学课。
fēicháng chǒng gǒu māo yú niǎo tù shù

二 我不太喜欢运动。我会唱歌，也会说法文和英文。我非常喜欢上网。
fēicháng

三 我有一点喜欢运动。我常常跑步。我网球打得不好。
chángcháng de

四 我喜欢打电话、和朋友喝茶。我也喜欢骑自行车。我会跳舞。我不喜欢看电影。

五 我很喜欢科学课和数学课。我也喜欢吃饭！
kē shù

六 我打球打得非常好。网球、篮球、羽毛球，我都打得很好。
de fēicháng de

3.26 Reading activity — A day out with the family

You have just received the following email from your friend Chen Hong:

你好！

今天是我叔叔的生日。我要跟我爸爸妈妈一起去我叔叔家。我们也
Jīn shūshu shēngrì shūshu

要去东方明珠塔玩儿。东方明珠塔很有意思，那里能看上海的风
fāng zhū tǎ fāng zhū tǎ si

景，也能学习上海的历史。上边还有‘太空舱’，那里可以看宇航
jǐng lìshǐ hái kōng cāng yǔháng

员在太空工作！东方明珠塔还有很多商店和饭馆，都很好。
kōng fāng zhū tǎ

你想跟我们一起去吗？

1) What is special about today?
2) What can you see from the Oriental Pearl Tower?
3) What can you learn about there?
4) What can you see in the 'space capsule'?
5) What else is there to do at the Oriental Pearl Tower?

Glossary

东方明珠塔	Dōngfāng Míngzhū Tǎ	= Oriental Pearl Tower
风景	fēngjǐng	= scenery
太空舱	tàikōng cāng	= space capsule
宇航员	yǔhángyuán	= astronaut
太空	tàikōng	= outer space

3.27 Writing activity — Response to Chen Hong

Here is your reply to Chen Hong. Copy the note in your notebook and replace the pinyin with the correct characters to complete the email:

你好 ！

东方明珠塔 __ __ __ __ __ ！ 我 __ __ __ 。你叔叔 __ __ __ __ ？
fāng zhū tǎ fēicháng yǒu yìsi hěn xiǎng qù shūshu jiā zài nǎr

__ __ __ __ __ ？ 我 __ __ __ 怎么走 。__ __ __ ？ 我们 __ __ 在东方明珠塔 __ __ 。
Zài shìzhōngxīn ma bù zhīdào Jǐ diǎn jiàn kěyǐ fāng zhū tǎ chī fàn

__ __ __ __ __ 贵吗？
Nǎlǐ de fànguǎn

再见！

Chinese Weddings

Chinese weddings are typically lavish affairs. They are usually held in a large venue such as a hotel reception room or restaurant and involve a banquet and a ceremony. The venue will often seat hundreds of people who sit at round tables, watching the ceremony which takes place on a stage. The ceremony is conducted by an MC, who could be a friend or family member of the couple. Guests are expected to bring a gift of money for the bride and groom, which is accepted and immediately counted at a table at the entrance to the wedding. There will often be a large number of guests, including important colleagues of the parents, friends and extended family.

The day starts as the groom goes to the bride's house to pick her up. There are various rituals which take place here. For example, the bride's girlfriends will guard the door and will not allow the groom to enter until he has either performed a forfeit or given them some money.

Nowadays the wedding ceremony blends elements of traditional Chinese and Western style weddings. Chinese elements include tying a knot and bowing to the parents. Western aspects could include wedding vows (saying "I do") and a bridal party. The wedding photographs are taken well before the wedding, and feature the couple in a beautiful location. These photos are then shown at the wedding itself. The bride will wear more than one dress at different points during the ceremony, including a white wedding dress and a traditional red Chinese wedding dress.

Wedding banquets involve a lot of fine food, some of which has symbolic meaning. For example, dates, peanuts, longans and lotus seeds all are symbolic. If you say the names of each of these four foods together, it sounds the same as a common goodwill phrase: 早生贵子 – 'have a child soon!'

Reading Challenge

王先生

这是王先生。他37岁。王先生是中国人。他住在日本。虽然他在日本工作，但是他的公司是美国公司，不是日本公司。公司叫东京电脑公司。东京电脑公司的电脑很新，也很快。王先生在那里卖电脑。他很喜欢他的工作。王先生上午8点去公司，下午4点半回家。他12点吃午饭。王先生很喜欢在公司吃饭。王先生的老板叫田中先生。虽然田中先生是日本人，但是他会说日文、中文和英文。田中先生也看英文书和美国电视。他2月14日去英国，2月21日回日本。他去英国看英国的商店。王先生说英国的天气很不好。今天8点王先生和田中先生去中国饭馆。饭馆里很热闹，人很多，所以他们只能在外边吃。

Answer the questions in English

1) Where does Mr Wang live?
2) What company does he work for?
3) How are the products described?
4) What time does Mr Wang start and finish work?
5) Where does Mr Wang like to have lunch?
6) Who is Mr Wang's boss and what ability does he have?
7) What country will the boss go to and when?
8) What does Mr Wang say about that place?
9) Where will they go today and how is it described?
10) What is the problem?

Glossary

公司	gōngsī	= company
老板	lǎobǎn	= boss
热闹	rènao	= lively

Research exercise

Research online to find the top 5 companies in China by size or fame. Had you heard of any of these companies before? What do they specialise in?

我会

Now you can...

...introduce yourself and others.

我姓王，叫王宾。	Wǒ xìng Wáng, jiào Wáng Bīn.	My surname is Wang; my full name is Wang Bin.
我来介绍自己。我叫陈洪。	Wǒ lái jièshào zìjǐ. Wǒ jiào Chén Hóng.	I will introduce myself. I'm called Chen Hong.
这是陈先生。	Zhè shì Chén xiānsheng.	This is Mr Chen.
这是我的父母。	Zhè shì wǒ de fùmǔ.	These are my parents.

...talk about family and pets.

那是谁？	Nà shì shéi?	Who is that?
那是陈刚，是陈洪的爷爷。	Nà shì Chén Gāng, shì Chén Hóng de yéyé.	That is Chen Gang, Chen Hong's grandfather.
你有没有宠物？	Nǐ yǒu méi yǒu chǒngwù?	Do you have any pets?
有，我有一只猫。它叫咪咪。	Yǒu, wǒ yǒuyī zhī māo. Tā jiào Mīmi.	Yes! I have one cat. It's called Mimi.

...describe how often something happens.

我天天都上网。	Wǒ tiāntiān dōu shàngwǎng.	I go online every day.
他常常听音乐。	Tā chángcháng tīng yīnyuè.	He often listens to music.

...say what jobs people do.

她做什么工作？她是经理。	Tā zuò shénme gōngzuò? Tā shì jīnglǐ.	Was does she do for work? She is a manager.
她在哪儿工作？她在工厂工作。	Tā zài nǎr gōngzuò? Tā zài gōngchǎng gōngzuò.	Where does she work? She works in a factory.
你将来想做什么工作？我想当演员。	Nǐ jiānglái xiǎng zuò shénme gōngzuò? Wǒ xiǎng dāng yǎnyuán.	What do you want to do for work in the future? I would like to be an actor.

我会 Now you can...

...describe how someone does an activity.

我打篮球打得非常好。	Wǒ dǎ lánqiú dǎ dé fēicháng hǎo.	I play basketball extremely well.
她英文说得不太好。	Tā Yīngwén shuō dé bú tài hǎo.	She doesn't speak English very well.

...use more adverbs to communicate degrees.

这本书非常贵。	Zhè běn shū fēicháng guì.	This book is extremely expensive.
这本书有一点贵。	Zhè běn shū yǒu yìdiǎn guì.	This book is a bit expensive.
这本书不太贵。	Zhè běn shū bú tài guì.	This book isn't too expensive.

...write the following characters:

只 叫 姓 名 字 知 道 还 先 年 非 常 画 商
得 员 太 鱼 鸟 条 当

欢迎来西安!

Welcome to Xī'ān!

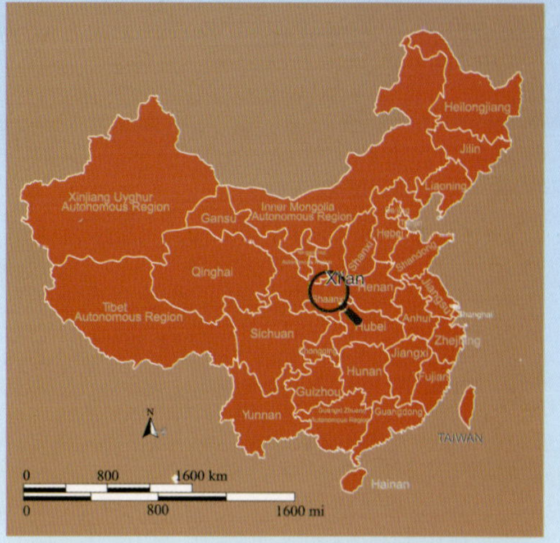

Main languages:
Mandarin, local Shaanxi dialect

Terracotta Army 兵马俑 (Bīngmǎyǒng)

人口 5 500 000

Mutton Stew 羊肉泡馍 (yángròu pào mó)

Forest of Stone Steles Museum 碑林 (Bēilín)

Xi'an was the capital during the Tang dynasty, famous for poetry.

购物 Shopping

Objectives

In this unit, you will learn…

…how to talk about clothes.
…how to communicate in a shop.
…about money and quantities.
…about traditional Chinese clothing.

Section 1: Talking about Clothes

Vocab

衣服	yīfu	clothing
衬衫	chènshān	shirt
毛衣	máoyī	jumper
T恤衫	T-xùshān	T shirt
裙子	qúnzi	skirt/dress
裤子	kùzi	trousers
短裤	duǎnkù	shorts
鞋	xié	shoes
袜子	wàzi	socks
帽子	màozi	hat
件	jiàn	measure word for clothing worn on the top
双	shuāng	measure word meaning 'pair'

4.1 Listening activity — Clothes

Listen to the recording and match the question number with the letter for the article of clothing as you hear it. Write the answers in your notebook.

4.2 Pair activity — Do you sell...?

With a partner, take turns 'entering a shop' and asking if they have what you need. The 商人 should use the prompts below to see what is currently in stock.

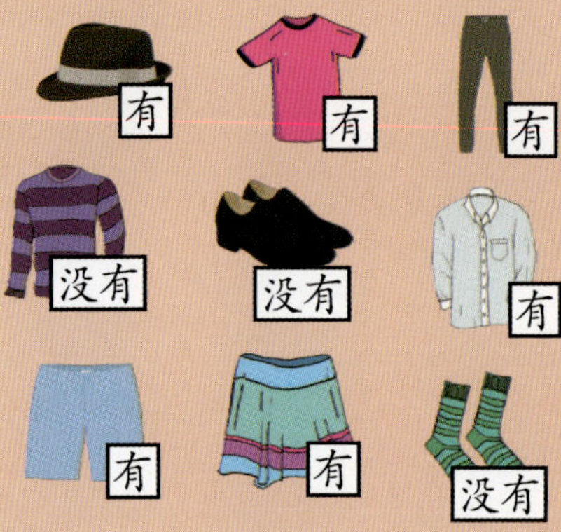

Vocab

穿	chuān	to wear (main articles)
戴	dài	to wear (accessories)
颜色	yánsè	colour
棕色	zōngsè	brown
舒服	shūfu	comfortable
便宜	piányi	cheap
号	hào	size

'Wear'

The word for 'wear' in Chinese changes depending on the type of clothing. 穿 (chuān) literally means 'go through' and is used for most clothes. 戴 (dài) means 'to put on' and is used for accessories such as hats, earrings, glasses, watches and bracelets.

Colours

When referring to the names of colours, you must say the colour name + sè: 红色(hóngsè), 绿色 (lǜsè), 蓝色 (lánsè), etc. The colour name is usually not used alone (i.e., 红, 绿, 蓝) unless accompanied by the noun it describes.

For clothing size, you use the words 小号 (xiǎohào, small), 中号 (zhōnghào, medium), 大号 (dàhào, large).

号 (hào) in dates

Also note that 号 (hào) can be used instead of 日 in dates: 一月九号 is the same as 一月九日.

那么便宜？我也要！

4.3 Listening activity — Which one do you like?

Listen to the recording as people express their preferences. Copy the table below, circle the preference and write (in English) the reason for each.

Preference		Reason given
1) This book	That book	
2) This phone	That phone	
3) Basketball	Badminton	
4) Small trousers	Medium trousers	
5) Brown one	Green one	
6) Beef	Fish	

4.4 Pair activity — Getting your friend's opinion

Imagine you are shopping with a friend. Take turns asking each other's preferences as you browse, giving a choice between "this" and "that". Don't forget to use the correct measure words (indicated)!

一  条 舒服 shū

二  件 jiàn 便宜 piányi

三  双 shuāng 颜色很好 yánsè

四  条 舒服 shū

五  双 shuāng 便宜 piányi

六  件 jiàn 颜色很好 yánsè

Listen to the recording and match the picture letter to the question number in your notebook.

A 

B 

C 

D 

E 

F 

4.6 Pair activity — Things in common

In pairs or small groups, practise the dialogue below to see what you have in common with each other.

Use 都 (dōu) when you find something you've got in common. You can ask about:

1) 看电视
2) 坐火车
3) 放风筝
4) 打太极拳
5) 吃肉
6) 拍照片
7) 学习英文

About the language: 还是，adj + 的，list + 都

还是

还是 means 'or'; it is used when asking 'A or B?' questions. Note you do not say 吗 in these questions.

你要喝茶还是咖啡？	Do you want to drink tea or coffee?
我们打网球还是乒乓球？	Shall we play tennis or ping pong?
图书馆在左边还是在右边？ (图 tú)	Is the library on the left or the right?
他喜欢大狗还是小狗？	Does he like big dogs or small dogs?

adj + 的

We have so far met the word 的 as showing possession:

爸爸的书	Dad's book
我的吉他	My guitar
小李的手机 (李 Lǐ)	Xiao Li's mobile phone

的 is also used when we describe something with adjectives:

很好的书	good book
很大的书	big book
很贵的书	expensive book

As you can see, the order is: adjective + 的 + noun.

Sometimes the noun is omitted from this structure when we know what is being talked about:

好的	a good one
绿的 (绿 lǜ)	a green one
贵的	an expensive one

For example, when browsing in a bookshop, you might say (in English) 'This is a good one!' instead of saying 'This is a good book!' because it is understood from context you are looking for books. The same is true in Chinese; you could say 这是好的！rather than 这是好的书！

都 (dōu)

The word 都 (dōu) is a way of expressing 'all' or 'both' in Chinese. However, it is sometimes used differently to the word 'all' in English.

他们都想去。	They all want to go.
我的朋友都喜欢唱歌。	All of my friends like singing.
我们都听中国音乐。	We both listen to Chinese music.

You can see that 都 (dōu) is put before the verb.
When the sentence has several objects, the objects may be listed before the verb:

中国菜、日本菜我都喜欢吃。	I like eating both Chinese and Japanese food. (Chinese food, Japanese food, I like both.)
羽毛球、乒乓球我都会打。	I can play both badminton and ping pong. (Badminton, ping pong, I can play both.)
北京、上海、香港我都想去。 (香港 Xiāng Gǎng)	I want to go to Beijing, Shanghai and Hong Kong. (Beijing, Shanghai, Hong Kong, I want to go to all.)

4.7 Writing activity — A bit of practice!

A Create full questions using 还是 and the words below. Write in your notebook and use characters when you can; otherwise use pinyin.

Example: 哥哥/弟弟 那是你哥哥还是你弟弟？

1) 裙子/裤子 (qún kù)
2) 篮球/足球
3) 看电影/看电视
4) 公共汽车/出租车

B Describe the pictures using the structure 'adjective + 的 + noun'.

Example:  很大的马。

1) 
2) 
3) 
4) 

C Translate the following into Chinese using 都 (dōu):

1) They are all Chinese.
2) We all study English.
3) None of us take the train. (We all do not take the train.)
4) I want to go to both Xi'an and Shanghai.
5) She can read both Chinese books and Chinese newspapers.

Language in action — Removing shoes

It is normal in China to remove your shoes in the home and wear slippers (拖鞋 tuōxié) instead. When you enter the house, your Chinese hosts are likely to say to you: "穿拖鞋 (chuān tuōxié)!"

Writing Characters

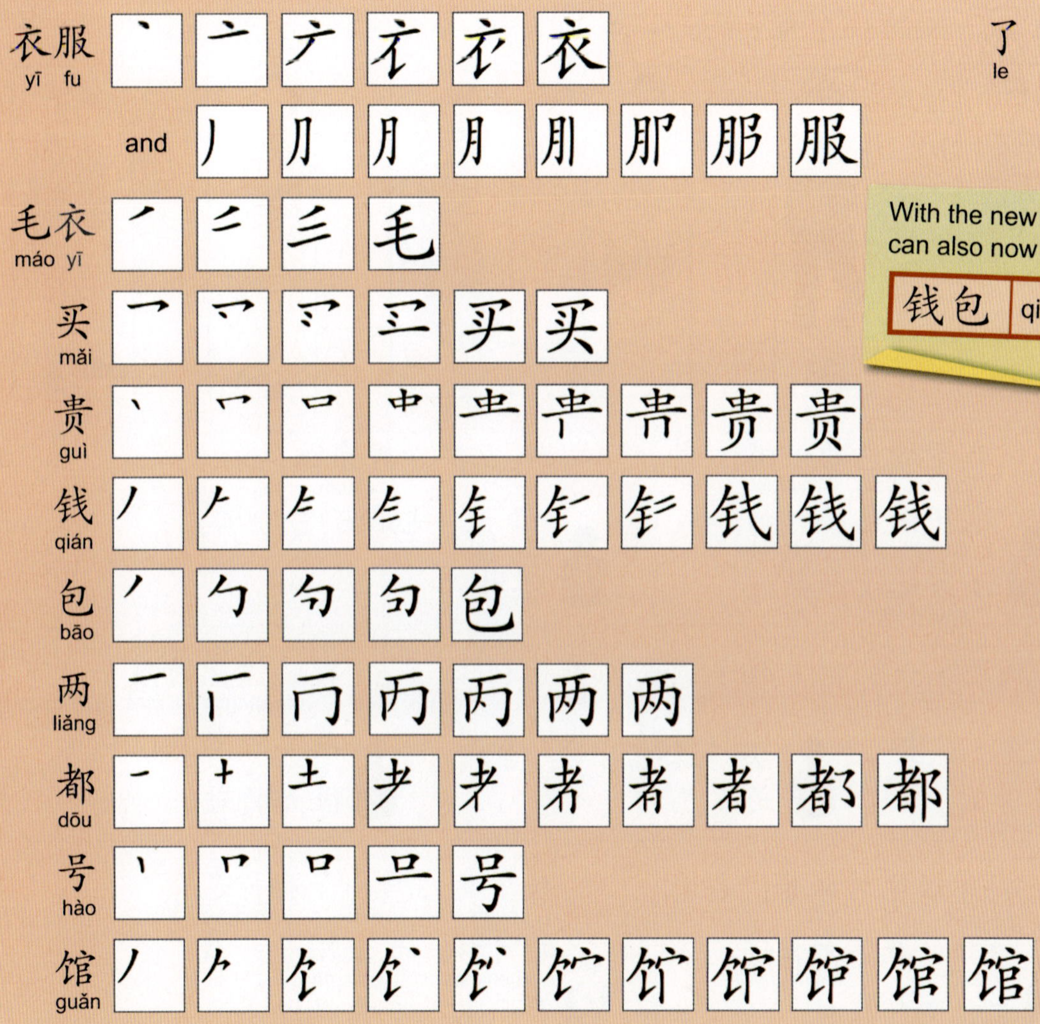

With the new characters, you can also now write:

钱包	qiánbāo	wallet

About the language: 是……的

This construction is used to talk about how something happened in the past. Unlike 了, it emphasises the way the verb was completed, rather than the verb itself.

我昨天买了一个包。	I bought a bag yesterday. *(Focus on action).*
这是昨天买的。	This was bought yesterday. *(Focus on time).*

是……的 is typically used in asking and answering questions about how things happened. For example:

你是几点来的？	What time did you arrive?
我是十点来的。	I arrived at 10.
你是跟谁一起去的？	Whom did you go with?
我是跟我哥哥一起去的。	I went with my brother.

The 的 in this construction can sometimes appear before a final object, if the object is a single word. The following two sentences mean the same thing:

我是昨天买包的。	I bought a bag **yesterday**.
我是昨天买的包。	I bought a bag **yesterday**.

This can be confusing, because the second sentence appears to say “I am a bag which was bought yesterday.”

4.8 Reading activity — Who am I?

Read the descriptions and match them to the correct people. Write your answers in your notebook.

一 我穿绿色的短裤。我
chuān lǜsè duǎnkù
也穿白色的衬衫。我
chuān sè chènshān
不穿袜子和鞋。
chuān wà xié

二 我五岁。我穿红色的
chuān sè
裙子，吃很好吃的冰
qún
淇淋。

三 我戴帽子。我还穿一
dài mào chuān
条很好看的裙子。我
qún
穿袜子， 不穿鞋。
chuān wà chuān xié

四 我穿黑色的裤子和绿
chuān sè kù lǜ
色的衬衫。我的鞋也
sè chènshān xié
是黑色的。
sè

五 我戴棕色的帽子，穿
dài zōngsè mào chuān
蓝色的毛衣。我还穿
lánsè chuān
很大的鞋。
xié

六 我穿红色的袜子，棕色
chuān sè wà zōngsè
的鞋。我不戴帽子。我
xié dài mào
有黄色的钱包。
sè

七 我穿黄色的裤子和棕色
chuān sè kù zōngsè
的衬衫。我戴帽子。我
chènshān dài mào
看一本很有意思的书。
si

4.9 Speaking activity — Easy to please

You are with your Chinese host family and want to make a good impression. When given two options, you always respond that you like both.

For example:

A: 你喜欢咖啡还是茶？

B: 咖啡、茶我都喜欢！

Now continue the conversation with the following:

- where to go today 我们去  还是  ?
- what to do together 我们  还是  ?
- how to get there 我们  还是  去?
- where to eat 你喜欢在  还是  吃饭?
- what to eat 你想吃 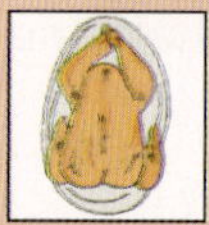 还是  ?

Reverse roles and ask the same questions (but give options different from the prompts above).

4.10 Reading activity – A recent shopping trip

Read the email from your friend, Ma Yunfei, and complete the sentences. Write the answers in your notebook.

你好！

昨天我和我朋友一起去市中心买衣服。我们是走路去的。我买了一件蓝色的毛
Zuó yī jiàn lánsè
衣和一条黑色的 裤子。一件毛衣二十八块钱，很便宜，也非常舒服。我喜欢买
yī sè kù jiàn yī kuài piányi shū
大号的衣服，因为大号很舒服。我朋友买了两个钱包。钱包都不便宜，三十块
hào yī hào shū piányi kuài
钱一个！她还买了一条裙子和一双袜子。
qún shuāng wà
我喜欢买衣服，常常去商店买。你喜欢不喜欢买衣服？你在哪儿买？
yī yī
马云飞
Yúnfēi

1) Yesterday Ma Yunfei went with her friend to ____________________ to buy clothes.
2) She bought a blue ____________________ and a ____________________.
3) She likes to buy large clothes because ______________________________.
4) Her friend also bought two ____________________.
5) Each one cost ____________________. Yunfei thought the price was very __________.
6) At the end of the email, Ma Yunfei asks where you like to shop for ______________.

4.11 Writing activity – National dress

First read the description of the clothing traditionally worn by men of the Huí (Muslim) ethnic group in Xi'an.

Then, using this as model, write a short description of what traditional clothing looks like in your country. List all the clothes and their colours.

他戴白色的帽子，穿白色的衬衫和白色
dài sè mào chuān sè chènshān sè
的裤子。他还穿黑色的坎肩。
kù chuān sè kǎnjiān

Glossary

坎肩 kǎnjiān = waistcoat

Study skills — Using a dictionary

Nowadays it is easier than ever to look up a Chinese character you don't know using a device with a touch screen. Many devices allow you to write the character and select the one you want from a range of similar looking characters. However, it is still useful to know how characters are arranged in a conventional dictionary so you can look words up when you need to.

Do you know how to pronounce the character for which you are searching? In a Chinese dictionary, characters are usually arranged by alphabetical order in pinyin. If you know the pronunciation, you can simply look it up in this way.

If you don't know the pronunciation, turn to the character index at the front of the dictionary and follow these steps:

一 Identify the radical

Characters are indexed at the start of the dictionary by radical. By this point, you should be familiar with many of the more common radicals; for example, water (江, 海, 洪) or mouth (叫, 吃, 喝). With most characters it is easy to work out the radical, but with some it is harder; for example, in the character 先 the radical is 儿. Also, in some characters you may not know which component is the radical; in 功, for example, both 工 and 力 are radicals. In such cases you just have to look in both sections.

二 Count the remaining strokes

Not including the radical, count how many strokes are required to write the character. For example, in 江 the number of strokes is 3, in 海 it is 7 and in 洪 it is 6. This is where a knowledge of writing characters becomes useful; for example, when writing the box shape 口 you use three strokes, not four. The lesson? Know your strokes!

三 Look up the character in the index

Now knowing the radical and the number of strokes, you can look up the character in the index. Characters are grouped by radical (部 bù) so the mouth radical is 口部. Within each radical, characters are grouped by remaining stroke count (画) so five strokes is 五画. When you find your character in the index, you will see the page number so you can look up its pronunciation and meaning in the dictionary.

4.12 Dictionary activity

Using the directions above, look up the following characters in a dictionary:

1) 怕	3) 实	5) 洗
2) 如	4) 草	6) 慢

Section 2: Money and measures

VOCAB

人民币	rénmínbì	Chinese yuan
百	bǎi	hundred
千	qiān	thousand
万	wàn	ten thousand
零	líng	zero
毛	máo	colloquial word for 1/10 of a Chinese yuan
一些	yìxiē	some

Language note — Big numbers

- Note that 10,000 is not written 十千(shíqiān); it has its own special word, 万 (wàn).
- Very large numbers are expressed in multiples of 10,000, or 万. So 100,000 is 十万 (shíwàn; literally, ten 10,000s) and 1,000,000 is 百万 (bǎiwàn).
- One 元 (yuán) is officially divided up into ten 角 (jiǎo); however, usually the word 毛 (máo) is used instead of 角 (jiǎo) when speaking.

4.13 Listening activity — Numbers

Listen to the recording and write the words you hear in your notebook.

1) 1999 2000 2006 2009
2) 500 1000 2000 4000
3) many books / some books / a few books / no books
4) ¥100 ¥200 ¥300 ¥400
5) ¥31 ¥3 ¥0.38 ¥1.3
6) ¥1000 ¥5000 ¥10,000 ¥50,000

4.14 Pair activity — Say the number

A With a partner, practise reading the following:

1) 500
2) 3,400
3) 43,000
4) 78,300
5) 60,500
6) 4,000
7) 300,000
8) 1,200,000

B Now write down three large numbers, keeping your numbers hidden from your partner. Read out your numbers and see if he/she can write them correctly; then swap roles.

4.15 Listening activity — How much?

Copy the table below. Then listen to the recording and fill in the table according to what you hear.

买什么？	多少钱？	
pens	元	毛
fish	元	毛
notebooks	元	毛
batteries	元	毛
newspapers	元	毛

4.16 Pair activity – Getting the right price

In pairs, act out customer and shopkeeper roles and practise bargaining a price. Use the dialogue below and swap in the items you want to buy (see the prompts); make sure you use the right measure words.

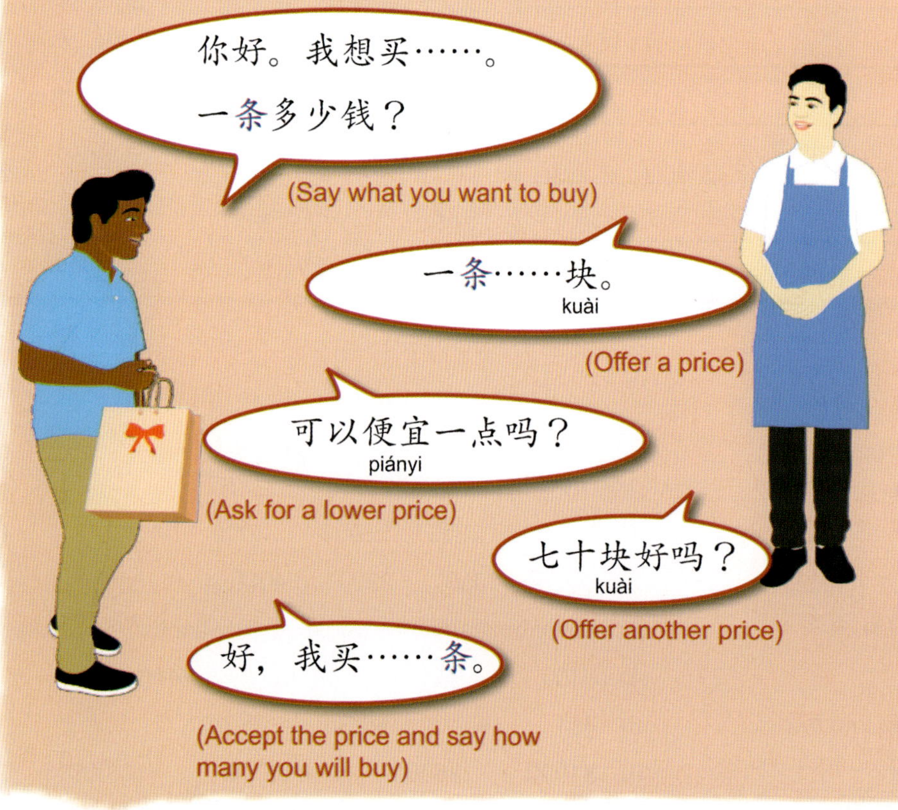

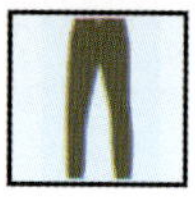	条	100元
	件 jiàn	60元
	本	5.5元
	个	48元
	个	30元

Describing Products

Vocab

东西	dōngxi	thing; stuff
买东西	mǎi dōngxi	'buy things' (go shopping)
卖	mài	to sell
新	xīn	new
旧	jìu	old (for objects)
给	gěi	give; to; for
一共	yígòng	in total
只	zhǐ	only

4.17 Listening activity – A new hat!

A husband and wife are discussing clothes. Listen and note what item of clothing is mentioned in each exchange. There are four exchanges.

Language notes

- This is an important time to be careful with your tones! 买 (mǎi) means 'buy' and 卖 (mài) means 'sell'.
- 只 (zhǐ) always goes before the verb. For example: 我只会说英文。

4.18 Pair activity — I need new shoes!

Now practise the following dialogue, swapping in different items and shops each time.

Item	Shop name
	热风 Rè
	百盛 Bǎichéng
	电脑先生
	小小毛衣店 yī
	百佳商店 Bǎijiā

4.19 Pair activity — In the shop

Here is an entire dialogue between customer and shopkeeper. See how fluent you can make it.

About the language: 给 (gěi) and 太……了

给

给 has two functions. It can be a verb meaning 'to give', and it can be a coverb (similar to preposition) meaning either 'to' or 'for'. As you learnt with 跟 in Unit 1, the sentence order with 给 is often different to English, with 给 being put before the verb.

Examples of 给 as a verb:

我给他一个包。 (gěi)	I give him a bag.
爸爸给我一辆自行车。 (gěi, liàng)	Dad gives me a bicycle.
老师给我们很多作业。 (gěi)	Teacher gives us a lot of homework.

Examples of 给 as a coverb:

我给她买一本书。 (gěi)	I buy a book for her.
我给老师介绍我的爸爸。 (gěi)	I introduce my dad to my teacher.
姐姐给妈妈唱歌。 (gěi)	Older sister sings for Mum.
我给朋友打电话。 (gěi)	I call (to) a friend.

太……了

To say something is 'too big', 'too many', 'too expensive', etc. you use the word 太. If the phrase comes at the end of a sentence, you often add 了 (le).

人太多了。	There are too many people.
那太好了！	That's great! (Literally, 'too good'.)
这台电脑太贵了。 (tái)	This computer is too expensive.
这件衬衫太小了。 (jiàn chènshān)	This shirt is too small.
他买了太多的书。	He bought too many books. (No 了 because the 太 phrase is not at the end of the sentence.)

4.20 Writing activity — Using 给 and 太……了

Translate the following into Chinese in your notebook. Use characters when you can; otherwise use pinyin:

1) He gives me ice cream.
2) I gave the teacher my homework.
3) I bought the new car for him.
4) I phoned him.
5) That's too old.
6) This is too expensive.
7) This music is great!

Writing Characters

东西 dōng xi

and

西安 Xī ān

一些 yì xiē

一共 yí gòng

给 gěi

百 bǎi

千 qiān

万 wàn

新 xīn

旧 jiù

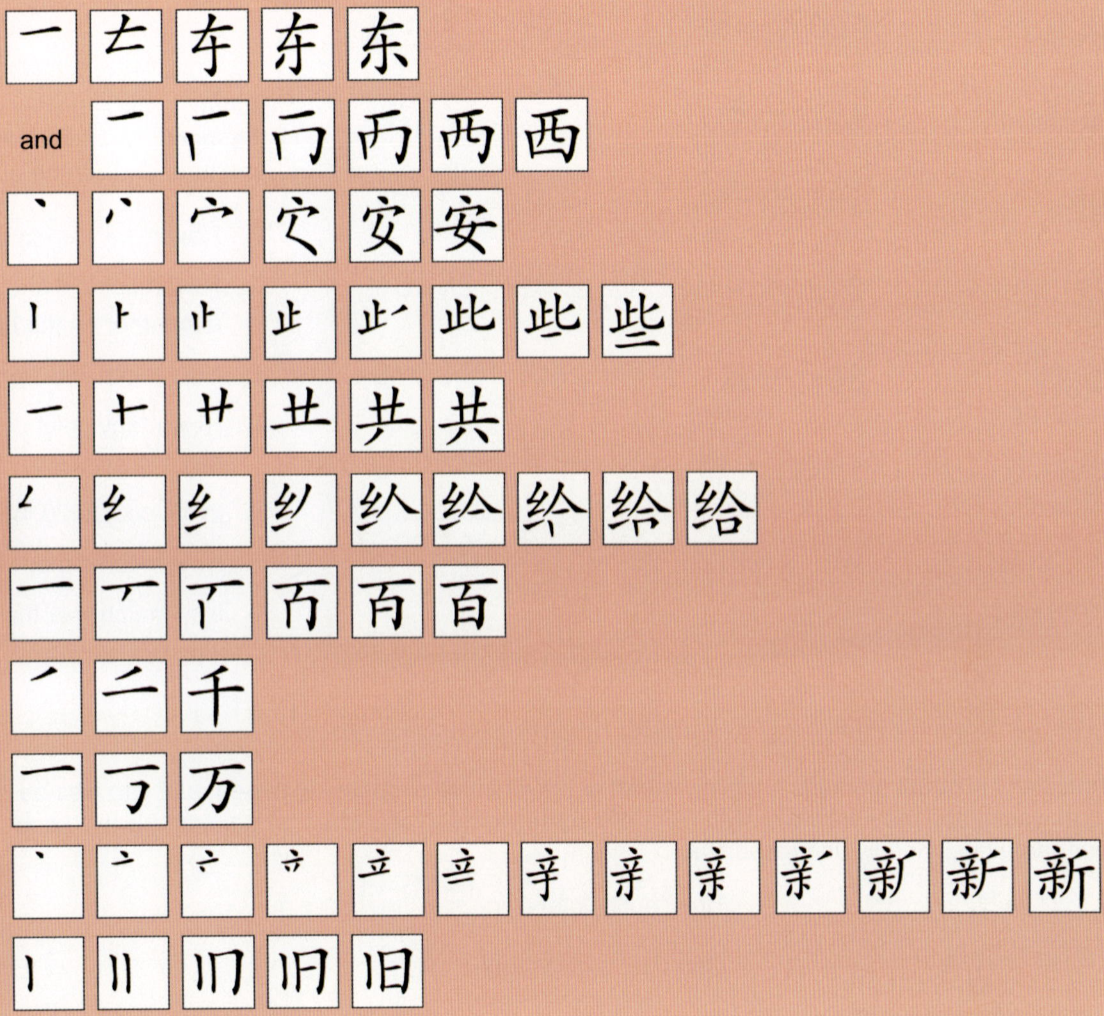

Did you know?

As you know, the people of China are ethnically diverse; one local culture may be very different from a neighboring culture, even if geographically close. One element that distinguishes different cultures is the dress customs and traditional costumes.

This is a photo of a Hmong woman in her traditional dress, characterised by dazzling silver headdress and necklaces. Her clothing is elaborately embroidered and includes many layers and pleats.

Cultural affiliation and ethnic labelling is complicated for any group of people anywhere in the world; however, if you do an internet search on minority costume in China, you can find lots of examples of beautiful traditional dress like this one and the Huí dress on page 80.

两辆自行车 liàng	600元一辆 liàng	一共：1200元
三本书	45元一本	一共：135元
手机	398元一台 tái	一共：398元
电脑	2420元一台 tái	一共：2420元
两双鞋 shuāng xié	80元一双 shuāng	一共：160元
两条裙子 qún	140元一条	一共：280元
		一共：4593元

4.21 Reading – Expenses

This was an expensive month for Yunfei! Look at the list she made of the most expensive things she bought and then answer the questions below.

1) How many bicycles did Yunfei buy?
2) How much did she spend altogether on the bicycles?
3) How much was her mobile phone?
4) How many pairs of shoes did she buy?
5) What cost 2420元?
6) How much did one dress cost?
7) How much was the grand total?

Cultural note – Haggling

Particularly in street markets, haggling is part of the Chinese shopping experience. It can also be fun to watch, and may draw a crowd! Here are some words to use when bargaining. Always keep your bargaining friendly and respectful.

多少钱？	How much is this?
可以打折吗？ zhé	Can I get a discount?
买两个可以打折吗？ zhé	Can I get a discount if I buy two?
给你十五，行吗？ Gěi	I'll give you 15 for it, OK?

4.22 Sketch – Shopping

Using *Cultural note – Haggling* above for inspiration, create a shopping sketch with a partner. Both sides should haggle for the best deal possible.

Here are some ideas for language you can use in your sketch:

- 你好！买什么东西？ (dōngxi)
- 我想买……
- 我给 (person) 买…… (gěi)
- 你喜欢什么颜色？ (yánsè)
- 你喜欢这件还是那件？ (jiàn … jiàn)
- 这个多少钱？
- 太好了！or 太贵了！
- 一共(cost)

How many new words from this unit can you include in your sketch?

4.23 Reading — Shopping for a birthday gift

The following dialogue takes place in 热风 (Rèfēng) clothing shop in Xi'an. Read the dialogue and complete the sentences. Write the answers in your notebook.

A: 您好！您买什么东西？
Nín dōngxi

B: 我买袜子。你有没有红色的？
wà sè

A: 对不起，没有红色的袜子，我们只有白色的和棕色的。
sè wà sè zōngsè

B: 是吗？明天是我爷爷的生日。我想给他买红色的衣服。
gěi sè yī

A: 红色的T恤衫、红色的衬衫、红色的裤子我们都有。
sè xùshān sè chènshān sè kù

B: 请给我看衬衫，好吗？
gěi chènshān

A: 好，您爷爷穿中号还是大号？
chuān hào hào

B: 爷爷穿中号。
chuān hào

A: 好，给你中号的。这是很舒服的衬衫。
gěi hào shū chènshān

B: 太好了！我喜欢。这件多少钱？
jiàn

A: 四十九块九毛。
kuài

B: 好，我给你五十。
gěi

1) The customer is hoping to buy ______________ for her ______________.

2) The shopkeeper says that the only colours in stock are ______________ and ______________.

3) The shopkeeper offers the alternatives of ______________, ______________ and ______________.

4) The customer needs a ______________ size.

5) The total cost is ______________.

4.24 Writing activity — A list of favours

It is Random Act of Kindness Day. Brainstorm a list of things you would like to do for other people. You will need to use the structure 给 (gěi) + person + verb. For example:

我想给爸爸买一本书。
gěi

I want to buy Dad a book.

我想去超市给奶奶买东西。
gěi dōngxi

I want to go to the supermarket for Granny.

List at least five things. Use characters whenever you can.

Character focus: 人，八，儿

Three characters that can easily be confused when writing are 人 (person), 八 (eight) and 儿 (son or -r ending). As well as appearing by themselves, these are also common as parts of other characters. It is useful to recognise the differences between them.

人

In this character the two strokes meet together at the top. In handwriting, the right-slanting stroke can start a little further down the left-hand stroke. Some examples you know are: 个 金 火 会 茶 给.

八

In this character the two strokes do not meet. In handwriting, the left stroke is often written shorter and slightly lower than the right stroke. An example you have learnt is: 公.

儿

In this character the two strokes do not meet. The left stroke is the same as in 八 but the right stroke goes vertically down, turns to the right, and flicks up, rather than sloping down. This character appears in these characters you have learnt: 元 玩 先.

Putting it together

4.25 Pair activity — Comparing clothing shops

You and a friend are visiting Xi'an and want to know the best place to go shopping for clothes. Compare the three shops below, then make a decision about which you would visit.

百盛
Bǎishèng

- 衣服都很便宜，可是不太好看。
  Yī piányi
- 有很多的衣服，还有帽子、鞋、包、钱包。
  yī mào xié
- 商店不在市中心。
- 服务不太好。

热风
Rè

- 衣服有一点贵，可是很好看。
  Yī
- 商店只有衣服，没有帽子、鞋、包、钱包。
  yī mào xié
- 商店在火车站对面 。
- 服务非常好。

百佳商店
Bǎijiā

- 便宜的衣服、贵的衣服，都有。
  Piányi yī yī
- 商店只有衣服，没有帽子、鞋、包、钱包。
  yī mào xié
- 商店在市中心。
- 服务很好。

4.26 Reading activity — Ancient Cultural Street

Here is a map of 书院门 (Shūyuànmén), an old-fashioned shopping street in Xi'an. Look at the map and complete the sentences in Chinese in your notebook.

1) 在迎春阁(Yíngchūngé)可以买 __________ 和 __________。

2) 紫清阁(Zǐqīnggé)在 __________ 的左边。

3) 卖(Mài)风筝的商店是 __________。

4) 在溪岩(Xī yán)茶业可以买 __________。

5) 珍宝楼(Zhēn bǎo lóu)在溪岩(Xī yán)茶业的 __________。

6) 紫清阁(Zǐqīnggé)有 __________ 衣(yī)服。

7) __________ 在一品宣(pǐn xuān)的对面。

4.27 Writing activity — Clothing review

You've just bought some clothes and you are very dissatisfied. Write an online customer review telling others what you think of your purchase. Here are some ideas to help you.

- 我___月___日去 (name of shop) 衣(yī)服店买衣(yī)服。
- 我很不喜欢这……，因为……
- 我买了……
- 我不想去 (name of shop)，因为……
- ……很贵，一共……元

Culture — Chinese clothes

Ordinary clothes worn by most people in China are often not very different from those worn in the UK, although fashions may vary. For special occasions, traditional clothes may be worn. China has many types of traditional clothing reflecting its many cultures and long history. Here are some types of clothing to look out for:

旗袍 Qípáo – Known as the Cheongsam in English, this is a close-fitting Chinese dress often made out of silk. It is popular as a fashionable garment but is also worn as a uniform for flight attendants and waitresses.

汉服 Hànfú – This is China's traditional clothing worn by men and women. It characteristically has long sleeves and is fastened with a sash or belt.

棉袄 Mián'ǎo – These Chinese cotton padded jackets are very warm and often have beautiful floral embroidery. They are more often worn by older people in China nowadays.

'Guess Fingers'

This is a short and fast-paced game that is popular in China. It is usually played by two people. Similar to Rock, Paper, Scissors, both players show their hands at the same time, but in Guess Fingers, you also shout out a number.

When you show your hands, instead of rock, paper or scissors, you have a choice to show '0' (both hands closed), '5' (one hand open) or '10' (both hands open).

Both players show 0, 5 or 10 fingers at once, making a total between them of 0, 5, 10, 15 or 20 fingers. As they show their hands, both players shout their guess of the total number of fingers. For example, you can open one hand to show 5 fingers and shout '10'. If your opponent also shows 5 fingers, your call is correct.

The round ends when one player's call is correct and the other player's call is incorrect. For example, if you open two hands to show 10 and call '20', and the other player opens both hands to show 10 and calls '15', then you win the round.

Use 我赢了！(wǒ yíng le) to declare yourself the winner!

"我赢了！"
yíng

Reading Challenge

你喜欢看什么电视节目？

A 我喜欢看《舌尖上的中国》。这个电视节目介绍了很多中国的食物和饮料。我看《舌尖上的中国》以前，不知道中国有那么多好吃的东西。我最喜欢四川菜，很辣，很好吃。

B 我喜欢看《家有儿女》。这个电视节目介绍了一个中国家庭，有爸爸、妈妈和三个孩子。这家人都很好玩，很友好。

C 我喜欢看《爸爸去哪儿》。这个电视节目是一个比赛，有很多爸爸和孩子。这个节目让我笑，也让我哭，因为爸爸很爱自己的孩子。

D 我喜欢看《西游记》。这个电视节目讲了一个很老的故事。有孙悟空、猪八戒等人物。这个电视节目很好玩，孙悟空的功夫太好了。

E 我喜欢看《爱情公寓》。这个电视节目很搞笑，很像美国的《六人行》(*Friends*)。《爱情公寓》有七个年轻人，都追求生活的幸福，可是有时候不懂事。

F 我喜欢看《非你莫属》。在这个电视节目里，有很多人在找一份工作。在这个比赛中，只有一个人能得到这份工作。一些老板会问很难的问题。

G 我喜欢看《小时代》。这个电视剧里面的人物都很时尚，很好看。我也很喜欢爱情的故事，也喜欢看中国年轻人的生活怎么样。

Name the Chinese TV show that has the most to do with:

1) Kung Fu
2) Finding a Job
3) Romance
4) Parenting
5) Delicious Food
6) Comic situations
7) Family life

Writing piece

Using the internet, try to find a clip of one of the programs mentioned above. While watching the clip, listen out for words that you recognise. Write down your thoughts about this TV program and compare it to a program you have watched in the past.

Glossary

食物	shíwù	= food
饮料	yǐnliào	= drink
家庭	jiātíng	= family
笑	xiào	= to laugh
哭	kū	= to cry
故事	gùshi	= story
等	děng	= et cetera
搞笑	gǎoxiào	= hilarious
追求	zhuīqiú	= to pursue
幸福	xìngfú	= happiness
不懂事	bù dǒngshì	= immature
找	zhǎo	= look for; search for
老板	lǎobǎn	= boss
人物	rónwù	= character (in fiction)
时尚	shíshàng	= fashion

我会

Now you can...

...talk about clothes.

哥哥穿一件白色的毛衣。	Gēge chuān yí jiàn báisè de máoyī.	Older brother wears a white jumper.
我穿黄色的裤子和棕色的衬衫。	Wǒ chuān huángsè de kùzi hé zōngsè de chènshān.	I wear yellow trousers and a brown shirt.
她戴帽子。	Tā dài màozi.	She wears a hat.

...talk about shopping.

我要买一些书。	Wǒ yào mǎi yìxiē shū.	I want to buy some books.
你喜欢什么颜色？	Nǐ xǐhuān shénme yánsè?	What colour do you like?
哪儿有卖鞋的？	Nǎr yǒu mài xié de?	Where sells shoes?
你要红的还是黑的？	Nǐ yào hóng de háishì hēi de?	Do you want red or black?
那个很便宜。	Nà gè hěn piányi.	That one is very cheap.
这是好的。	Zhè shì hǎo de.	This is a good one.

...communicate in a shop.

你有没有短裤？	Nǐ yǒu méiyǒu duǎnkù?	Do you have shorts?
这件衬衫太小了。	Zhè jiàn chènshān tài xiǎo le.	This shirt is too small.
一个多少钱 ？	Yí gè duōshǎo qián?	How much money for one?
可以便宜一点儿吗？	Kěyǐ piányi yìdiǎnr ma?	Can you lower the price?
可以打折吗？	Kěyǐ dǎzhé ma?	It there a discount?
三十块钱一个。	Sānshí kuài qián yí gè.	30 yuan for one.
一共三百块钱。	Yígòng sānbǎi kuài qián.	300 yuan in total.

我会

Now you can...

...use 都 for plurals

咖啡、茶，我都喜欢！	Kāfēi, chá, wǒ dōu xǐhuān!	I like coffee and tea!
我们都听中国音乐。	Wǒmen dōu tīng Zhōngguó yīnyuè.	We all listen to Chinese music.

...use 给 for indirect objects

我给你买吧。	Wǒ gěi nǐ mǎi ba.	I'll buy it for you.
我给老师介绍我的爸爸。	Wǒ gěi lǎoshī jièshào wǒ de bàba.	I introduce my father to the teacher.
我给她买一本书。	Wǒ gěi tā mǎi yì běn shū.	I buy a book for her.

...write the following characters:

买 钱 两 都 衣 服 给 些 东 西 共 包 毛 块
号 百 千 万 新 旧 安 了 贵

他怎么样？ Describing People

Objectives

In this unit, you will learn…

…how to describe a person's appearance.
…how to make comparisons.
…how to talk about personality.
…about the novel, Journey to the West.

Section 1: What is he like? What is she like?

Vocab

长	zhǎng	to appear, to grow
漂亮	piàoliang	beautiful
帅	shuài	handsome
高	gāo	tall
瘦	shòu	thin
胖	pàng	fat
可爱	kě'ài	cute
老	lǎo	old
年轻	niánqīng	young

'old'

老 and 旧 both mean 'old'. As you learnt, 旧 is used for objects and carries a sense of 'worn' or 'tattered'. By contrast, 老 is for people, animals and places, and simply refers to the age (not condition).

5.1 Listening activity — 他长得很胖
zhǎng pàng

Listen to the recording and match each question number to the correct picture. Write the answers in your notebook.

A

B

C

D

E

F

G

H
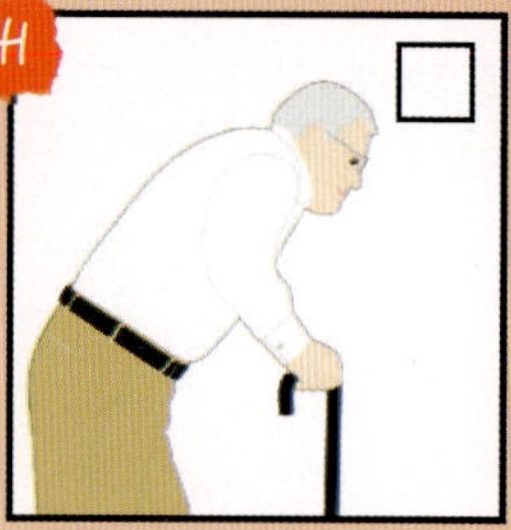

5.2 Pair activity — Celebrity brainstorm

With a partner, look at the list of new vocabulary on page 95. For each attribute, think of one famous person who has that attribute and one famous person who does not.

For example:

Yao Ming 长得很高。
zhǎng gāo

Daniel Radcliffe 长得不高。
zhǎng gāo

Brainstorm with your partner and write down your list.

Comparing People

Vocab

认识	rènshi	to recognise; get to know somebody
怎么样	zěnmeyàng	What's it like? How is...?
比	bǐ	(used for comparisons)
头发	tóufa	hair
长	cháng	long
短	duǎn	short
眼睛	yǎnjing	eyes
觉得	juéde	think, feel
最	zuì	most
对	duì	correct

Language notes

- 认识 (rènshi) and 知道 (zhīdào) both mean 'to know', but in different ways. 认识 means to recognise a person or an object; for example, 我认识她 = 'I know her'. 知道 means to know a fact or a situation; for example, 我不知道他在哪儿 = 'I don't know where he is'.
- 长 (zhǎng) is an example of a character with more than one pronunciation. You can tell how to read it only from context. Some English words have this feature; for example, 'bow' can be read in two ways: 'After the performance he gave a bow.'/'The ribbon was tied in a bow.' Look at the two vocabulary lists on these pages; can you see how the character is the same but the pronunciation and meaning are different?

5.3 Listening activity — What does she look like?

Listen and match each person to her descriptions. Three attributes are mentioned for each person.

1. Older sister
2. Younger sister
3. Aunt

A. Not as tall as me
B. Taller than me
C. Hair is longer than mine
D. Hair is shorter than mine
E. White hair
F. Green eyes, prettier than me
G. Chubbier than me
H. Thinner than me
I. Blue eyes

5.4 Pair activity — Do you know Tim?

Use the following dialogue to describe the people below. Use the new words on page 95.

A: 你认识萍萍吗？
rènshi Píngping
B: 不认识。她长得怎么样？
rènshi zhǎng yàng
A: 她很高，有一点儿瘦。她的眼睛是
gāo shòu yǎnjing
棕色的。

1) 萍萍
Píngping

2) Maria

3) 辰辰
Chénchen

4) Sam

5) Tim

6) 王浩
Wáng Hào

5.5 Listening activity — Which is better?

As you hear things compared, write the 2nd speaker's preferences in your notebook.

1) 可爱：  还是  ?

2) 好玩儿：  还是  ?

3) 有意思：  还是  ?
si

4) 好喝： 

还是  ?

5) 好看：  还是  ?

6) 好吃：  还是  ?

5.6 Pair activity — What do you think?

Now express your own opinions about the topics in *5.5 Listening activity* (above). With a partner, look at each topic and use the pattern below to say what you prefer.

我觉得 A 比 B 好。 你觉得怎么样？
jué jué yàng

I think A is better than B. What do you think?

我觉得 B 最好。
jué zuì

I think B is the best. ...or...

我也觉得 A 最好。
jué zuì

I also think A is the best.

5.7 Listening activity — Family reunion

Your Chinese friend has come to your family reunion and can't remember anybody's name! Listen to her asking who everyone is and write down how you would respond to each question.

Write in Chinese, 他/她是我的……。 他叫……。

他/她是我的……。

他/她叫……。

Did you know?

Getting personal

Ideas of what is polite and what is rude vary from culture to culture and from generation to generation. If you are an English speaker travelling in China, you may be surprised by the way Chinese talk about physical appearance. Topics which are sensitive or even taboo in English are often much more readily discussed in Chinese. For example, your friend might greet you with the words:

你胖了！ (pàng) You have got fatter (since the last time I saw you).

This is something that may cause offence in English, but in Chinese it is unlikely to be intended to hurt, and could be simply a friendly greeting. You may hear similar remarks about skin colour, eyes or height. As you make closer friends with Chinese speakers, you will also find topics that make them uncomfortable too; be aware that this phenomenon works both ways!

About the language: 的 for relative clauses and comparisons

的 for relative clauses

You learnt in Unit 4 that 的 is used to mark descriptions, such as 很好的书 or 很多的钱. The pattern for this was *adjective* + 的 + *noun*. In addition to adjectives, you can also put whole phrases before 的 to describe the noun in more detail. In English, this is a relative clause: longer descriptions of a noun that start with 'that', 'which' or 'who'. Here are some examples of English sentences that have relative clauses:

This is the book that I bought yesterday.

I want to buy the hat that my friend made.

The friend who I told you about is going to China.

In Chinese, relative clauses are treated like adjectives. The word order is:

Relative clause + 的 + noun

这是我昨天买的书。	(This is I bought yesterday 的 book.)
我要买我朋友做的帽子。	(I want to buy my friend made 的 hat.)
我跟你说的朋友要去中国。	(I told you about 的 friend is going to China.)

Notice that in both languages, you can take out the relative clause (in English) or the relative clause + 的 (in Chinese) and the sentence will still make sense:

这是书。	This is the book.
我要买帽子。	I want to buy a hat.
朋友要去中国。	A friend is going to China.

It is very important to pay attention to 的 as it can change the whole meaning:

他喜欢衣服。	He likes clothes.
他喜欢的衣服	the clothes that he likes

Notice that the first is a full sentence, while the second is a phrase.

Comparisons

Making comparisons in Chinese is easy! The order is: **Noun + 比 + noun + adjective**

For example:

他比(bǐ)我高(gāo)。	He is taller than me. (Literally: 'He compared to me is tall')
这件衬衫比(bǐ)那件贵。	This shirt is more expensive than that one.
他的头发(tóufa)比(bǐ)我的好看。	His hair looks nicer than mine.

Important! Never use 很 in comparison sentences! You can't say 他比(bǐ)我很高(gāo)。

About the language (continued)

Negative comparisons are similar to the structure just explained; you simply replace 比 (bǐ) with 没有. The word order is:

Noun + 没有 + noun + adjective

我没有他瘦。 shòu	I'm not as thin as him.
他没有他哥哥帅。 shuài	He's not as good-looking as his brother.

To say biggest, smallest, most expensive, etc. replace 很 with 最 (zuì):

这个很好。	This is good.	→	这个最好。 zuì	This is the best.
她的头发很长。 tóufa cháng	Her hair is long.	→	她的头发最长。 tóufa zuì cháng	Her hair is the longest.

5.8 Writing activity — relative clauses and comparisons

A Translate the following sentences into English.

1) 穿红毛衣的人是谁？
2) 他是喜欢法文的学生。
3) 我昨天买的衣服很不好。
zuó
4) 他穿的袜子很不好看。

B Below are some simple sentences, each followed by a relative clause. Put each relative clause into its sentence and write out the new, more descriptive sentence.

For example:

这是老师。（说中文）
This is the teacher. (speaks Chinese)

→ 这是说中文的老师。
This is the teacher who speaks Chinese.

1) 那是公共汽车。（去北京的）
2) 这是游戏。（我弟弟喜欢的）
3) 衣服很漂亮。（你买的）
piàoliang
4) 你喜欢牛肉吗？（我妈妈做的）
5) 那个人叫什么名字？（弹吉他的）

C Write sentences comparing the following:

1) 好听：中国音乐 / 美国音乐
2) 好吃：中国菜 / 法国菜
3) 高：我 / 我的老师
gāo
4) 可爱：兔子 / 鸟
5) 漂亮：我的衣服 / 我朋友的衣服
piàoliang

Writing Characters

怎么样 zěn me yàng

觉得 jué de

高 gāo

年轻 nián qīng

穿 chuān

比 bǐ

最 zuì

头发 tóu fa

长 cháng

Read the text about Ma Yunfei's family and label each person in the picture using the choices below. Write the matches in your notebook. (Note that three options are not needed.) The relative clauses have been highlighted to make reading easier.

请你看这张照片。这是我家。

1) 看书的孩子是我阿姨的女儿。她五岁，非常可爱。

2) 戴黄色帽子的人是我叔叔。你觉得他帅不帅？
jué shuài shuài

3) 穿红色裙子的女人是我妈妈。她的头发比我的短。
tóufa bǐ

4) 坐在椅子上的男人是我爸爸。他是作家，天天都很忙。
yǐ

5) 穿白色衬衫的老人是我爷爷。爷爷比爸爸胖。
bǐ pàng

6) 坐在椅子上的女人是我阿姨。她很瘦。
yǐ shòu

7) 你认识爸爸左边的人吗？那是我！
rènshi

Possible family members:

A. Ma Yunfei
B. Father
C. Mother
D. Grandad
E. Granny
F. Uncle
G. Aunt
H. Brother
I. Sister
J. Cousin

5.10 Pair activity — Who is he?

Your class is on an exchange with Number 26 High School in Xi'an and this is your first day at the school. While the class is on break, you and a classmate try to remember some of the Chinese students' names.

Ask your partner about:

- 跳舞的人
- 打篮球的人
- 做作业的人
- 打电话的人
- 戴红色帽子的人
- 看书的人
- 玩手机的人

5.11 Reading activity — Email from Ma Yunfei

You've just received an email from Ma Yunfei. Read it and look at the statements that follow, selecting the correct answer for each. Write the answers in your notebook.

你好！

你觉(jué)得西安怎么样(yàng)？我们一起去饭馆吃午饭吧！你知道老孙(Sūn)家饭馆吗？我觉(jué)得那家饭馆是西安最(zuì)好的饭馆。菜很好吃，也不贵。服务员穿的衣服都很漂亮(piàoliang)。你想去吗？饭馆在图书馆对面。我们可以坐公共汽车去，也可以走路去。我觉(jué)得走路比(bǐ)坐车好。你觉(jué)得怎么样(yàng)？我们十一点见，好吗？

云飞
Yúnfēi

1) Ma Yunfei is inviting you to eat breakfast / lunch / dinner with her.
2) According to her, the restaurant is the biggest / best / cheapest in Xi'an.
3) She says the food is cheap / abundant / salty.
4) She says the waiters and waitresses are good / are good-looking / wear nice clothes.
5) The restaurant is next to the bank / in the city centre / across from the library.
6) She would prefer to walk / take a taxi / take the bus to get there.
7) She asks you what you think / what you will wear / what time you would like to meet.

Re-write the response below in your notebook using Chinese characters.

Tài hǎo le! Wǒ hěn xiǎng hé nǐ yìqǐ qù chī wǔfàn. Wǒ zhīdào nà jiā fànguǎn. Wǒ zài xuéxiào rènshi le xīn péngyou, tā yě shuō nà jiā fànguǎn hěn hǎo. Tā māma shì fànguǎn de 经理. Tā hěn gāo, tóufa hěn cháng. Wǒmen kěyǐ qù kàn tā! Zǒu lù, zuò chē, dōu kěyǐ. Wǒmen shíyī diǎn jiàn 吧!

Achieving really beautiful handwriting in Chinese is an art, and it takes time and practice to get right. Here are a few tips for working on your handwriting at an early stage.

Blocks of equal size

Regardless of how complex they are, characters should always fill up the same sized space. For more complex characters, the strokes have to be smaller to fit in the box. Take a look at these, for example, and see how the simple element becomes squashed when it appears in more complex characters.

母 → 敏 → 繁

月 → 骨 → 髓

寸 → 尉 → 熨

A common mistake is to make simple characters too small and complex characters too big. Try to make them all the same size.

Horizontal strokes

一 二 三

Horizontal strokes are not quite level; they tilt up slightly. There are two types of horizontal stroke: long and short. Long ones flatten off at the end and short ones stay straight. In 二 and 三 the bottom stroke is long and the others are short. Also, in 三 the middle stroke is shorter than the top one. Once you can write these characters beautifully, it will help you write more complex characters well, too. Can you see 一, 二 or 三 inside the following characters?

生 些 工 元 去 天 共 样 音 万 坐

5.13 Writing activity — Missing person!

Make a missing person poster! Draw a picture and use the template to make the poster. Write the description of the person below the picture.

寻人启事
Xún qǐshì

姓名：　　　　他住在：

他有 [colour] 的眼睛 (yǎnjing)、[colour] 的头发 (tóufa)。他的头发 (tóufa) 很（长 (cháng) / 短）。

他（很 / 不）高 (gāo)。 他很 [adjective]，也很 [adjective]。

他很（老 / 年轻 (qīng)），生日是 [year] 年 [month] 月 [day] 日。

他会 [skill]，不会 [skill]。

他常常穿 [colour] 的 [clothing] 和 [colour] 的 [clothing]。

你知道他在哪儿吗？请给我打电话: [phone number]

Section 2: Personality

vocab

酷	kù	cool
聪明	cōngming	clever
努力	nǔlì	hard-working; to make an effort
真	zhēn	real; really

5.14 Listening activity — He's so cool!

Listen to the recording and label the pictures with the corresponding question number in your notebook.

聪明

酷

努力

可爱

5.15 Pair Activity — Describing a friend

Decribe one of your closest friends to a classmate. Use the dialogue below and answer your classmate's questions using 非常，有一点儿 and 不太.

Ask whether your classmate's friend is:

- 酷 kù
- 聪明 cōng
- 好玩儿
- 高 gāo
- 努力 nǔlì
- 漂亮/帅 piàoliang shuài
- 可爱

VOCAB

每	měi	every
有时候	yǒu shíhou	sometimes
虽然	suīrán	although
可是	kěshì	but
但是	dànshì	but

每 (měi)

- 每 usually requires a measure word. For example 'every person' is 每个人.
- 天 and 年 do not need measure words (you say 每天and 每年), but 月 takes the measure word 个 (so you say 每个月).
- When 每 is used, 都 is often put before the verb (e.g. 我每天都看他).

5.16 Listening activity — Talking about frequency

Listen to Ma Yunfei talk about how often she does certain things and then select the frequency, writing your answers in your notebook.

	每天 měi	常常	有时候 shíhou
1. 买东西	○	○	○
2. 喝中国茶	○	○	○
3. 跟朋友唱歌	○	○	○
4. 看电视	○	○	○
5. 吃面包	○	○	○
6. 去邮局	○	○	○
7. 走路上学	○	○	○
8. 放风筝	○	○	○

5.17 Pair activity — Getting around

Below is a survey showing how Ma Yunfei's classmates usually travel around Xi'an. In pairs, comment on each method of transport using one of the following options:

姓名	走路	骑自行车	坐公共汽车	坐出租车	坐地铁	坐父母的车
张博 Zhāng Bó	✓	✓			✓	
杨丹丹 Yáng Dāndān	✓		✓			
赵和光 Zhào Héguāng	✓	✓	✓		✓	✓
白鸿羽 Bái Hóngyǔ	✓	✓	✓			
魏力言 Wèi Lìyán	✓		✓			

5.18 Listening activity — Although...

Listen to the recording and complete the sentences in English. Write the answers in your notebook.

1) Although I don't like wearing skirts, ________________.
2) Although ____________________, he isn't hard working.
3) Although _______________, he doesn't work in a hospital.
4) Although she is old, ______________________.
5) Although _______________, I sometimes buy it for her.
6) Although _______________, he can't speak English.

5.19 Pair activity — Debating pros and cons

In pairs, discuss buying a car using the prompts below. One person should argue the pros while the other person argues the cons. With each argument, start off by acknowledging what your partner just said. Finish each argument with the last point in the 'cons' column.

Pros	
好看	很贵
很舒服 shū	太大了
颜色很好 yánsè	我不喜欢

我想买这辆车，
liàng
它很好看。

虽然很好看，可是很贵。
Suīrán

虽然很贵，可是很舒服。
Suīrán

虽然很舒服，……
Suīrán

Now discuss eating lunch with 马云飞 (Mǎ Yúnfēi) in the school canteen:

我们跟马云飞一起
Yúnfēi
吃午饭吧，她很酷。
kù

虽然她很酷，
Suīrán kù
可是……

	Cons
她很酷 kù	她不好玩儿
她很可爱	我不太喜欢她
她是我朋友	她不是我朋友

Now discuss buying a pair of shoes:

我想买这双鞋，
很好看！

虽然很好看，
Suīrán
可是……

Pros	
很好看	颜色不好
很便宜	你家里已经有很多鞋 yǐ
可以给朋友买	他不会喜欢

已经 = already

About the language: 真(zhēn) and 虽然 (suīrán) ……可是……

真(zhēn)

真 is usually used instead of 很 when making an exclamation. For example:

他真帅！ (zhēn shuài)	He's really handsome!
那真好！ (zhēn)	That's fantastic!

虽然……可是…… (Suīrán)

This structure is used when we say 'although' in English. For example:

虽然我很忙，可是我还要去看电影。 (Suīrán)	Although I'm busy, [but] I'm still going to see a film.

Notice in the Chinese, you need to say 可是, but in English we don't say 'but' in the second half of the sentence.

While we may use 'but' in English to state simple differences, in Chinese the two clauses have to be contradictory. For example, you can say in English, 'He studies French but I study Chinese', but you could not use 可是 for a sentence like this in Chinese because there is no contradiction.

他学法文，我学英文。	He learns French [but] I learn English.
虽然他学法文，可是他不想去法国。 (Suīrán)	He learns French but he doesn't want to go to France.

The first sentence states a difference between two things which aren't particularly related. The second sentence states two things which are contrary to one another.

Note that 可是 and 但是 (dàn) can be used interchangeably.

Translate the following into Chinese in your notebook. Use characters when you can; otherwise use pinyin.

1) Although that restaurant's food is not good, it's cheap.
2) Although he's handsome, he plays basketball badly.
3) Although that sweater is old, it is comfortable.
4) Although my little sister is young, she likes drinking coffee.

Writing Characters

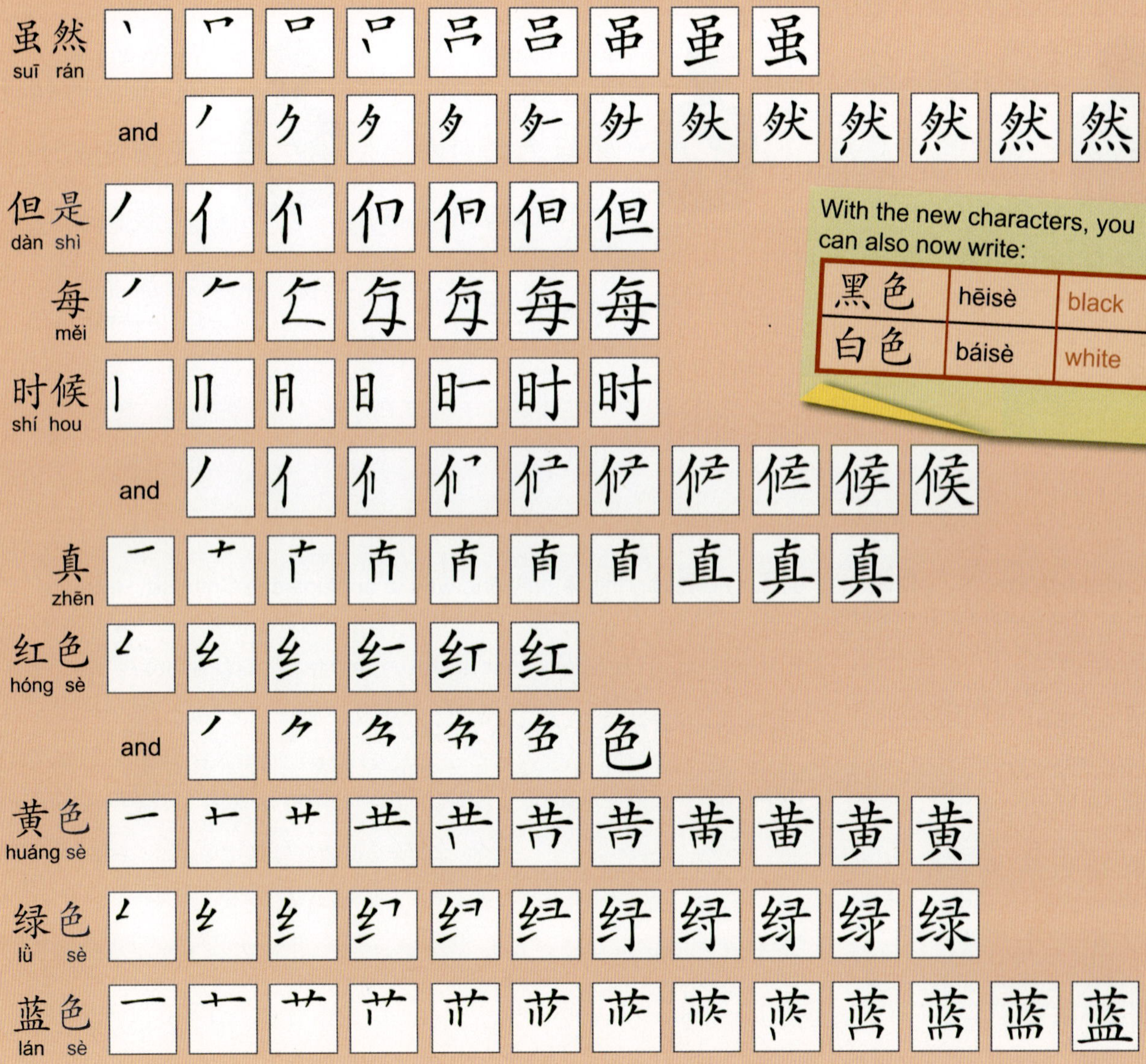

With the new characters, you can also now write:

黑色	hēisè	black
白色	báisè	white

5.21 Writing Activity — How often do you...?

Using 每天都 (měitiān dōu), 常常(chángchang) and 有时候 (yǒu shíhou), list how often you do the following things. For example, 我常常打篮球。 If you don't do something, say 我不……。

- 看书
- 上网
- 坐汽车去上学
- 游泳
- 打网球
- 去市中心
- 吃鱼
- 买衣服

5.22 Reading activity — Sketch to the descriptions

Make a sketch of these three people according to the statements.
You'll need different coloured pencils to complete this activity.

Steven

- 很胖
  pàng
- 头发比李强短
  tóufa bǐ Lǐ Qiáng duǎn
- 穿蓝色的衣服
- 有黑色的头发和棕色的眼睛
  tóufa yǎnjing

李强 (Lǐ Qiáng)

- 非常瘦
  shòu
- 穿绿色的衬衫
- 穿白色的裤子和红色的袜子
- 眼睛比王梅大
  yǎnjing bǐ Wáng Méi

王梅 (Wáng Méi)

- 穿黄色的裙子
- 比李强高
  bǐ Lǐ Qiáng gāo
- 有绿色的包
- 很漂亮
  piàoliang

Cultural notes — Apologising and forgiving

You already know 对不起 means 'sorry'; however, this is only one way to apologise in Chinese. Here are several other useful expressions.

不好意思！ si	Excuse me! (This is for minor mistakes and for getting people's attention)
真抱歉！ Zhēn bàoqiàn	I apologise! (This is for major mistakes)
麻烦你…… Máfan	Sorry, but would you mind... (Used when asking people to do things for you)
麻烦你给我一张纸？ Máfan	Could you give me a piece of paper?
没事儿！ shì	No problem.
不要紧！ jǐn	No big deal.

Did you know?

The Terracotta Army is made up of life-sized figures which vary in height, uniform, and hairstyle, as well as facial features. In addition to thousands of military men, horse and chariot statues are included in the ensemble, making it very impressive indeed! The sculptures were buried with Emperor Qín Shǐhuáng (秦始皇) in 210-209 BCE and were intended to serve him in his afterlife. The details of how the army was created and discovered is fascinating.

5.23 Pair game — Guess the person

Find a partner. Describe somebody you both know without saying that person's name; your partner must guess the person you are thinking of. You can mention:

Hair length/colour	（他有黑色的头发。他的头发很短，可是比我的长。） tóufa tóufa bǐ cháng
Eye size/colour	（她的眼睛不大。她有蓝色的眼睛。她的眼睛很漂亮。） yǎnjing yǎnjing yǎnjing piàoliang
Height/weight	（她不胖，也不瘦。她比较高。） pàng shòu bǐjiào gāo
His/her character	（他很酷。他非常聪明。） kù cōng
Hobbies	（他喜欢买东西。他有很多钱。）
What you do with him/her	（我有时候跟他一起打网球。我们一起上科学课。） shíhou

Vocab

东	dōng	East
南	nán	South
西	xī	West
北	běi	North
部	bù	part
成都	Chéngdū	Chengdu
南京	Nánjīng	Nanjing
天津	Tiānjīn	Tianjin
香港	Xiānggǎng	Hong Kong

Language note — Cardinal Directions

Northeast is 'eastnorth' in Chinese. So we have:

西北 = Northwest

东北 = Northeast

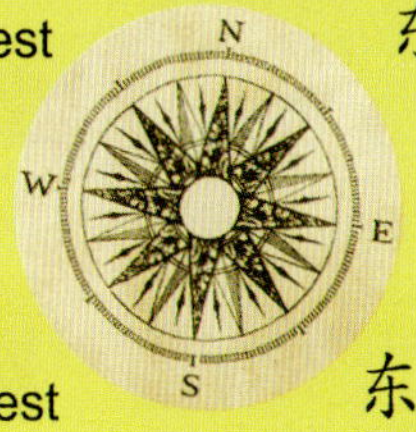

西南 = Southwest

东南 = Southeast

5.24 Listening activity — Where in China?

Seven cities are highlighted on the map below. Listen to the recording and match the cities with the question numbers, writing the answers in your notebook.

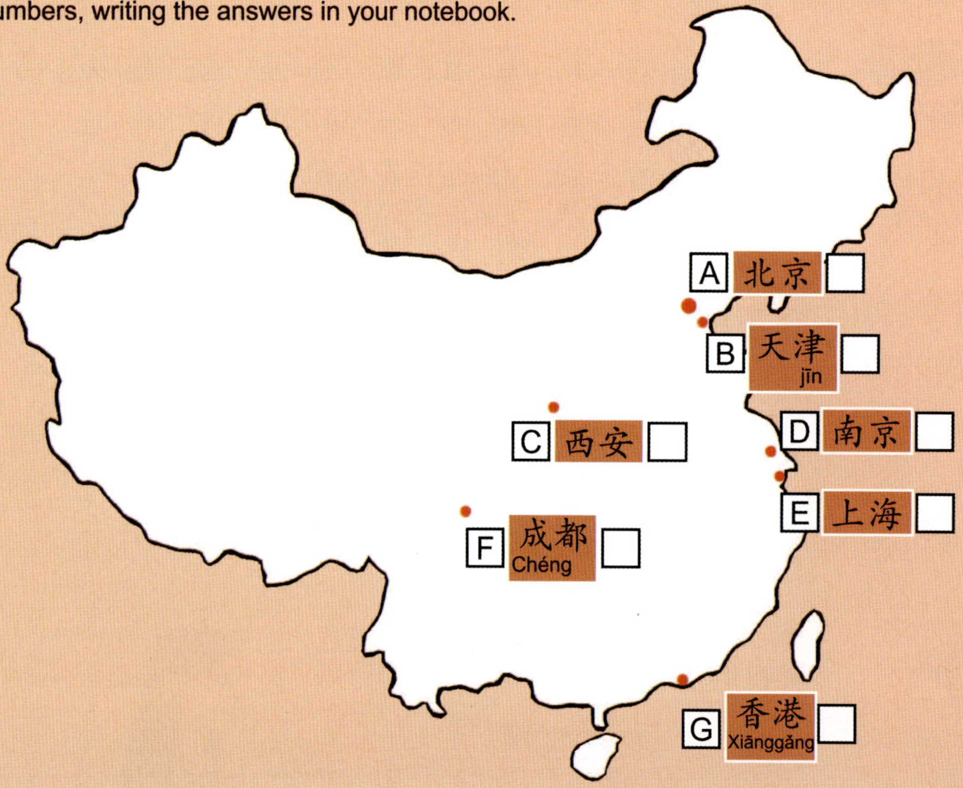

5.25 Pair activity — Important Chinese cities

With a partner, look at the map below and see who can find each of the following cities first. When you find one, you can say ……在这儿，在中国……部(bù)!

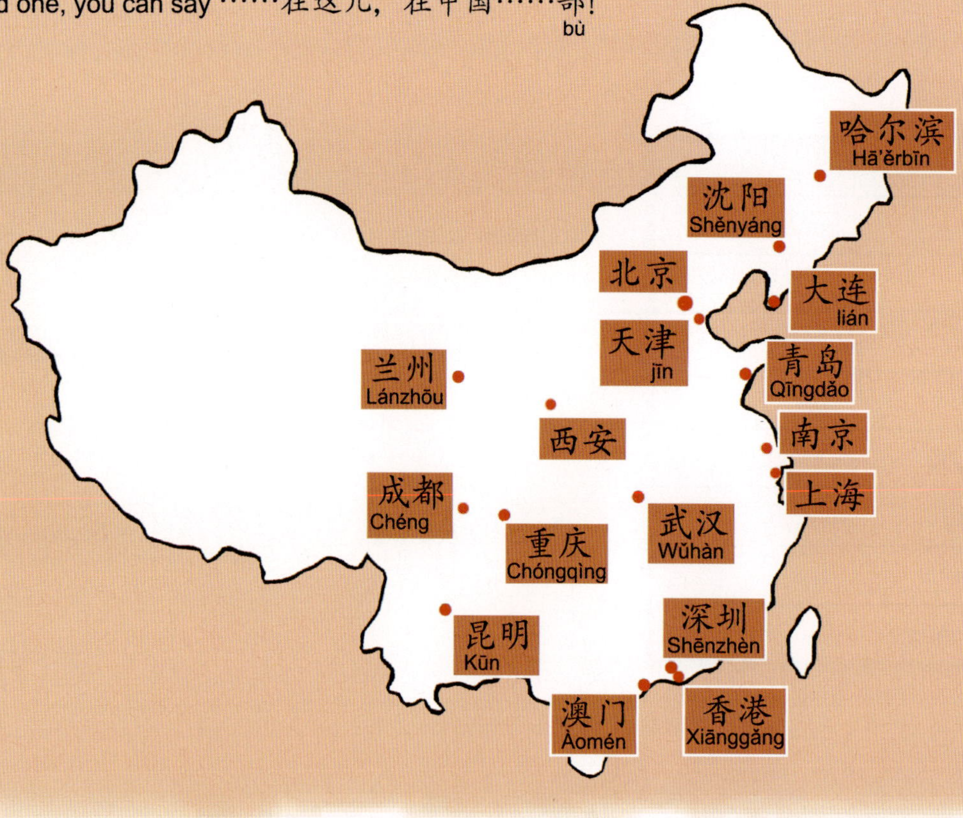

Can you find...

1) 兰州 Lánzhōu
2) 哈尔滨 Hā'ěrbīn
3) 昆明 Kūn
4) 澳门 Àomén
5) 大连 lián
6) 武汉 Wǔhàn
7) 深圳 Shēnzhèn
8) 沈阳 Shěnyáng
9) 重庆 Chóngqìng
10) 青岛 Qīngdǎo

5.26 Reading and writing activity — Match-making

Below are profiles of three men and three women who would like to be matched for a date. Read their profiles and decide how best to match them. Write a couple of sentences explaining why you have matched them in this way.

姓名：黄建　　工作：作家
Jiàn
最喜欢的颜色：红色。我觉得自己
Zuì　jué
非常好玩儿。我不老，可是我也不
太年轻。我最喜欢练书法。我住在
niánqīng　zuì
天津，可是我想住在中国南部。我
jīn　bù
有一只鸟。

姓名：白天飞　　工作：经理
fēi
最喜欢的颜色：蓝色。我觉得自己
Zuì　jué
很帅，也很酷。我不胖，也不瘦。
shuài　kù　pàng　shòu
我很高。我喜欢打篮球，不喜欢看
gāo
电视。我有很多钱，住在市中心。
shì
我是成都人。我不喜欢宠物。
Chéngdū

姓名：赵红　　工作：商人
Zhào
最喜欢的颜色：黄色。我觉得自己
Zuì　jué
很漂亮。我不喜欢长头发的男人。
piàoliang　cháng tóufa
我想认识一个很帅的男人。我最喜
rènshi　shuài　zuì
欢看电视，我每天都看。我住在香
měi　Xiāng
港，可是我常常去天津工作。
gǎng　jīn

姓名：高光明　　工作：医生
Gāo Guāng
最喜欢的颜色：绿色。我的头发比较
Zuì　tóufa　bǐjiào
长，是棕色。虽然我不聪明，可是
cháng　Suīrán　cōng
我很努力。我每天都在医院工作，很
nǔlì　měi
忙！我想认识一个漂亮的女人。虽然
rènshi　piàoliang　Suīrán
我没有宠物，但是我很喜欢动物。
dàn

姓名：徐芳芳　　工作：工人
Xú Fāngfāng
最喜欢的颜色：红色。我唱歌唱得
Zuì
很好。我想认识一个有钱的男人。
rènshi
虽然我在市中心的工厂工作，可是
Suīrán
我不想住在市中心。我住在成都。
Chéngdū
我没有宠物。

姓名：张兰　　工作：艺术家
Lán　yìshù
最喜欢的颜色：绿色。我的朋友说我
Zuì
很聪明。我的眼睛是蓝色的。我最喜
cōng　yǎnjing　zuì
欢画画。我不喜欢运动。我在家里
工作。我住在中国西部。我有时候
bù　shíhou
去成都玩儿。我有两只猫。
Chéngdū

5.27 Writing activity — First encounter

Imagine the six people above pair up as you've matched them. Choose one of your pairs and write the dialogue they have when they meet for the first time. Use the information in the profiles on page 114 as a starting point for your dialogue. You can use the following to help your pair get to know each other:

- 虽然……可是……。
  Suīrán
- 我觉得……比……好。
  jué bǐ
- 你觉得……怎么样？
  jué yàng

Character focus

Here are some characters you learnt in the last two chapters, together with similar characters from before. Can you spot the elements in common? Is there a sound link or a meaning link? Copy and fill this table in your notebook.

	Element	Sound or meaning link?
觉 — 学		
轻 — 车		
时 — 日		
红 — 工		
蓝 — 篮*		
钱 — 银*		
衣 — 衬*		
块 — 土		
百 — 白		

*Hints
篮球 = basketball
银行 = bank
衬衫 = shirt

Putting it together

5.28 Class game — Find somebody who...

Everyone in the class must walk around and find one person for each of the points below. When you find somebody who matches a description, write his or her name down in your notebook. Win the game by filling the list first!

- 不吃肉的人
- 短头发的人
  tóufa
- 黄色头发的人
  tóufa
- 有新鞋的人
- 有时候放风筝的人
  shíhou
- 会游泳的人
- 走路上学的人
- 喜欢吃甜的人
  tián
- 有弟弟的人
- 没有手机的人
- 喜欢看报纸的人
- 穿裙子的人
- 有宠物的人
- 会打网球的人
- 有蓝色眼睛的人
  yǎnjing
- 喜欢买东西的人

Glossary
甜 = sweet

西安的历史人物

西安的历史非常长。在西安，你可以看到很多历史。
cháng dào

下面是三个西安的历史人物。

这是杨贵妃。她是中国皇帝的一
Yáng Fēi huángdì
个太太。她有一点儿胖，也很漂
pàng piào
亮。皇帝很爱她。在华清池前面
liang Huángdì Huáqīng chí
可以看到杨贵妃的塑像。
dào Yáng Fēi sùxiàng

这是玄奘。他是和尚。他穿红
Xuánzàng shang
色的衣服，戴金色的帽子，骑
白色的马。他去印度学习佛
sè Yìndù Fó
教。他很努力。在大雁塔前面
jiào nǔlì Yàn
可以看到玄奘的塑像。
dào Xuánzàng sùxiàng

这是秦始皇。他是中国的第一个
Qín Shǐhuáng dì
皇帝。他戴很大的帽子。他很聪
huángdì cōng
明。在兵马俑前面可以看到秦
bīng yǒng dào Qín
始皇的塑像。
Shǐhuáng sùxiàng

5.29 Reading activity – Three statues in Xi'an

Read about the three famous people above and answer the questions in English in your notebook.

1) Who rode a white horse?
2) Whose statue can be seen at the Terracotta Warriors?
3) Who was loved by the emperor?
4) Who was a monk?
5) Who was China's first emperor?

Glossary

历史	lìshǐ	= history
人物	rénwù	= character; figure
皇帝	huángdì	= emperor
华清池	Huáqīng chí	= Huaqing Pool
塑像	sùxiàng	= statue
和尚	héshang	= monk
印度	Yìndù	= India
佛教	Fójiào	= Buddhism
大雁塔	Dà Yàn Tǎ	= Great Goose Pagoda
秦始皇	Qín Shǐhuáng	= Emperor Qin Shihuang
第一个	dì yí gè	= first
兵马俑	bīng mǎ yǒng	= Terracotta Warriors

5.30 Writing activity — Pre-interview form

In China, joining a school club or activity group usually requires an interview or audition. Imagine you are auditioning for a dancing club. In your notebook, copy and fill in the pre-interview form below. See if you can use 虽然……可是……, and don't forget to say what you do well (for example, 我网球打得很好). Use complete sentences whenever you can.

Glossary

号码	hàomǎ	= number
性格	xìnggé	= character
参加	cānjiā	= to join
俱乐部	jùlèbù	= club

姓名： 1)

手机号码： 2)
mǎ

生日： 3)

性格： 4)
xìnggé

最喜欢的颜色： 5)
zuì

最喜欢的菜： 6)
zuì

最喜欢的电影： 7)
zuì

最喜欢的音乐： 8)
zuì

爱好： 9)

你为什么想参入我们的俱乐部？
cānrù jù bù

10)

Did you know?

Journey to the West

A modern depiction of the monkey king.

《西游记》(xīyóujì), also known in English as *Monkey* or *Journey to the West*, features one of China's most beloved characters, 孙悟空 (Sūn Wùkōng) the Monkey King. Many legends exist about this semi-divine figure, but the most famous collection of stories came to be written down as a novel in the Míng dynasty, in around 1592. The novel tells the story of a group of characters who journey together from China to India in search of Buddhist scriptures. The main character is the monk 唐三藏 (Táng Sānzàng), who is protected by Sūn Wùkōng and his friend 猪八戒 (Zhū Bājiè), half man, half pig. Along the way, they have many adventures and meet many demons who they need to fight.

Sūn Wùkōng always gets into trouble, and loves fighting. He fights with a magic staff and can transform into various animals and objects. The stories of Xīyóujì have entertained people for generations through plays, street performances, shadow puppets, and more recently, movies and video games.

This is one of China's most famous and popular folk songs. Its title is Jasmine Flower.

茉莉花
mò lì huā

好一朵美丽的茉莉花
duǒ lì mò lì huā

芬芳美丽满枝桠
fēn fāng lì mǎn zhī yā

又香又白人人夸
yòu xiāng yòu kuā

让我来将你摘下
ràng zhāi

送给别人家
sòng bié

茉莉花呀茉莉花
mò lì huā ya mò lì huā

Jasmine Flower

What a beautiful Jasmine flower,

A spray of fragrance and lovely petals,

Everyone loves your snow-white buds,

Let me pick a Jasmine flower,

And give it to others,

Jasmine flower! Oh! Jasmine flower!

In the poem, can you find...

- a measure word?
- a colour?
- an exclamation?

Reading Challenge

我的中国朋友

我最好的朋友是中国人，他的名字叫张军。他是广州人。广州是中国的一座城市，在广东省。广东省在中国南部。他会说英语，也会说汉语。他说广东话，可是我学习普通话，所以他说的汉语跟我学习的汉语不一样。我跟他在伦敦中学一起上学。他的数学很好，可是他觉得英语很难。我跟他不一样。我觉得英语很容易，可是我觉得数学很难。因为张军的家离英国很远，所以他在学校住。有时候他很想家。有一天，他很不开心。

我问他："今天你为什么不开心？"

他说："今天是中秋节，是中国的节日。"

我说："我觉得节日应该很开心吧？"

他："中秋节的时候，中国人跟家人一起吃晚饭，看月亮。可是今天我不能跟我爸爸、妈妈在一起，所以我想家。"

我："你不要难过了，你十二月可以回国看家人。"

张军问我："你去过中国吗？"

我："我没去过中国。中国跟英国有什么不一样？"

他："中国有很多不一样的东西。中国菜不一样。我觉得，中国菜比英国菜好吃。"

我："广州怎么样？"

他："广州比这个城市大，可是没这儿漂亮。广州离香港很近，从广州到香港坐火车两个小时。很多广州人喜欢在香港买东西。广州也有白云山，那里很漂亮，可以去散步。广州天气很热，夏天气温32度，冬天也不冷，气温15度。广州菜非常有名，你吃过吗？"

我："我吃过点心，那是广东菜吗？"

他："是，你喜欢吗？"

我："我很喜欢，我也想去广州旅游。"

他："欢迎来我家！"

Glossary

广州	Guǎngzhōu	= Guangzhou
省	shěng	= province
广东话	Guǎngdōnghuà	= Cantonese
普通话	pǔtōnghuà	= Mandarin
容易	róngyì	= easy
离……很远	lí ... hěn yuǎn	= far from ...
开心	kāixīn	= to feel happy
中秋节	Zhōngqiūjié	= mid-Autumn festival
节日	jiérì	= festival
难过	nánguò	= sad
不一样	bùyíyàng	= different
散步	sànbù	= to take a walk
气温	qìwēn	= temperature

Answer the questions in Chinese

1) 张军从哪儿来？
2) 广州在哪儿？
3) 张军觉得英语好学吗？
4) 张军住在哪儿？
5) 中秋节是什么？
6) 张军为什么不开心？
7) 张军喜欢英国菜吗？
8) 广州人去哪儿买东西？
9) 广东冬天冷不冷？
10) 我喜欢广东菜吗？

Writing piece

Using the internet, choose a Chinese city which is unfamiliar to you and find out about its famous sights, festivals, foods and people. Create a short travel brochure in Chinese describing the city, complete with pictures and references.

我会

Now you can...

...describe a person's appearance.

他长得很胖。	Tā zhǎng de hěn pàng.	He is fat.
她长得很漂亮。	Tā zhǎng de hěn piàoliang.	She is beautiful.
她的头发比我短。	Tā de tóufa bǐ wǒ duǎn.	Her hair is shorter than mine.
她的头发是白色的。	Tā de tóufa shì báisè de.	Her hair is white.
她的眼睛是棕色的。	Tā de yǎnjing shì zōngsè de.	Her eyes are brown.

...make comparisons.

你觉得怎么样？	Nǐ juéde zěnmeyàng?	What do you think?
我也觉得看电影最有意思。	Wǒ yě juéde kàn diànyǐng zuì yǒu yìsi.	I think that watching films is the most interesting, too.
他没有他哥哥帅。	Tā méiyǒu tā gēge shuài.	He is not as handsome as his older borther.
她的头发最长。	Tā de tóufa zuì cháng.	Her hair is the longest.

...talk about personality.

你认识萍萍吗？	Nǐ rènshi Píngping ma?	Do you know Pingping?
他不太努力。	Tā bú tài nǔlì.	He is not so hard-working.
他非常聪明。	Tā fēicháng cōngming.	He is very clever.
虽然他很聪明，但是他不努力。	Suīrán tā hěn cōngming, dànshì tā bù nǔlì.	Desite being very clever, he his not very hard-working.

我会

Now you can...

...use 的 for relative clauses.

这是我昨天买的书。	Zhè shì wǒ zuótiān mǎi de shū.	This is the book I bought yesterday.
我跟你说的朋友要去中国。	Wǒ gēn nǐ shuō de péngyǒu yào qù Zhōngguó.	The friend I spoke to you about is going to China.
穿红色裙子的女人是我妈妈。	Chuān hóngsè qúnzi de nǚrén shì wǒ māma.	The woman wearing the red skirt is my mother.

...talk about a place's location.

西安在中国西北部。	Xī'ān zài Zhōngguó xīběi bù.	Xi'an is in the Northwest of China.

...write the following characters:

最 样 觉 高 轻 穿 头 发 比 长 虽 然 但 每 时
候 真 色 黄 绿 红 蓝

欢迎来台北!

Welcome to Táiběi!

Main languages:
Mandarin, Taiwanese (Hokkien)

Shilin Night Market

人口 7 400 000

Oyster Omlette 蚵仔煎 (Hézǐ jiān)

National Palace Museum
国立故宫博物院
(Guólì Gùgōng Bówùyuàn)

Taipei is pronounced "Táiběi," but is written with 'p' because Taiwan uses a different Romanisation system for Chinese.

出去吃饭 Eating Out

Objectives

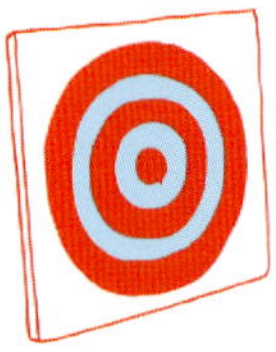

In this unit, you will learn…

…more words for food and drink.
…how to order food in a restaurant.
…how to talk about completed actions.
…how to soften the tone of a sentence.
…about food around East Asia.

Section 1: I'll try some of that!

Vocab

羊肉	yángròu	lamb
猪肉	zhūròu	pork
虾	xiā	shrimp / prawn
包子	bāozi	filled steamed bun
饺子	jiǎozi	dumpling
鸡蛋	jīdàn	egg
蛋糕	dàngāo	cake
西瓜	xīguā	watermelon
苹果	píngguǒ	apple
果汁	guǒzhī	juice
豆浆	dòujiāng	soya milk
珍珠奶茶	zhēnzhū nǎichá	bubble tea

6.1 Listening activity — What will you have?

Listen to the recording and label the correct group of pictures with the corresponding question number in your notebook.

6.6 Writing activity — Recommendations

Translate the following into Chinese in your notebook. Use characters whenever you can.

1) This book is good, have a look!

2) This pork is good, have a taste!

3) This soya milk is good, have a taste!

4) This music is good, have a listen!

5) Why not take the train?

6) Why don't we go swimming?

7) Why not use chopsticks?

Writing characters

菜 cài

豆 dòu

羊肉 yáng ròu

猪肉 zhū ròu

鸡肉 jī ròu

果汁 guǒ zhī

鸡蛋 jī dàn

昨天 zuó tiān

今天 jīn tiān

明天 míng tiān

台北超市

Tái

+886 3945 2341

2017年9月14日

猪肉 (zhū)	73 元
鸡肉 (jī)	50 元
鸡蛋 (jīdàn)	30 元
红豆 (dòu)	25 元
苹果 (píngguǒ)	60 元
面条	20 元
面包	30 元
可口可乐	10 元
果汁 (guǒzhī)	24 元
绿茶	80 元
一共	402 元

6.7 Reading activity – Supermarket receipt

Your Chinese friend, Wang Chun, went shopping. Have a look at her receipt (left) and then write down what she spent on the following items. Write the answers in your notebook.

1) Pork
2) Eggs
3) Apples
4) Coke
5) Red beans
6) Chicken
7) Noodles
8) Juice

Many international products and companies have created a Chinese version of their names in order to appeal to the Chinese market. Here are a few familiar brands with their Chinese versions. Notice how they have tried to keep the name sounding similar while choosing characters that will create a good impression.

Characters	Pinyin	Literal Meaning
可口可乐	kěkǒukělè	Delicious-happy
宝马	bǎomǎ	Precious horse
雀巢	quècháo	Sparrow's nest
乐事	lèshì	Happy event
家乐福	jiālèfú	Family happiness and prosperity

6.8 Sketch – Please eat it!

With a partner, act out this sketch as a parent and young child. The parent is trying to get the child to eat dinner, but the child refuses.

爸爸：我给你做了饺子(jiǎo)，你尝尝(chángcháng)吧！
孩子：我不吃！
爸爸：很好吃。
孩子：我要吃蛋糕(dàngāo)。
爸爸：明天可以吃蛋糕(dàngāo)。
孩子：我不喜欢饺子(jiǎo)。
爸爸：你的朋友都喜欢吃。
孩子：不要！不要！
爸爸：你吃。吃吃吃！
孩子：好吧。

6.9 Reading activity — What I ate today

Read what Wang Chun and her mum Li Mei ate today and answer the questions below in your notebok.

今天我吃了很多好吃的菜。我在家里吃了早(zǎo)饭，我吃了饺(jiǎo)子，喝了一杯豆浆(bēi dòujiāng)。我在学校(xiào)吃了午饭。羊(Yáng)肉、猪(zhū)肉、牛肉，我都喜欢吃。今天午饭我只吃了猪(zhū)肉包子和一碗(wǎn)米饭。今天是我朋友的生日，他和我一起去了饭馆吃晚(wǎn)饭。我们吃了面条，喝了珍(zhēn)珠奶茶，也吃了蛋糕(dàngāo)。

我是经理，每天都很忙。今天我没有在家吃早(zǎo)饭，我去小商店买了三个包子，在公共汽车上吃。我在公司吃了午饭。我吃了米饭和菜。我最喜欢吃鸡(jī)肉。我晚上六点回家，给我家人做了一碗虾(wǎn xiā)和两个菜。我们都喜欢吃西瓜(guā)。

1) What did Wang Chun have for breakfast?
2) What did she have for lunch?
3) Why didn't she eat at home for dinner?
4) Where does Li Mei normally eat breakfast?
5) What is her favourite food?
6) What did she make for dinner tonight?

6.10 Writing activity — Sorting meals

In your notebook, make three columns: 早(zǎo) 饭、午饭、晚 (wǎn) 饭. Then sort the foods and drinks into the columns based on what you think might make a nice combination for each meal. You can add other foods and drinks, too! When you are done, answer the questions below.

早饭 (zǎo)	午饭	晚饭

1) 你最喜欢的菜是什么？
2) 你吃不吃肉？
3) 你最喜欢喝什么？
4) 你在学校(xiào)还是在家里吃午饭？
5) 你每天和谁一起吃晚饭？

6.11 Writing activity — Your preferences!

Write sentences comparing the following foods, saying which you prefer of the pair. You can write in the format:

我觉得(A)比(B)好吃。

or...

我觉得(B)没有(A)好吃。

1) 羊肉 (yáng) VS 鸡肉 (jī)

2) 绿茶 VS 豆浆 (dòujiāng)

3) 猪肉 (zhū) VS 牛肉

4) 面条 VS 米饭

5) 红豆 (dòu) VS 鸡蛋 (jīdàn)

6) 苹果 (píngguǒ) VS 西瓜 (guā)

7) 果汁 (guǒzhī) VS 茶

Eating a large and varied meal with friends or family is a big part of Chinese culture

Study skills — Fluency

Gaining fluency in Chinese can be something of a challenge because of the need to pay attention to the tones. A really useful method to gain fluency in a long sentence is to start at the end of the sentence and work slowly towards the beginning. For example, if the sentence is:

昨天我跟我朋友一起去商店买了很多衣服。
Zuó

You can build up your fluency in this way:

衣服。
很多衣服。
买了很多衣服。
去商店买了很多衣服。
一起去商店买了很多衣服。
我朋友一起去商店买了很多衣服。
我跟我朋友一起去商店买了很多衣服。
昨天我跟我朋友一起去商店买了很多衣服。

Section 2: In a restaurant

Vocab

台北	Táiběi	Taipei
餐厅	cāntīng	restaurant; dining hall
欢迎	huānyíng	"Welcome!"; to welcome
请	qǐng	please; to ask; to invite
进	jìn	to enter
等	děng	to wait
点菜	diǎn cài	to order food
不客气	bú kèqi	"You're welcome."
开门	kāi mén	(of a restaurant/business) to be open
关门	guān mén	(of a restaurant/business) to be closed

Language note — 请 (qǐng)

请 (qǐng) has various related meanings:

一 'Please'

请给我一杯水。(bēi) Please give me a glass of water.

二 To ask someone to do something

他请老师帮助他。(bāngzhù) He asks the teacher to help him.

三 To invite someone out (and pay the bill)

明天我请你吃饭。Tomorrow I'll take you out to eat.

6.12 Listening activity — What did he say?

You are eating out and have a series of exchanges with the waiter. What does he say to you? Match each recording number on the left with the English translation on the right. Write the answers in your notebook.

一	A	Welcome! Come in. Please sit down.
二	B	We open at 6am.
三	C	Do you like Taipei?
四	D	Please wait a moment.
五	E	How are the Chinese restaurants in the UK?
六	F	We're out of pork!
七	G	Would you like to order?
八	H	We close at 8pm.

6.13 Pair activity — In the restaurant

With a partner, act out the following restaurant dialogue. One of you should be the waiter (A) and the other person should be the customer (B).

A: 欢迎！请进！你们几位？
yíng jìn wèi

B: 只有我。

A: 好，里面请。请坐吧。点什么菜？
cài

B: 我想吃台北菜。这里有什么好吃的菜？
Tái

A: 这里的牛肉面很好吃。

B: 好，来一碗牛肉面。
wǎn

A: 还有吗？

B: 再来一杯珍珠奶茶。
bēi zhēn

A: 好，请等一下。
děng

……

A: 一碗牛肉面。一杯珍珠奶茶。
wǎn bēi zhēn

B: 太好了！谢谢。

A: 不客气！你会不会用筷子？
kèqi yòng kuài

B: 会！

……

B: 服务员！埋单！
Máidān

A: 好，给你。

B: 牛肉面真好吃！明天我和朋友会来吃早饭，几点开门？
zǎo kāi

A: 好！我们餐厅早上五点开门，晚上九点关门。
cāntīng zǎo kāi

VOCab

已经	yǐjīng	already
应该	yīnggāi	should
三杯鸡	sānbēijī	three cup chicken
红烧豆腐	hóngshāo dòufu	braised tofu
点心	diǎnxīn	dim sum
韩国烧烤	Hánguó shāokǎo	Korean barbeque
寿司	shòusī	sushi

6.14 Listening activity — Bought!

Wang Chun is preparing for her friend's birthday party. She asks Li Qing what food has already been bought. Listen and note down the foods they have in your notebook.

	Bought	Not bought
1) Sushi	○	○
2) Chicken	○	○
3) Watermelon	○	○
4) Three cup chicken	○	○
5) Eggs	○	○
6) Apples	○	○
7) Cake	○	○

6.15 Pair activity — 你买苹果了吗？
píngguǒ

Your friend kindly offered to go shopping for you. Together you made a shopping list, but she forgot it before she left for the 超市! Ask your friend whether she bought the items below. (If there is a number, that's how many she bought; an 'X' means she forgot the item.)

6.16 Pair activity — What have we already ordered?

You and a friend are in a restaurant and another friend will join you. You have already ordered a few things but need to review your order so you can decide what else you need. With a partner, practise the following dialogue:

A: 我们已经点了什么菜？
yǐ

What have we ordered?

B: 已经点了两碗饺子：一碗猪肉的、一碗牛肉的。
Yǐ zhū

We've already ordered two bowls of dumplings: one with a pork filling and one with beef.

A: 好，我们再点两碗豆浆吧。
wǎn dòujiāng

OK, we should order two bowls of soya milk.

---

1) 饺子和两个菜
jiǎo

绿茶

2) 韩国烧烤和两碗米饭
Hán shāokǎo wǎn

果汁
guǒzhī

3) 很多寿司
shòu

茶

4) 红烧豆腐和一个菜
shāo dòufu

一碗汤
wǎn tāng

5) 牛肉面和蛋糕
dàngāo

两杯可口可乐
bēi

6) 两杯果汁
bēi guǒzhī

点心

Did you know?

"Happy Birthday (and thanks for dinner)!"

In China, friends will often celebrate a birthday by going out to eat. But if it's your birthday, don't expect to be treated; you will most likely treat everyone else, as is customary! For all restaurant meals – everyday and special occasions included – it is normal for one person to foot the whole bill rather than to split.

Unit 6 | 第六单元

About the language: Completed actions

Using 了

The word 了 is used to indicate that an action has been completed. It usually gets put after the verb. Here are a few simple examples:

我吃了。	I have eaten / I ate.
他看了。	He has seen / He saw.
你买了吗？	Did you buy it? / Have you bought it?

The placement of 了 in a sentence depends on the object of the verb. If the object is short (one word only) then 了 goes at the end of the sentence. If the object is long (more than one word) then 了 goes directly after the verb. Here are some examples; the objects are highlighted:

Short objects:

我回家了。	I returned home.
妈妈去北京了。	Mum went to Beijing.
饭馆关门了。	The restaurant closed.
我的朋友点菜了。	My friend ordered food.

Long objects:

我们吃了中国菜。	We ate Chinese food.
他看了三本书。	He read three books.
她认识了一个朋友。	She made a new friend.
弟弟买了一件衬衫。	Younger brother bought a shirt.

The most important thing to remember about 了 is when it **cannot** be used. 了 generally cannot be used in the following cases:

- In negative sentences
- With modal verbs (要，应该 (yīnggāi)，能，可以，会，喜欢)
- For repeated or continuous actions in the past
- With verbs 是，有，觉得

没有 for negative past sentences

We have learnt the word 不 to make negative sentences. If you want to talk about things that did not happen in the past, you must replace 不 with 没有. For example:

我不打网球。	I don't play tennis.
我没有打网球。	I didn't play tennis.
她不去中国。	She is not going to China.
她没有去中国。	She did not go to China.

Often 没有 is shortened to just 没, so alternative sentences are:

我没打网球。 and 她没去中国。

Each sentence below has been scrambled. Unscramble the sentences and write each with correct word order in your notebook.

一 这 — 书 — 看 — 没 — 我 — 本 ……………

二 吃 — 鸡蛋 (jīdàn) — 三 — 他 — 了 — 个 ……………

三 我喜欢的 — 妈妈 — 买 — 没 — 有 — 包子 ……………

四 吗 — 你 — 果汁 (guǒzhī) — 了 — 喝 ……………

五 没 — 买 — 有 — 羊肉 (yáng) — 爸爸 ……………

六 几 — 了 — 个 — 买 — 你 — 包子 — 猪肉 (zhū) ……………

Now write answers to the following questions. Use complete sentences.

你今天上了什么课？

你昨(zuó)天去商店了吗？

你昨(zuó)天玩儿了什么游戏？

你今天早(zǎo)饭吃面包了吗？

Writing characters

饺子 jiǎo zi — 饺

等 děng — 等

进 jìn — 进

关门 guān mén — 关 and 门

开门 kāi mén — 开

欢迎 huān yíng — 迎

已经 yǐjīng — 已 and 经

台北 Tái běi — 台

吧 ba — 吧

6.18 Reading activity — Where are these dishes from?

Below is a list of some East Asian cities, along with the signature dishes from those cities. Using your knowledge of geography from Unit 5, match each dish with its location on the map. Write the answers in your notebook.

一 天津 → 包子

二 北京 → 北京烤鸭 (kǎoyā)

三 兰州 (Lánzhōu) → 牛肉面

四 成都 → 四川火锅 (chuān guō)

五 香港 → 点心

六 台北 (Tái) → 三杯鸡 (bēijī)

七 南京 → 南京盐水鸭 (yán yā)

八 首尔 (Shǒu'ěr) → 韩国烧烤 (Hán shāokǎo)

九 东京 → 寿司 (shòu)

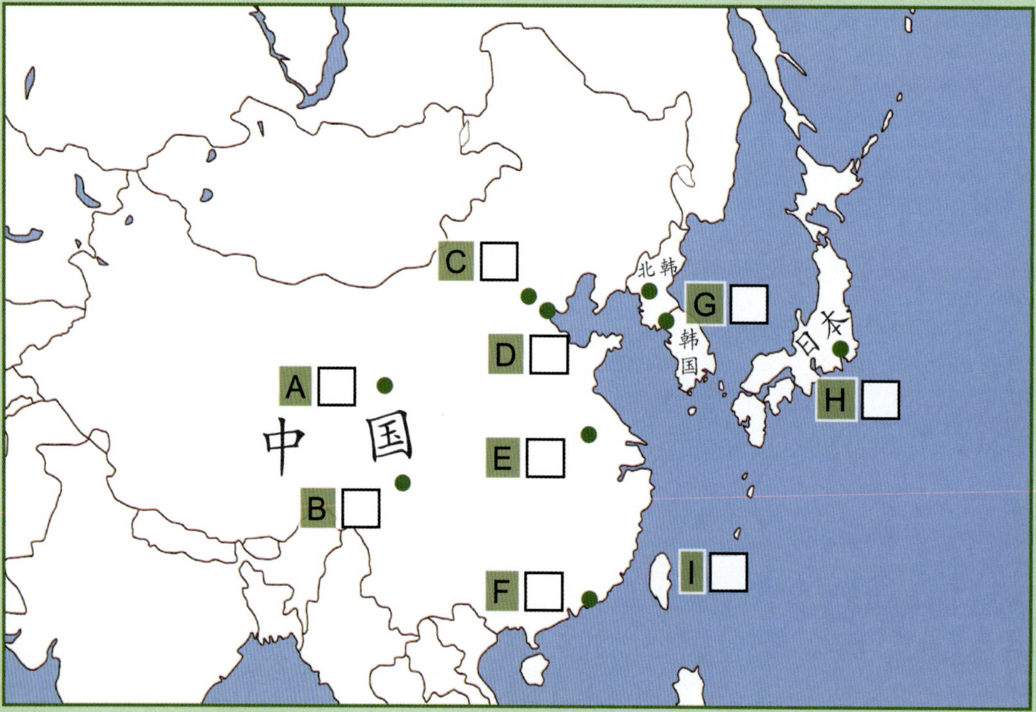

Language in action — Expressing thanks

You have learnt 谢谢 to mean 'thank you'. Here are some other common ways to say 'thank you' and 'you're welcome':

Ways to say 'thank you'

辛苦你了 (Xīnkǔ)	I gave you hard work (I troubled you to do something)
非常感谢 (gǎn)	Extremely heartfelt thanks

Tapping the table with two fingers is a way to thank someone for pouring you tea.

Ways to say 'you're welcome'

这是我应该的 (yīnggāi)	It's what I should do
不用谢 (yòng)	No need to thank me
不用客气 (yòng kèqi)	No need to be polite

6.19 Sketch — Eating out

In groups of two or three, create a restaurant sketch. Look at pair activity 6.13 on page 132 as a model and include the following:

- A warm welcome from the waiter（欢迎！请进！）
  Huān jìn
- A suggestion（你们坐这儿吧！我们吃……吧！）
- Preferences（我喜欢……！我不喜欢……。A 比 B 好吃。我不喜欢很……的菜。）
  cài
- A small dispute（虽然……，可是……。）
- Your order（来一碗……和一杯……）
  wǎn bēi
- An exclamation of how hungry/thirsty somebody is（我很饿！我很渴！）
  è kě
- An introduction to a new dish（这个很好吃，你尝尝吧！）
  chángcháng
- A comment on the dish(es)（这个太……了！）
- A request for the bill（服务员！埋单！）
  Máidān
- The restaurant's opening/closing times （我们……开门，……关门。）
  kāi

You may want to use these flavours:

甜 tián	辣 là	苦 kǔ	咸 xián
sweet	spicy	bitter	salty

Pop songs for learning Chinese

One of the best ways for improving your vocabulary in Chinese is by learning songs. The following pop songs are well known in China and can be found online with their lyrics. Karaoke is a popular pastime in China, where it is known as KTV. You will impress your Chinese friends by singing in Chinese! Beware that the lyrics in karaoke videos are almost always written in traditional characters. Here are nine great songs to try, in order of complexity.

Easy — just warming up

《月亮代表我的心》，邓丽君
《朋友》，周华健
《天堂》腾格尔

Fairly Challenging — guaranteed to impress

《我的歌声里》，曲婉婷
《橄榄树》，齐豫
《失落沙洲》，徐佳荣

Extremely hard — kudos for even attempting

《那些年》，胡夏
《北京一夜》，陈昇/刘佳慧
《爱在西元前》，周杰伦

6.20 Reading activity — 我们应该在哪儿吃饭？
yīnggāi

Below are the profiles of four restaurants/food stalls. Look at each profile and answer the questions in your notebook.

老四川
chuān

- 只有四川火锅；菜都很辣
  chuān guō là
- 11:00 – 21:00开门
  kāi
- 走路、坐车、坐地铁去，都可以
- 好吃，可是有一点贵

韩国美食
Hán shí

- 有韩国烧烤，也有寿司
  Hán shāokǎo shòu
- 10:00 – 23:00开门
  kāi
- 可以走路去
- 很好吃，可是非常贵

饺子王
Jiǎo Wáng

- 只有饺子：猪肉、羊肉、牛肉、白菜
  jiǎo zhū yáng
- 07:00 – 20:00开门
  kāi
- 可以走路去
- 很好吃，也不贵

家常菜

- 有很多中国菜；宫保鸡丁是这家饭馆最好的菜
  cài gōngbǎojīdīng
- 05:00 – 17:00开门
  kāi
- 只能坐车去
- 不太好吃，可是非常便宜

1) 我想去饭馆吃早饭。我不喜欢吃饺子，我想吃面条。我应该去哪儿吃饭？
   zǎo jiǎo yīng gāi
2) 我是成都人。我想吃很辣的菜。我应该去哪儿吃饭？
   là yīnggāi
3) 我七点走路上学。我想在路上买早饭。我应该去哪儿？
   zǎo yīnggāi
4) 今天是我朋友的生日，我想请他去饭馆吃饭。我们想尝尝好吃的菜。我们应该去哪儿吃饭？
   chángcháng yīnggāi
5) 我没有很多钱。我可以坐车去饭馆。我应该去哪儿吃饭？
   yīnggāi
6) 我是商人，工作太忙了。我十点回家。有没有饭馆晚上十点还开门？
   kāi

6.21 Writing activity — Restaurant dialogue

You are an exchange student in Taiwan and your host family has invited you out to dinner. Write a dialogue similar to the one you acted out with your classmates in the sketch on page 138. You can use the following to help you get started.

妈妈：我们今天晚上一起去吃饭吧！
我：好。我们去哪儿？
妈妈：你喜欢 [name of country] 菜吗？
我：喜欢！
妈妈：我知道一家很好的 [country] 饭馆，叫 [name of restaurant]。
我：太好了！我们几点去？
妈妈：[time] 怎么样？

...continue the dialogue, mentioning how you go to the restaurant and what you plan to eat and drink.

6.22 Listening activity — Taking orders

You are a waiter in a little restaurant. Listen to what the customers want to eat and write down their orders in Chinese in your notebook. Write in pinyin if you don't know a character. There are six orders.

Did you know?

Pulled Noodles, or 拉面 (lāmiàn)

The method for noodle-making described earlier in this chapter is a special drying technique. However, making fresh "pulled" noodles is still a common practice in restaurants all over China. The chef starts by rolling a little snake of dough, then stretching and doubling, stretching and doubling, until the strands are very thin.

Character focus — Traditional characters

In Hong Kong, Taiwan, Macao, and Chinese communities around the world, people often use traditional Chinese characters to write. These are different to those you are learning in this book, which are simplified characters. Although it requires special study to be able to read traditional characters, sometimes the traditional and simplified forms of a character look similar and you can work out the meaning. Here are some examples of radicals that look similar:

Simplified	Traditional
讠	言
饣	食
纟	糸
钅	金
贝	貝

繁体字

VS.

简体字

Using the patterns above, can you convert the following traditional characters into simplified characters?

誰，飯館，說，員，給，紅，請，餃子

Sometimes, you can also figure out a character's meaning by looking at the characters around it and thinking about words you know that use the character. With this method, can you convert the following traditional characters into simplified characters?

老師，喜歡，市場，學生，火車，覺得

Putting it together

6.23 Speaking activity — Did you remember?

A parent is reminding a forgetful child to do various things. In each case the child forgot, but her older sibling remembered. Act out the conversation in threes.

1) 穿鞋了吗？
2) 早饭吃了吗？ (Zǎo)
3) 关门了吗？
4) 买课本了吗？
5) 作业做了吗？
6) 给奶奶打电话了吗？
7) 阿姨的生日蛋糕做了吗？ (dàngāo)

6.24 Reading activity — Shopping in the night market

You are walking around a night market in Taipei with your friends and come across this stall selling drinks and snacks. Although you don't know all of the characters, use what you know to guess answers to each question. Write the answers in your notebook, then look up the items to check your answers.

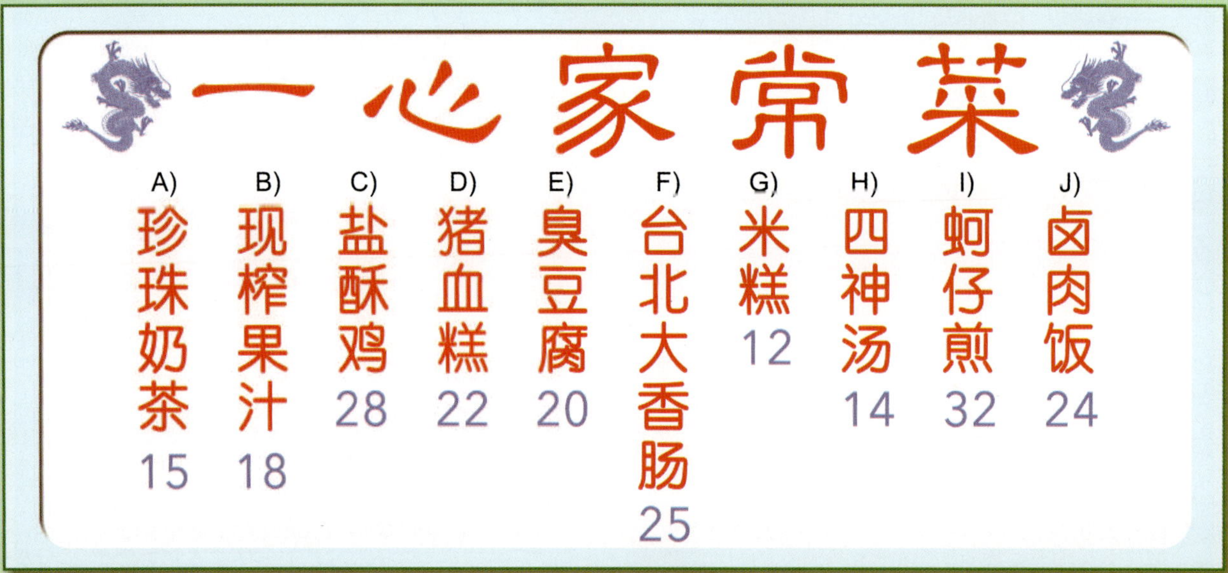

1) Which items are drinks?
2) Which items contain meat?
3) Which food items do not contain meat?
4) Which item contains fruit?
5) Which item is a type of soup?

Now, search for pictures of each item online and see if you were correct.

6.25 Writing activity — Email to your Chinese teacher

While on holiday in Taipei, you write the following email to your Chinese teacher in the UK. Complete the email by filling in the blanks in your notebook.

__ __ 好！
Lǎo shī

我在 __ __ 。台北 __ __ __ ， __ 漂亮！ __ __ __ 认识了 __ __ __ __ __ ，
Táiběi hěn hǎo wán hěn Wǒ yǐjīng yí gè xīn péngyou

__ __ 王春。王春 __ __ __ 。 __ __ __ __ 。她很瘦， __ __ __ __ 。她的 __ __ __
tā jiào Wáng Chūn Wáng Chūn shì xuésheng Tā shí sān suì yě bǐ wǒ gāo tóu fa hěn

短， __ __ __ __ 。 王春的 __ __ 是经理， __ __ __ __ 电脑公司 __ __ 。
shì hēi sè de Wáng Chūn mā ma zài hěn dà de gōngzuò

__ __ 我和王春 __ __ __ __ __ 早饭。王春 __ __ __ __ __ __ ，我吃了 __ __ __ __ 。
Zuó tiān Wáng Chūn qù fàn guǎn chī le zǎo Wáng Chūn chī le yáng ròu bāo zi jī ròu jiǎo zi

__ __ __ __ __ 了豆浆。 __ __ __ __ __ __ 豆浆 __ __ ， __ __ __ __ 很贵！
Wǒ men yě dōu hē dòujiāng Wǒ jué de guǒ zhī bǐ dòujiāng hǎo hē kě shì guǒ zhī

__ __ __ __ __ __ __ __ __ __ __ __ __ 。 __ __ __ 红烧豆腐、三杯鸡 __ __ __ __ __ 。
Wǒ zài Tái běi chī le hěn duō hěn hǎo chī de cài Wǒ chī le shāo dòufu bēi jī hé hěn duō miàntiáo

__ __ __ __ __ __ __ __ __ ？你叔叔是台湾人， __ __ __ ？ __ __ __ __ 台湾 __ ？
Nǐ zuì xǐ huan de cài shì shén me Tái shì bú shì Tā hái zhù zài Táiwān ma

__ __ 我和王春 __ __ __ __ __ __ 。 __ __ __ __ __ __ __ __ __ 。 __ __ __ __ __ ！
Míngtiān Wáng Chūn yì qǐ qù dǎ wǎngqiú Tā shuō tā wǎng qiú dǎ de hěn hǎo Wǒ xiǎng qù kàn kan

祝好！
Zhù

Did you know?

Chinese Tea

Tea has always been an extremely popular drink in China, and China has some of the world's most famous types of tea. Everything about tea in China is a refined art form: from cultivating the tea, picking the best leaves, making the tea set, through to the art of tea drinking. The art of tea is called 茶艺.

China has many different types of tea. Here are a few of the most popular kinds to look out for and try.

龙井茶 (lóngjǐng) The classic green tea, Dragon Well, is grown at one of China's famous scenic spots: West Lake in Hangzhou. It is perhaps China's most famous tea.

茉莉花茶 (mòlì huā) Jasmine tea is green tea infused with jasmine flowers.

菊花茶 (júhuā) Chrysanthemum tea actually has no tea leaves; it is simply a flower and sugar infusion.

铁观音 (guān) Tie Guanyin is a famous Oolong tea from Fujian province. Oolong is half-way between green tea and black tea. It has a buttery aroma.

普洱茶 (pǔ'ěr) Pu'er is a black tea from Yunnan province. It is unusual because it is pressed into hard, round tea-cakes and left to mature before drinking.

Reading Challenge

谈谈购物、打算

今天我和我朋友一起去中央广场买了很多衣服。我的朋友想买一条裙子，我想买一件衬衫。我们十二点半在“好买商店”前边见面，然后我们去了很多商店。我喜欢在“物美价廉”买衣服，因为很便宜。可是我的朋友说“物美价廉”的衣服真难看，我应该去“时尚”。我觉得，“时尚”的衣服很贵。我买了一件蓝色的衬衫，很漂亮，也不贵。我的朋友买了一条红色的裙子，很好看，可是很贵。现在是春天，天气不热，我们应该穿很多衣服。可是，夏天的时候，我不会穿很多衣服，因为天气很热。

明天是我朋友的生日，我要去参加他的晚会。我想买礼物送给他，可是今天我没有买，因为明天我要去商店给他买电脑游戏。晚上回到家，我爸爸妈妈说我不可以去晚会，因为我姑姑明天要来我家。爸爸妈妈说我要和家人一起吃晚饭，不可以去晚会。我很不高兴，我的朋友都会去，我为什么不可以去？

Answer the questions in Chinese

1) What did my friend want to buy?
2) Which shop do I like and why?
3) What did I buy?
4) What's happening tomorrow?
5) What do I plan to buy tomorrow and why?
6) What am I not allowed to do, and why?
7) What do I think about it?

Glossary

中央	zhōngyāng	= central
广场	guǎngchǎng	= public square
晚会	wǎnhuì	= evening party
礼物	lǐwù	= present
姑姑	gūgu	= paternal aunt

Writing piece

In Chinese, write about an experience you had shopping. Write at least 75 characters. Make sure to describe what you bought and say how much it cost.

我会

Now you can...

...talk about food and drink.

你最喜欢的菜是什么？	Nǐ zuì xǐhuān de cài shì shénme?	What is your favourite dish?
我喜欢吃羊肉。	Wǒ xǐhuān chī yángròu.	I like to eat lamb.
今天我吃了很多好吃的菜。	Jīntiān wǒ chīle hěn duō hǎo chī de cài.	Today I ate lots of delicious food.
我很饿！	Wǒ hěn è!	I'm hungry!

...order food in a restaurant.

请进！你们几位？	Qǐng jìn! Nǐmen jǐ wèi?	Come in! How many are you?
里面请。请坐吧。点什么菜？	Lǐmiàn qǐng. Qǐng zuò ba. Diǎn shénme cài?	Inside please. Please have a seat. What would you like to order?
服务员！来一个猪肉面和一个羊肉面。	Fúwùyuán! Lái yígè zhūròu miàn hé yígè yángròu miàn.	Waiter! Please bring one pork noodles and one lamb noodles.
来一碗猪肉饺子。	Lái yì wǎn zhūròu jiǎozi.	Bring a bowl of pork dumplings.

...talk about completed actions.

我买了三个苹果。	Wǒ mǎile sān gè píngguǒ.	I bought three apples.
我没有买羊肉。	Wǒ méiyǒu mǎi yángròu.	I didn't buy lamb.
我们点了什么菜？	Wǒmen diǎn le shénme cài?	What have we ordered?
妈妈去北京了。	Māma qù Běijīng le.	Mum went to Beijing.
她认识了一个朋友。	Tā rènshí le yígè péngyǒu.	She made a friend.
我没有打网球。	Wǒ méiyǒu dǎ wǎngqiú.	I didn't play tennis.

我会 Now you can...

...soften the tone of a sentence.

我用一下你的笔，好吗？	Wǒ yòng yíxià nǐ de bǐ, hǎo ma?	Is it okay if I use you pen for a bit?
你看看。	Nǐ kàn kàn.	Have a look!
我打一下电话。	Wǒ dǎ yíxià diànhuà.	I make a quick phonecall.
你尝一尝吧。	Nǐ cháng yì cháng ba.	Have a taste!
你喝一碗汤吧。	Nǐ hē yì wǎn tāng ba.	Drink a bowl of soup!

...write the following characters:

菜 豆 羊 饺 猪 鸡 进 关 开 门 果 汁 昨 今
明 蛋 迎 已 经 台 吧 等

我的一天 My Day

Objectives

In this unit, you will learn…

…how to tell the time precisely.
…how to talk about your daily routine.
…how to describe what you do at school.
…about the Three Kingdoms.

Section 1: Daily Routine

vocab

起床	qǐ chuáng	to get up
出门	chū mén	to go out; to leave
休息	xiūxi	to rest
放学	fàngxué	to finish school for the day
洗手	xǐ shǒu	to wash hands
做饭	zuò fàn	to cook
跟……见面	gēn ... jiàn miàn	to meet ...
聊天	liáo tiān	to chat
睡觉	shuì jiào	to sleep

Using 跟 to meet up with someone

To say you meet someone in Chinese, you need to use the word 跟. For example, if you want to say 'I met my friend' you say 我跟我朋友见面。

You can't say *我见面我的朋友。

7.1 Listening activity — Wang Chun's day

Listen to Wang Chun say what she does in a day and order the activities as you hear them in your notebook.

7.2 Pair activity — Re-tell

With a partner, look at the pictures on page 146 and take turns retelling Wang Chun's typical day. Use the same order of items that you just heard and point to each picture as you say it.

Time

现在	xiànzài	now
半	bàn	half
刻	kè	quarter of an hour
分	fēn	minute
以前	yǐqián	before
以后	yǐhòu	after
什么时候	shénme shíhou	when
时间	shíjiān	time
上一个	shàng yí gè	previous
下一个	xià yí gè	next
周末	zhōumò	weekend

Expressing 'next' and 'previous'

To say 'next' and 'last' in Chinese requires a measure word. The measure word changes depending on the object. So, 'next week' is 下一个星期 but 'next class' is 下一节(jié) 课.

Often 一 is left out of the phrase, so 上一个 becomes 上个 and 下一个 becomes 下个.

7.3 Listening activity — 现在几点？
Xiǎn

Listen to the recording and write the time you hear in your notebook.

1)	8:15	8:45	8:00
2)	9:30	6:30	4:30
3)	6:12	7:10	6:10
4)	5:27	5:28	5:29
5)	12:15	11:45	11:10
6)	2:30	5:30	6:15
7)	11:15	10:45	1:15
8)	12:56	2:56	4:30

7.4 Pair activity — 现在几点？
Xiàn

Draw clock faces like the ones below and fill them in with times. Practise reading each clock aloud without showing your partner, who should write down the times she hears. Compare her answers with your clocks. Then change roles.

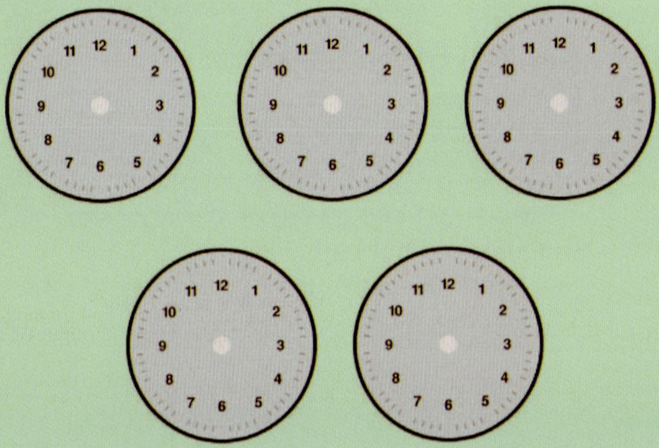

7.5 Listening activity — Aren't you going to...?

In each recording, somebody mentions doing two things, one after another. Copy the table below into your notebook, then fill in the missing information according to what you hear.

	Time	First...	Then...
1)	8:30	Eat breakfast	
2)		Finish class	Take a break
3)	6:10	Wash hands	
4)			Go to sleep

7.6 Pair activity — 我睡觉以前要看书。
shuì

Working with a partner, use the speech pattern below to make sentences with the prompts.

现在10:05。我看书以后要睡觉。
Xiàn shuì

You can use 以前 or 以后, as long as you get the order correct. In other words, you could say:

我睡觉以前要看书。 (shuì)	Before I sleep, I'll read a bit.
我看书以后要睡觉。 (shuì)	After reading for a bit, I'll sleep.

一 05:30 PM
看朋友 → 回家

四 04:30 PM
放学 → 去公园玩儿

七 02:00 PM
去银行 → 去邮局

二 07:20 AM
穿上衣服 → 吃早饭

五 12:30 PM
吃午饭 → 上中文课

八 05:45 PM
回家 → 看报纸

三 08:45 PM
看电视 → 给叔叔打电话

六 06:15 PM
洗手 (xǐ) → 做晚饭

Unit 7 | 第七单元

7.7 Listening activity — Arranging to meet

Listen to the recording and answer the questions below in your notebook.

1) When do they arrange to go swimming?
2) When do they arrange to watch a film?
3) When do they arrange to play football?
4) When do they arrange to go dancing?

Badminton in the park

7.8 Pair activity — Arranging to meet

In pairs, practise the dialogue below, proposing the various activities and times. If the time is crossed out, that means it is not convenient for the other person, in which case the second time should be proposed.

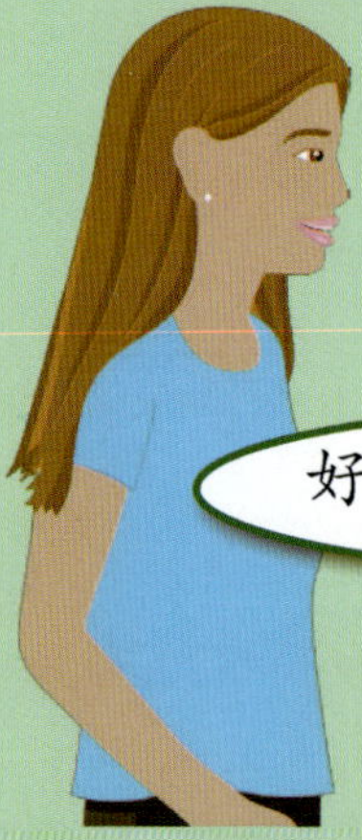

我们去唱歌吧！

好，你什么时候有时间？ (jiān)

下个周末可以吗？ (zhōumò)

Either: 好，下个周末我不忙。 (zhōumò)

or: 下个周末我没有时间。星期二好吗？ (zhōumò, jiān)

一 Next weekend

二 Next Thursday

三 ~~Next weekend~~ Next Tuesday

四 ~~Next Friday~~ Next Thursday

五 Next weekend

六 ~~——~~ Next Sunday

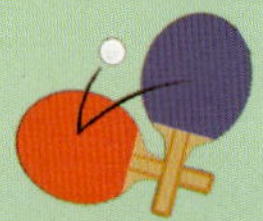

About the language: Telling the time / 以前 / 以后

Telling the time in Chinese

Here are some examples of how to tell the time in Chinese:

9:00	九点		
9:30	九点半 (bàn)	or	九点三十分 (fēn)
9:15	九点一刻 (kè)	or	九点十五分 (fēn)
9:45	九点三刻 (kè)	or	差一刻十点 (chà, kè)
9:10	九点十分 (fēn)		
9:55	九点五十五分 (fēn)	or	差五分十点 (chà, fēn)

以前，以后

The position of 'before' and 'after' in a Chinese sentence is different to English. For example:

九点以前	before nine o'clock
九点以后	after nine o'clock

Phrases with 'before...' and 'after...' are time phrases, which go before the main verb in the sentence. Here are some examples:

上学以前我会吃早饭。	Before starting school I have breakfast.
上课以前我常常跟朋友聊 (liáo) 天。	Before class I often chat with my friends.
吃午饭以后我们上历史课。	After eating lunch we have history class.
九点以后没有公共汽车。	After nine o'clock there are no buses.

7.9 Writing activity

Translate the following sentences into Chinese in your notebook. Use characters whenever you can; otherwise, use pinyin.

1) After I go to the shop, I will go to the hotel.

2) After I wash my hands, I will make supper.

3) Before I watch television, I will do my homework.

4) Before I go to meet him, I will go shopping.

5) I go to bed after 10 o'clock.

6) I go to work before 7:30.

Writing characters

时间 shí jiān

半 bàn

分 fēn

周末 zhōu mò

and

起床 chuáng

睡觉 shuì

见 jiàn

手 shǒu

现在 xiàn

课 kè

With the new characters, you can also now write:

床	chuáng	bed
见面	jiànmiàn	to see somebody
上课	shàngkè	to go to class
下课	xiàkè	to get out of class

Did you know?

炕 (kàng) — Bed-stoves

How would you like to sleep on a heated brick oven bed? The *kang* is just that: a brilliant, 3-in-1 solution to heat the home, cook your meals and provide a cosy space to work and relax. Made of bricks or clay, a *kang* is a platform, usually about waist height, which is often wall-to-wall and takes up less than half of the room. People can sit on it during the day and sleep on it at night. Beneath it, the smoke from the cooking fire (usually in the kitchen, adjacent) circulates and keeps it warm. *Kangs* have been an essential element of traditional Chinese homes, especially in the North.

觉

Notice that 觉 in 觉得 (juéde) also appears in the word 睡觉 (shuìjiào). This is another case of a character that has multiple readings.

床

床 (chuáng) on its own means 'bed', and the measure word is 张 (zhāng).

7.10 Reading activity — My day

Read the text about Wang Chun's day and answer the questions in your notebook.

我今天七点半(bàn)起床(chuáng)，八点一刻(kè)出门了。我坐火车去学校(xiào)，九点上了艺术课。上个星期我们学习了画画；这个星期，我们要学习拍照片。我十二点半(bàn)吃了午饭。今天我吃了猪肉饺子和两个菜。吃饭以后，我上历史课。历史不好学，可是我喜欢上历史课。我们三点放学。下课以后，我和朋友见面聊(liáo)天。我五点回家了。做作业(zuòyè)以前，我听音乐。我六点四十分(fēn)和父母(fùmǔ)一起吃了晚饭。我们吃了牛肉面。我十点半睡(bàn shuì)觉。

1) What time did Wang Chun wake up?
2) How did she get to school?
3) What class did she attend at 9:00?
4) What did she learn in art class last week?
5) What time did she have lunch?
6) What did she eat for lunch today?
7) What did she do after classes finished?
8) What did she do before starting her homework?

Language in action — Greetings through the day

You have learnt that 你好 means hello, but it is also a little formal: it's often used when you meet strangers for the first time. Here are some other ways to greet people in Chinese:

早！	Good morning!
晚上好！	Good evening!
晚安！	Good night!
你吃了吗？	Have you eaten? (Used as a greeting around mealtimes.)
你去哪儿？	Where are you going? (Used as a greeting for people who are walking.)

7.11 Writing activity

Jot down an outline of a typical day for you, including various activities and the times you do them. Look at the reading exercise 7.10 above as an example. Once you have had enough practice saying what you do, present your day to a classmate. Be sure to include 以前 and 以后 in your presentation!

7.12 Reading activity – Texting with Wang Chun

Read the text exchange between you and Wang Chun and answer the questions in your notebook.

晚上好！你现在忙吗？我有东西想给你，我想要跟你见面。
xiàn
王春
Wáng Chūn

什么东西？谢谢，你真好！今天晚上我没有时间，可是明天我能去看你。明天上午可以吗？
jiān

不可以，明天是星期六，起床以后我要去看奶奶。她住在市中心。我晚上八点半回家。下个星期怎么样？
chuáng, bàn

下个星期一好吗？我们三点放学以后见面吧。
fàng, jiàn

好，我三点五分在学校门口等你！
fēn, xiào

Glossary
门口 ménkǒu = entrance

1) Why does Wang Chun want to see you?
2) When does she want to see you?
3) What is the day today?
4) What is Wang Chun doing tomorrow?
5) What time will she return home tomorrow?
6) Where do you finally agree to meet?

7.13 Writing activity – Thank you email

When you finally met Wang Chun, she gave you a little present. A few days have passed and you would like to write an email thanking her for her gift. Copy and complete the note below in your notebook.

__ __ __ __
Wáng Chūn nǐ hǎo
Hello, Wang Chun:

__ __ __ __ __ __ __ __ __ __ ，__ 漂亮， __ __ __ __ ！ __ __ __ __ __ __ 。 谢谢__ ！
Nǐ gěi wǒ de xīn máoyī fēicháng hǎo, hěn piàoliang. Wǒ hěn xǐhuan! Wǒ zuì xǐhuan lánsè. Xièxie nǐ!
The jumper you gave me is really good... very beautiful! I like it! Blue is my favourite colour. Thank you!

__ __ __ __ __ __ __ __ __ __ __ __ 。 __ __ __ __ __ __ __ __ __ __ 。 __ __
Zuótiān wǒ shàngkè yǐqián hé yí gè péngyou jiànmiàn. Tā shuō tā yě hěn xǐhuan wǒ de máoyī. Xià ge
Yesterday I met up with a friend before starting class. She said she also really likes my jumper. Next

__ __ __ __ __ 。 __ __ __ __ __ __ __ 件。 __ __ __ __ __ __ __ __ __ __
yuè shì tā de shēngrì. Wǒ yě xiǎng gěi tā mǎi yí jiàn. Wǒmen kě bù kěyǐ yìqǐ qù nà jiā shāngdiàn
month is her birthday. I would also like to buy her one. Can we go to that shop together

__ __ ？ __ __ __ __ __ ？ __ __ __ __ __ __ ？
mǎi yīfu? Xià ge zhōumò hǎo ma? Nǐ shénme shíhou yǒu shíjiān?
to buy clothes? Is next weekend okay? When do you have time?

__ __ __ __ ， __ __ __ __ ！ __ __ __ ！
Xiànzài shí diǎn bàn, Wǒ qù shuìjiào le! Míngtiān jiàn!
It's half ten now. I'm going to sleep. See you tomorrow!

7.14 Writing activity – Best timetable ever!

Make the perfect weekly timetable for yourself – in Chinese! In your notebook, model your timetable on the table below. Include the classes you would take, mealtimes, relaxation time (and what you do to relax), as well as the times you would ideally wake up and go to sleep.

	星期一	星期二	星期三	星期四	星期五	星期六	星期天
八点半 bàn							
九点							
十点十分 fēn							

Study Skills – Flashcards

A useful way to keep track of all the Chinese words you are learning is to make a flashcard of each one. This is a good format to use:

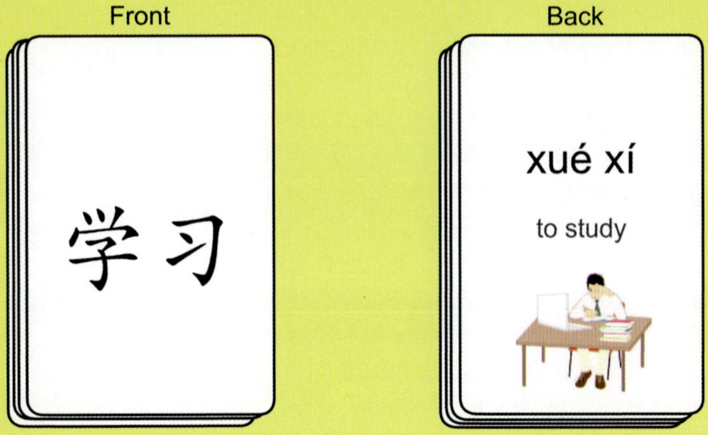

One benefit of flashcards is that you can bring them with you and practise them when you have brief periods of free time. In general it is more effective to study a few words frequently in small chunks of time than to try to study more material in one long session.

Flashcards are also good for playing games!

Flashcard game 1: **Snatch**

For three or more players. Put 10-20 cards face up on a table. One person is the caller and says a card. The other players attempt to take the card that was called. The caller may not take the card. The person who took the correct card keeps it and scores one point. Then the role of caller moves to the next person. When all the cards have been taken, whoever has the most, wins.

Flashcard game 2: **Quick draw**

For two players. Each player starts with a shuffled pack of flashcards. At the same time, both players reveal a card to each other. The first person to correctly call the Chinese word they see (held by the other person) scores a point. This is a good game for players of mixed levels, as the two packs can contain a different set of vocabulary based on the personal goals of each player.

First player to 10 points wins.

Section 2: In class

Vocab

节	jié	measure word for class periods
班	bān	a class (group of students)
教室	jiàoshì	classroom
本子	běnzi	exercise book; notebook
写	xiě	to write
汉语	Hànyǔ	Chinese
英语	Yīngyǔ	English
练习	liànxí	to practise

Class
The word 'class' can be translated as 班 (group of students) or 课 (lesson).

Language
In Chinese, 文 and 语 both mean 'language' and are both used in names of languages. So 英语 and 英文 both mean 'English', and 汉语 and 中文 both mean 'Chinese'. Note that you can't say *汉文 and *中语.

7.15 Listening activity — Touring Wang Chun's school

Listen and imagine Wang Chun is taking you on a tour of her school. In your notebook, match the number of each recording with the English translation on the right.

一
二
三
四
五
六
七
八

a) Would you like to see my notebook?
b) My class has 20 students.
c) My teacher has written many books.
d) This is my English classroom.
e) I practise English every day.
f) My English teacher is American; he can't speak Chinese.
g) I have six class periods every day.
h) English is my favourite class.

7.16 Pair activity — Interviewing a student in Taiwan

	Subject	# Students
8:00-8:45	数学	43
8:50-9:35	英语 (yǔ)	61
9:40-10:10	休息 (xiū xi)	–
10:15-11:00	艺术	45
11:10-11:55	汉语 (hànyǔ)	39
12:00-12:45	吃午饭	–
12:50-1:35	科学 (kē)	44
1:45-2:30	历史	52

With a partner, act out the following scenario:
You are doing a project about the school life of students in Taiwan and you have arranged an online interview with a Taiwanese student to get some information. Ask about his classes using the following questions:

1. 你今天上几节课？ (jié)
2. 你的班里有多少个学生？ (bān)
3. 你几点上英语课？你几点下课？ (yǔ)
4. 你喜欢练习英语吗？ (yǔ)

VOCab

所以	suǒyǐ	therefore; so
生气	shēngqì	angry
高兴	gāoxìng	happy; in high spirits
累	lèi	tired; exhausted
总是	zǒngshì	always
正在	zhèngzài	in the middle of (doing something)
帮	bāng	to help (verb)
帮忙	bāng máng	help (noun)

Tired

累 (lèi) usually refers to physical exhaustion. 'Sleepy' tired is a different word: 困 (kùn).

7.17 Listening activity — 我很累！
lèi

Listen to the recording and match the sentences below. Write the answers in your notebook.

一	I'm tired because...	a) ...the teacher doesn't like me.
二	I'm happy because...	b) ...I go swimming every morning.
三	I'm angry because...	c) ...I have new clothes.
四	I'm happy because...	d) ...I walked here.
五	I'm tired because...	e) ...the dog ate my homework.
六	I'm angry because...	f) ...my dad gave me money.
七	I'm happy because...	g) ...we are going to the park.

7.18 Listening activity — 你正在做什么？
zhèng

Listen to the recording. In your notebook, write what the boy is doing and whether or not he accepts help.

What is he doing?	Does he accept help? Yes	No

7.19 Pair activity — Offering Help

In pairs, practise offering help using the following dialogue and the prompts below.

你正在做什么？
zhèng
What are you in the middle of?

我正在做作业呢。
zhèng
I'm doing my homework.

要我帮你吗？
bāng
May I help you?

Either: 好，谢谢！
OK, thanks!

Or: 不用，我自己来。
No need, I'll do it myself.

1) 做晚饭
2) 买本子
3) 写汉语 (xiě Hànyǔ)
4) 上网买衣服
5) 做作业
6) 看法语(yǔ)书

About the language: 因为…… 所以 …… / 正在

suǒ / zhèng

因为 (reason), 所以 (result)。

This structure is used to give reasons when speaking or writing more formally; note that 因为 comes first in the sentence since that is a more natural order in Chinese.

For example:

因为我没有时间，所以我不去买东西。 jiān suǒ	Because I don't have time, I won't go shopping.
因为数学不好学，所以我不喜欢数学。 suǒ	Because maths is hard, I don't like it.
因为今天是我的生日，所以我很高兴。 suǒ xìng	Because today is my birthday, I'm happy.

As you can see, you need to put 所以 (suǒ) ('therefore') in the second half of the sentence in Chinese.

正在 (action) 呢。

正在 is put before the verb to say 'in the middle of' doing something. Often 呢 is also added at the end of the sentence. Here are some examples:

我正在看书呢。 zhèng	I am in the middle of reading a book.
王春正在做作业呢。 Wáng Chūn zhèng	Wang Chun is in the middle of doing homework.

In this structure, you can omit 正, 正在 or 呢. So, there are multiple ways to say the same thing. All of the following mean 'I'm watching a film':

我看电影呢。 我正在看电影。(zhèng) 我正在看电影呢。(zhèng) 我在看电影。 我在看电影呢。

Writing characters

正在 zhèng zài
呢 ne
节 jié
放学 fàng xué
本子 běn zi
写 xiě
汉语 hàn yǔ
因为 yīn wèi
所以 suǒ yǐ
学习 xí

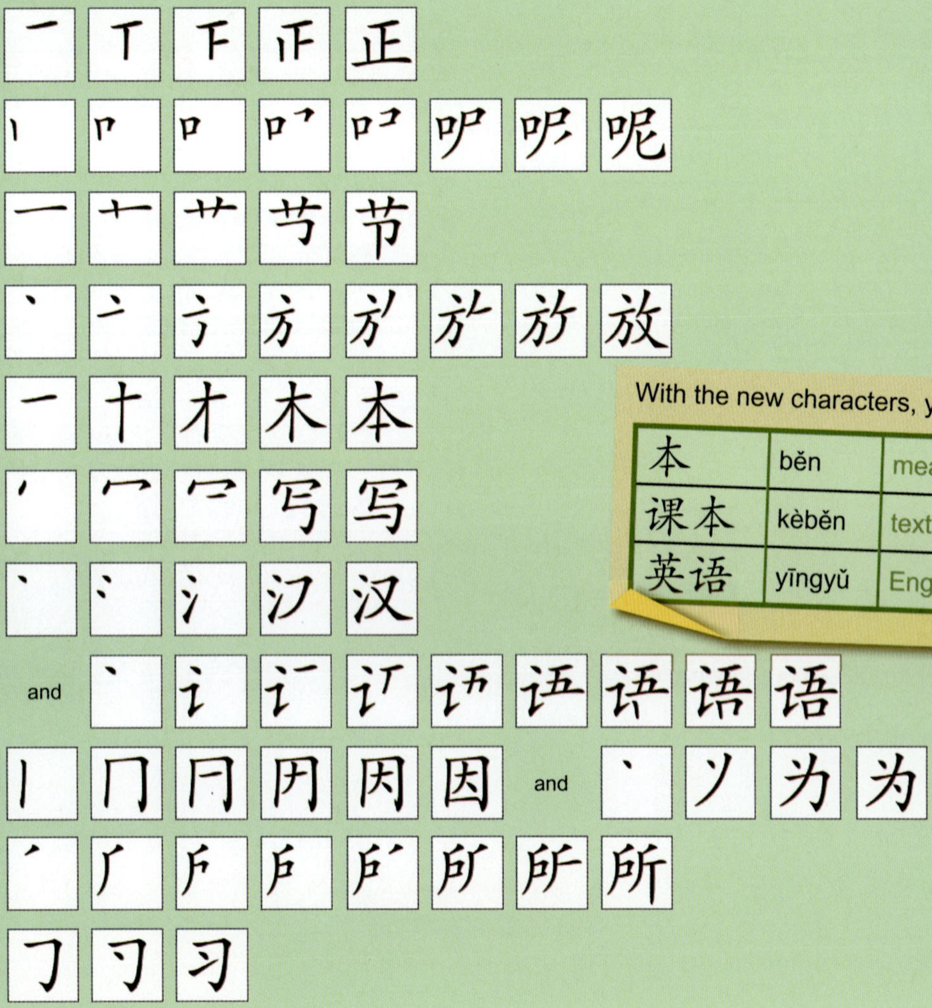

With the new characters, you can also now write:

本	běn	measure word for books
课本	kèběn	textbook
英语	yīngyǔ	English language

7.20 Writing Activities

一 Translate the following into Chinese in your notebook. Use characters whenever you can; otherwise, use pinyin.

1) I am not hungry, so I won't eat now.
2) I don't have a car, so I will take the train to school.
3) I bought a lot of green tea because I like it!
4) He is happy because he has a new bicycle.

二 Use the words from the word bank to fill the blanks below so that you produce five correct ways of saying 'I am browsing online'. Not all the blanks will be filled. Write in your notebook.

1) 我— —上网—。
2) 我— —上网—。
3) 我— —上网—。
4) 我— —上网—。
5) 我— —上网—。

Word bank: 呢 呢 呢 在 在 在 在 正 zhèng 正 zhèng

三 What are five ways to say 'I am (in the middle of) cooking lunch'? List them in your 本子, using the notes above to help.

7.21 Reading Activity – A Bad Day

Today Wang Chun had a tough morning. Read her account of the day, matching the first half to the second half of each sentence below. Write the answers in your notebook.

一 因为我想买书……

二 因为我上午十点一刻出门……

三 因为书店里的人太多了……

四 因为那家饭馆的菜都很贵……

五 因为我吃得不多……

六 因为我有一点累……

七 我没有去书店，也没有吃午饭。可是，因为我在台北……

a) ……所以我去市中心的书店。

b) ……所以我回家休息。

c) ……所以我只喝了一杯珍珠奶茶。

d) ……所以我还是很高兴！

e) ……所以我不能坐十点的车，只能等下一辆。

f) ……所以我不想进去。我要去书店左边的饭馆。

g) ……所以我很饿。

Glossary

辆	liàng	= measure word for wheeled vehicles

Did you know?

Chinese Riddles

In the Chinese speaking world, 谜语 (míyǔ) riddles are associated with festivals, especially 元宵节 (yuánxiāo jié, the Lantern Festival), which occurs 15 days after Chinese New Year.

Riddles are typically written on slips of paper which are attached to lanterns in the streets. The challenge is to 猜 (cāi, 'guess') the right answer.

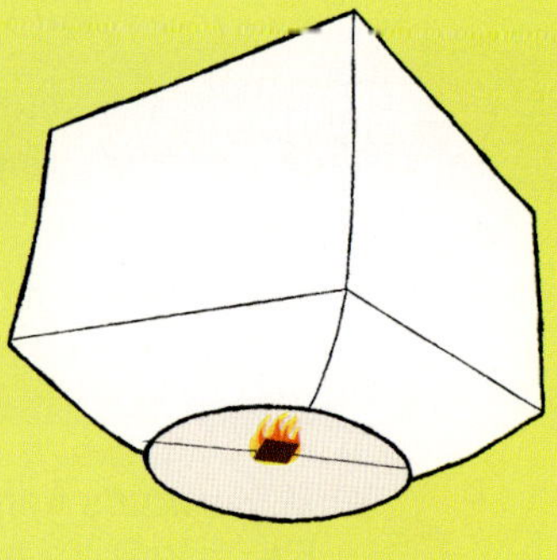

Chinese riddles usually tell you the category of the thing you are guessing. For example, 'guess an animal' or 'guess a Chinese character'. The hint is written with the word 打 ('to hit').

Can you solve the following riddles?

1) 五个兄弟，住在一起，名字不同，高矮不齐。
Five brothers live together. Their names are different, and they are of different heights.

2) 年纪不算大，胡子一大把，不管见到谁，总爱叫妈妈。
(Although) its age is not great, it has a large beard. No matter who it sees, it always says 'mama.'

3) 一加一（打一字）
One plus one. (Guess a character)

Language in action — Exclamations

The Chinese words and sounds for exclaimations are different to English. Here are some you might hear.

哇！	(wā)	Wow!
哎呀！	(āiyā)	Oh no!
啊！	(ā)	Oh!
嗯。	(èn)	Yup. Uh-huh. (Informal word meaning 'yes')

7.22 Pair activity — 你为什么想上数学课？

You are choosing your classes for next year and your friend is asking you why you've chosen each class. Look at the list of reasons below (you can add some of your own) and practise the conversation, then present to the class.

因为中文很有意思，所以……
si suǒ

因为我想要多练习英语，所以……
yǔ suǒ

因为我朋友都想上科学课，所以……
suǒ

因为美术教室很漂亮……
jiàoshì

因为数学老师很好……

因为历史作业很少，所以……
suǒ

7.23 Reading activity — 你放学以后做什么？

Here are some responses students have posted on an online forum about how they spend their time after school. Have a look and then answer the questions below in your notebook.

金娜(nà)	2017年9月14日	07:49	回复 (fù)	分享 (fēnxiǎng)
	在韩国，我们学习很累。放学以后，我还要去上课。可是我也很喜欢弹吉 lèi. 它，我天天都弹。我星期二晚上也上艺术课。周末我会跟朋友见面。 Zhōumò			
小丽 (lì)	2017年9月12日	15:32	回复 (fù)	分享 (fēnxiǎng)
	我是上海人。我的作业也很多，可是我有很多爱好。上学以前，我有时候 去公园打羽毛球。放学以后，我常常跟我朋友唱歌。每天下午五点半我和 bàn 爷爷奶奶吃饭。我十点一刻睡觉。 kè shuì			
Ben	2017年12月23日	12:04	回复 (fù)	分享 (fēnxiǎng)
	我家在美国。我每天都很忙，但是我的作业比较少。我两点五分放学，坐 jiào fēn 车回家。我在家里看电视、吃饭。因为我星期一、三、四去踢足球，所以 suǒ 那三天我要穿运动服。我六点四十分回家。 fēn			

1) What fun activity does Jin Na do every day?
2) What does she do at the weekend?
3) What does Xiao Li do before school?
4) What does she do after school?
5) What time does Ben finish school?
6) What does he do three days per week?

7.24 Writing activity — Add your post!

Now it's your turn to post a response to the forum. What do you do after school? Copy the post below, filling in characters to make it relevant to you. See if you can add extra information to make it more personal.

名字：	日期：	时间 (jiān)：	回复 (fù)	分享 (fēnxiǎng)
	我是 [nationality] 。我家在 [country] 。我 [time] 起床， [transport] 上学。去学校以前，我有时候 [activity] 。我每天上 [number] 节课。我最喜欢的课是 jié [subject] 课。我们 [time] 放学。放学以后，我常常 [activity] 。我有时候也 [activity] 。我的作业很 [adjective] 。晚上我在 [place] 跟 [person] 吃晚饭。我最喜欢吃 [food] 。我晚上 [time] 睡觉。 shuì			

7.25 Writing activity — School brochure

Create a brochure for your school. Include the following information:

- The name of the school

  （学校的名字叫……）
  xiào

- The number of classrooms, teachers and students

  （学校有……个老师）
  xiào

- The courses offered

  （学校有……、……、……课）
  xiào

- Which meals are provided, and at what times

  （学生可以在学校吃……和……）
  xiào

- The dress code

  （学生应该穿……）

- When school starts and finishes

  （学生……点上学，……点放学）

- Activities offered after class

  （下课以后，学生可以……）

- How you can get to school

  （学生能……，也能……来学校）
  xiào

Character focus — Similar looking characters

Here are some characters you have learnt that are easily confused. Can you say which is which?

们 vs 门	有 vs 友
问 vs 间	走 vs 起
牛 vs 午	那 vs 哪
见 vs 现	西 vs 四
左 vs 右	大 vs 太
百 vs 白	北 vs 非
觉 vs 学	知 vs 和

Did you know?

The marble-sided Taroko Gorge has some of Taiwan's most stunning scenery. It can be visited in a weekend from Taipei.

Putting it together

7.26 Reading activity — 台北101

Read about Taipei 101 and in your notebook write whether the statements below are true or false.

台北101建于2004年。从2004年到2010年，它是世界上最高的建筑：一共有101
jiàn yú cóng dào shìjiè jiànzhú
层。因为中国人觉得"四"会带来不好的运气，所以台北101没有第四十四层，
céng dài yùnqì suǒ dì céng
只有第四十二、第四十三、第四十三A和第四十五层。台北101里面很漂亮，也
dì dì dì dì céng
很新。

台北101每天晚上有不一样的灯光。一天一个颜色：星期一是红色的灯，星期三
dēngguāng dēng
是黄色，星期四是绿色……很漂亮！

台北101里边有很多商店和饭馆，也有书店、服装店、银行，还有超市。台北
zhuāng
101里边的东西都很贵！

Glossary

建于	jiànyú	= built in (a time/place)
从……到……	cóng...dào...	= from... to...
世界	shìjiè	= the world
建筑	jiànzhú	= building
层	céng	= floors; levels
带	dài	= bring
运气	yùnqì	= luck
第	dì	= ordinal number marker (for example, 第一课 means 'first lesson')
灯光	dēngguāng	= light
服装店	fúzhuāng diàn	= clothing shop

	✔ 正	✘ 误
1) Taipei 101 is currently the tallest tower in the world.	○	○
2) There are 101 shops and restaurants in the tower.	○	○
3) There is no 44th floor.	○	○
4) The light on the tower is red on Thursdays.	○	○
5) There are many banks in Taipei 101.	○	○
6) Some shops are cheap, some are expensive.	○	○

7.27 Writing activity — Letter to Chinese teacher

You have an opportunity to do work experience in China! Now you are writing to your Chinese teacher to say you will be away. Convert the pinyin in the letter below to Chinese characters; write it in your notebook.

老师您好！
Lǎoshī nín hǎo!

厂 。
Yǒu yìjiā Zhōngguó gōngchǎng qǐng wǒ qù zuò liǎng gè yuè lǎoshī. Yīnwèi nàlǐ

， 厂 理 帮
de rén zhèngzài xuéxí yīngyǔ, suǒyǐ gōngchǎng de jīnglǐ qǐng wǒ qù bāng

。 兴， 。
gōngrén xuéxí. Wǒ fēicháng gāoxìng, yě hěn xiǎng qù. Tāmen yào wǒ liù

校 才
yuè yī hào dào nàr gōngzuò, kěshì wǒmen xuéxiào liù yuè èrshí hào cái fàng

假， 。请
jià, suǒyǐ liù yuè de qián sān gè xīngqī wǒ bù néng lái shàng kè. Qǐng

， ？ 业， 练
wèn, wǒ kěyǐ qù ma? Wǒ huì zuò zuòyè, yě huì měitiān liànxí

。 、 聊 ，
hànyǔ. Tiāntiān gēn Zhōngguó rén yìqǐ zhù, yìqǐ liáotiān, wǒ juéde wǒ de

！
zhōngwén huì xué de hěn hǎo!

您 ？
Nín juéde zěnme yàng?

祝好！
Zhù hǎo!

Glossary

才	cái	= particle meaning 'later than expected'
放假	fàngjià	= take a holiday

"你正在做什么呢？

……嗯！……

因为今天的天气非常好，所以我出去买东西。今天我太高兴了！"

三国 Three Kingdoms

From 220 to 280AD, China was divided up into three kingdoms: 魏 (Wèi) in the North, 蜀 (Shǔ) in the Southwest, and 吴 (Wú) in the Southeast. Each kingdom fought for control of all China and had famous generals leading their armies into battle. These generals have become popular characters in stories; they are cultural icons in China, just like Robin Hood or King Arthur are ancient cultural icons in Britain. Nowadays, films, TV dramas and videogames also tell the stories, but the most famous novel about the Three Kingdoms was written in the 14th century and is called 《三国演义》 (Sānguó Yǎnyì, *Romance of the Three Kingdoms*).

Cao Cao

Main Characters

There are three heroes, sworn as brothers. They fight for the kingdom of 蜀 (Shǔ).

刘备 (Liú Bèi)
关羽 (Guān Yǔ)
张飞 (Zhāng Fēi)

Their enemy: A brilliant, ruthless general, who fights for the kingdom of 魏 (Wèi).

曹操 (Cáo Cāo)

The Huarong Path

This game became popular in China in the 1930s and tells a story from the *Three Kingdoms*. Cao Cao has just been badly defeated at the Battle of Red Cliffs and tries to escape through a narrow valley, 华容道 (Huáróng Dào, the Huarong Path). However, Guan Yu is already in the valley and ambushes Cao Cao. Cao Cao is almost captured, but Guan Yu shows him mercy and allows him to escape.

The object of the game is to slide the blocks so that the large block (Cao Cao) can escape the box. The only exit is from the other side of the box. Notice that each of the blocks refers to a character in the story. It takes an incredible 81 moves to complete the puzzle!

The Huarong Path board game

Reading Challenge

你为什么上网？

Seven people have responded in a forum asking about their favourite websites, highlighted below beside the mouse icons.

万宁 — 天猫

我上网买东西。网上东西不贵。我喜欢上天猫买衣服。我上个星期买了一件蓝色的衬衫。

小雨 — 可可英语

我上网学习英文。我可以听英文新闻，看英文电影。我有时候上可可英语学习。

婷婷 — 微信

我上网跟朋友聊天。我有时候用手机上网，有时候用电脑。我喜欢上微信跟朋友聊天。

鹏鹏 — 新浪读书

我很喜欢在网上看书。坐地铁上班的时候我会看书，我也常常上新浪读书看最新的小说。

瑞敏 — 51玩网

我爱上网玩游戏。我最喜欢的游戏叫《魔兽世界》。51玩网站有很多游戏。我妈妈说我应该少玩游戏。

刘涛 — 百度

我上网看新闻。我每天看中国新闻、美国新闻和天气预报。我喜欢看百度新闻，因为网站很快。

李志 — 点评网站

我喜欢跟朋友去饭馆吃饭。我们上点评网站看看饭馆好不好。点评网站会说哪家饭馆很好，哪家饭馆不太好。

Glossary

新闻	xīnwén	= news
小说	xiǎoshuō	= novel
上班	shàngbān	= go to work
魔兽世界	Móshòu Shìjiè	= World of Warcraft

Match the following activities with the most suitable website:

1. Studying English
2. Reading reviews
3. Shopping
4. Reading novels
5. Chatting with friends
6. Reading the news
7. Playing online games

a) 天猫
b) 微信
c) 51玩
d) 点评
e) 可可英语
f) 新浪读书
g) 百度新闻

Chinese website focus

Try to access one of the Chinese websites above.

1) Can you spot any characters you know?
2) Can you work out how to navigate the website?
3) What similarities and differences do you see in the way Chinese websites are set up, compared to the websites you are used to?

我会

Now you can...

...tell the time precisely.

现在九点半。	Xiànzài jiǔ diǎn bàn.	It's half past nine now.
现在十一点三刻。	Xiànzài shíyī diǎn sān kè.	It's quarter to twelve now.
我们下课以后，就可以休息。	Wǒmen xiàkè yǐhòu, jiù kěyǐ xiūxi.	We can rest after we finish the lesson.
我看书以后要睡觉。	Wǒ kànshū yǐhòu yào shuìjiào.	After reading I go to sleep.
下个周末我不忙。	Xià ge zhōumò wǒ bù máng.	I'm not busy next weekend.
下个月是她的生日。	Xià ge yuè shì tā de shēngrì.	It's her birthday next month.

...talk about your daily routine.

我起床。	Wǒ qǐchuáng.	I get up.
我洗手。	Wǒ xǐshǒu.	I wash my hands.
我吃早饭。	Wǒ chī zǎofàn.	I eat breakfast.
我穿上衣服。	Wǒ chuānshang yīfu.	I get dressed.
我出门。	Wǒ chū mén.	I go out.
你正在做什么？	Nǐ zhèngzài zuò shénme?	What are you doing at the moment?
我正在做饭呢。	Wǒ zhèngzài zuò fàn ne.	I'm cooking now.
你什么时候有时间？	Nǐ shénme shíhòu yǒu shíjiān?	When do you have time?

...describe your life at school.

吃午饭以后，我们上历史课。	Chī wǔfàn yǐhòu, wǒmen shàng lìshǐ kè.	After we eat lunch we have history class.
下课以后，我和朋友见面。	Xià kè yǐhòu, wǒ hé péngyou jiànmiàn.	After class I meet with friends.
你每天上几节课？	Nǐ měitiān shàng jǐ jié kè?	How many classes do you take each day?
你的班里有多少个学生？	Nǐ de bān lǐ yǒu duōshǎo gè xuéshēng?	How many students are there in your class?
我的班有三十五个学生。	Wǒ de bān yǒu sānshíwǔ gè xuéshēng.	My class has 35 students.

我会

Now you can...

...ask why and give reasons.

你今天为什么很高兴？	Nǐ jīntiān wèishéme hěn gāoxìng?	Why are you happy today?
因为我们去公园玩儿，所以我很高兴！	Yīnwèi wǒmen qù gōngyuán wánr, suǒyǐ wǒ hěn gāoxìng!	I am happy because we're going to the park to play.

...write the following characters:

间 半 分 周 末 床 睡 见 手 现 课 本 正 节
放 写 汉 语 呢 因 为 所 习

放假 On holiday

Objectives

In this unit, you will learn…

…how to talk about the weather.
…how to say where you are going on holiday.
…how to talk about the scenery in different places.
…all about Taipei.

Section 1: What's the weather like?

Vocab

天气	tiānqì	weather
冷	lěng	cold
热	rè	hot
下雨	xià yǔ	to rain
下雪	xià xuě	to snow
刮风	guā fēng	windy
太阳	tàiyáng	sun
有太阳	yǒu tàiyáng	sunny
多云	duōyún	cloudy

8.1 Listening activity — How is the weather?

Listen to the recording and match the question number to the corresponding picture in your notebook.

With a partner, look at the pictures above and practise asking each other about the weather. If that becomes easy, ask about today's weather (今天的天气怎么样？) or yesterday's weather (昨天的天气怎么样？).

8.3 Listening activity — Weather forecast

You will hear a weather forecast for cities in China. Write the name of each city in your notebook and then match it to weather you hear.

1) 北京
2) 天津
3) 台北
4) 杭州
5) 广州
6) 上海
7) 西安

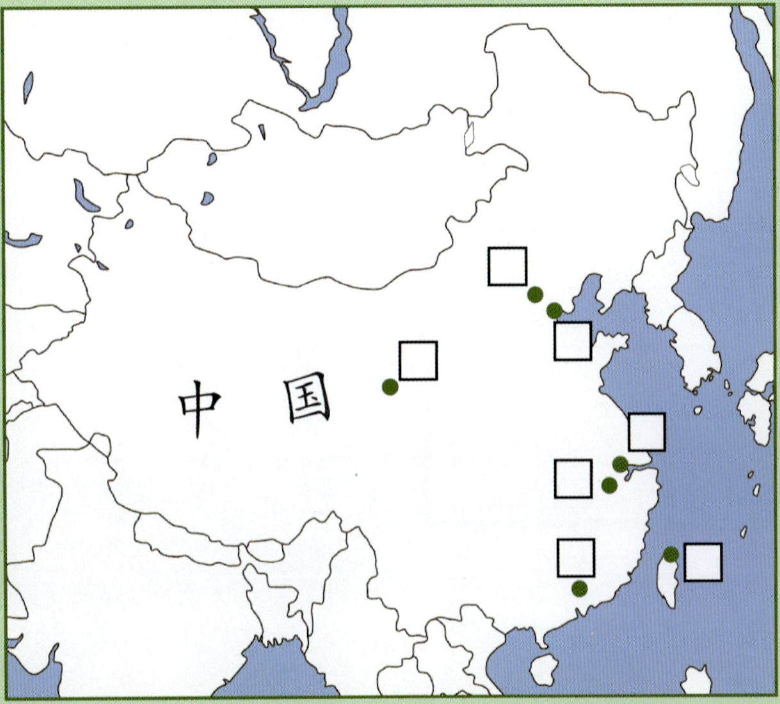

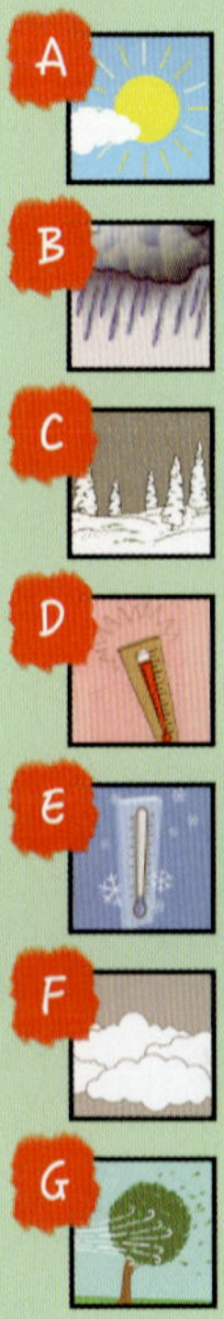

8.4 Pair activity — Tomorrow's weather

Work with a partner. Using the prompts below, practise asking and giving the forecast for tomorrow. The person giving the forecast should also make a weather-related suggestion.

台湾	Táiwān	Taiwan
杭州	Hángzhōu	Hangzhou, city near Shanghai
广州	Guǎngzhōu	Guangzhou, city near Hong Kong
韩国	Hánguó	South Korea
地方	dìfang	place
从	cóng	from
到	dào	to
去年	qùnián	last year
今年	jīnnián	this year
明年	míngnián	next year
然后	ránhòu	then, afterwards

This/last year vs. today/yesterday

Notice that 今年 and 明年 match 今天 and 明天; however, 'last year' is not *昨年, but rather 去年.

8.5 Listening activity — Where is he from?

A new student is asking where the other students are from. Listen and write down the place each person is from and the day he or she arrived in Taiwan for the start of term. Write the answers in your notebook.

8.6 Class activity — Where are you from?

Look at the map of China on page 170 and pick a city to represent. Go online to find out about today's weather in that city. Then stand and go around the class, interviewing your classmates to find out where they come from and the weather there today. Write down everyone's answers and share with the class.

8.7 Listening activity — Where did he go?

You will hear the itineraries of three trips. Copy the table below, then note all the cities mentioned.

	From...	To...
Last year	Beijing	
This year		Chicago
Next year		

Did you know?

China's climate varies a lot depending on where you are, ranging from a sub-arctic climate in the far northeast to tropical rainforest in the far south. In general, south China has much more rainfall than northern China; the northwest is especially dry. Look at these pictures of different landscapes in China to see the wide variation that exists.

Hainan Island

Xinjiang

East Chinese village

Jiuzhaigou, Sichuan

8.8 Pair activity — Tomorrow's weather

With a partner, practise talking about travel itineraries in the past and future. Use the prompts below to say where you go and in what order.

我明年要去中国，然后（ránhòu）从（cóng）中国去日本。

Next year I will go to China and then on to Japan.

我去年去了成都，然后（ránhòu）从（cóng）成都坐火车到（dào）香港，然后（ránhòu）从（cóng）香港飞到（fēi dào）南京。

Last year I went to Chengdu, then took the train to Hong Kong, then flew to Nanjing.

1) 我明年要: USA ✈ UK
2) 我去年: Shanghai ✈ Hangzhou
3) 我今年: Taipei ✈ Beijing ✈ Tianjin
4) 我明年要: Hong Kong ✈ Guangzhou ✈ Shanghai
5) 我去年: UK ✈ China ✈ Korea ✈ Japan
6) 我今年: Taipei ✈ Hong Kong ✈ Korea

Note that if you start from and return to the same place, you can say '回到（dào）'.

About the language: Future, 从 and 到
cóng dào

Future using 会 and 要

Unlike European languages, there is no future tense in Chinese. Instead, the future is often understood from context. So, 我去北京 could mean 'I go to Beijing' or 'I *will* go to Beijing'. Two words often used to indicate the future are 会 and 要, which both could be translated as 'will'.

要	Usually used when the sentence involves a need or desire to do something
我要回家	I will go home. (This implies I must go home or want to go home)
会	Usually used when the sentence describes a factual statement or prediction about the future
明天会下雨 (yǔ)	Tomorrow it will rain. (No implication that it must rain or that I want it to rain)

Sometimes, either 会 or 要 could be used in the same place, but the nuance will be slightly different.

今天晚上我要学习中文。	Tonight I will study Chinese (because I need to or want to).
今天晚上我会学习中文。	Tonight I will study Chinese (because that is the plan I have made).

从 and 到
cóng dào

从 (place/time A) 到 (place/time B)

从……到…… describes a starting and finishing point. The construction can be used either for time or physical location.

我明年要去中国，然后(ránhòu)从(cóng)中国飞(fēi)到(dào)英国。	I am going to China next year, and then I'll fly from China to the UK.
我去年去了成都，然后(ránhòu)去了香港，最后从(cóng)香港飞到(dào)了南京。	Last year I went to Chengdu, then I went to Hong Kong, and finally I flew from Hong Kong to Nanjing.

In some cases, you can simply use either 从 or 到.

他上课上到(dào)下午六点。	He has lessons until 6pm.
我从(cóng)台北来。	I come from Taipei.

Around the capital

Taipei is surrounded by mountains on all sides, including the volcanic Yangmingshan National Park, which lies within the city boundaries. Famous sights in the city include the Chiang Kai-shek memorial hall, the National Palace Museum, and Taipei 101.

The Chiang Kai-shek Memorial Hall

8.9 Writing activity

A Unscramble the characters below to make sentences and then translate each sentence into English. Write the new sentences in your notebook.

1) 会 — 我 — 他 — 看 — 明 — 天

2) 天 — 不 — 来 — 她 — 今 — 会

3) 我 — 要 — 明 — 去 — 天 — 家 — 友 — 朋

4) 年 — 去 — 他 — 明 — 的 — 师 — 老 — 要 — 海 — 上

B Translate the sentences below into Chinese. Use characters whenever possible; otherwise, use pinyin.

1) I come from Shanghai.
2) She has class from 3pm to 4:30pm.
3) He will go from the school to the supermarket.
4) Next year, I will go from the UK to China.

Writing characters

With the new characters, you can also now write:

雨	yǔ	rain
雪	xuě	snow
云	yún	cloud

8.10 Reading activity – Weather in Chinese cities

Read the text and write whether each statement below is true or false in your notebook.

A

我从北京来。今天的天气很好：
cóng
有太阳，也有风。不热，也不冷。
yáng rè lěng

B

我是英国人。去年我去了中国很多
地方。广州最好玩儿，可是天气太
Guǎngzhōu
热了！有时候下雨，也常常多云。
rè yǔ yún

C

我是南京人。南京今天很热，可
rè
是十二月会很冷，也会下雪。
lěng xuě

D

我从西安来到台北。西安很
cóng dào
热，可是没有台北这么热！
rè rè

E

我明年要去香港。我的香港朋友说，那儿的天气很好，可以不用穿太多衣服。

F

我住在天津。天津的天气跟北京的一样。每年四月会有大风，我不喜欢。

	✓ 正	✗ 误
1) Beijing is sunny today.	○	○
2) Nanjing can get both hot and cold during the year.	○	○
3) Right now, Xi'an is hotter than Taipei.	○	○
4) When the Englishman visited Guangzhou, it rained every day.	○	○
5) Weather in Hong Kong tends to be warm or hot.	○	○
6) Last April was especially windy in Tianjin.	○	○

Glossary

不用 búyòng = no need to

Did you know?

Taipei's fast and extensive metro system will take you anywhere you want to go in the city. It is not called 地铁 but 捷运 (jiéyùn) which means 'rapid transit'.

Language in action — Names of provinces

Now you know the points of the compass, it is easy to understand the names of many Chinese provinces. Look at the list of provinces below and the meaning of each province.

- 山东 Shān — East of the mountains
- 山西 Shān — West of the mountains
- 河北 Hé — North of the river
- 河南 Hé — South of the river
- 湖北 Hú — North of the lake
- 湖南 Hú — South of the lake
- 江西 Jiāng — West of the river
- 广东 Guǎng — East expanse
- 广西 Guǎng — West expanse
- 云南 Yún — South of the clouds

Now look online at a map of China and try to locate each of these provinces. Notice how they relate to each other in terms of name and location.

Taipei or Taibei?

The capital of Taiwan is typically written "Taipei". However, in pinyin (the romanisation system used in this book), it is correctly written Taibei. Although Taiwan officially adopted pinyin in 2008, in practice, it has several competing systems for romanising Chinese. This leads to a lot of confusion as to how to romanise Chinese. So, you might see a street sign for 中山(shān) 路 romanised as 'Zhongshan road', 'Chungshan road' or even 'Jhongshan road.'

8.11 Sketch — Comparing the weather in two places

With a classmate, prepare a sketch in which two acquaintances have just discovered that they have both been to China, but to different places. Discuss your itineraries and what the weather was like in each place.

北京　天津　台北　上海　成都

西安　杭州 Hángzhōu　广州 Guǎngzhōu　南京　香港

Start the sketch with the following dialogue:

A: 我去年去了中国。

B: 是吗？你去了什么地方(dìfang)？

A: 我去年去了……，然后去了……

从(Cóng)……到(dào)……坐飞(fēi)机要三个小时。

B: ……的天气怎么样？

……

You should make comparisons about the weather in the places you 'visited'. For example:

一 ……比……热(rè)。

二 ……的天气没有……好。

三 ……每天有太阳(yáng)，可是……天天都下雨(yǔ)。

Below are forecasts for six cities in China. In your notebook, match each weather picture on the right to the forecast described. There is one extra picture which will not be used.

1) 天津

明天天气会很好。会有一点风，也不会太热。
qì rè

2) 北京

上午会多云，下午三点以后会有太阳。
yún yáng

3) 西安

明天的天气会不好：上午、下午都会下雨。
qì yǔ

4) 上海

明天会是今年最热的一天。晚上会多云。
rè yún

5) 台北

明天会很热，也会有大风。
rè

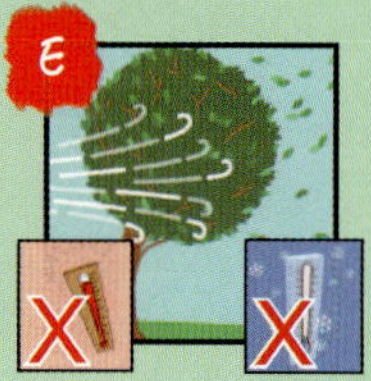

8.13 Reading and writing activity — Dream Destination

You are planning a dream adventure around the world. Look at the three small countries on the right and decide where to travel and when based on the climates and your weather preferences.

Use the template to write your itinerary:

我想去很多地方

- 我三月要去……，因为那时候 (weather comment)。我可以 (activity)。
- 我六月要去……，因为那时候 (weather comment)。我可以 (activity)。
- 我九月要去……，因为那时候 (weather comment)。我可以 (activity)。
- 我十二月要去……，因为那时候 (weather comment)。我可以 (activity)。

Country A — A

三月：不冷，也不热。现在是最舒服的时间。
lěng rè

六月：有一点冷。有太阳，有时候也下雨。
lěng yáng yǔ

九月：非常冷，常常下雪。
lěng xuě

十二月：有一点冷。每天有大风，不下雨。
lěng yǔ

Country B — B

三月：不冷，也不热。天天都下雨。
lěng rè yǔ

六月：很热。天天都有太阳。
rè yáng

九月：不冷，也不热。有太阳，也有风。
lěng rè yáng

十二月：不冷，也不热。有太阳，可是没有风。
lěng rè yáng

Country C — C

三月：有一点冷，可是不下雪，只下雨。
lěng xuě yǔ

六月：已经很热了，常常下雨。
rè yǔ

九月：很热，有时候有太阳，有时候下雨。
rè yáng yǔ

十二月：有一点儿冷。每天多云。
lěng yún

8.14 Writing activity — Weather forecast

Find the weather forecast in various towns around your country for this week. Then create your own weather map in Chinese using words from this unit. You can illustrate your map with pictures.

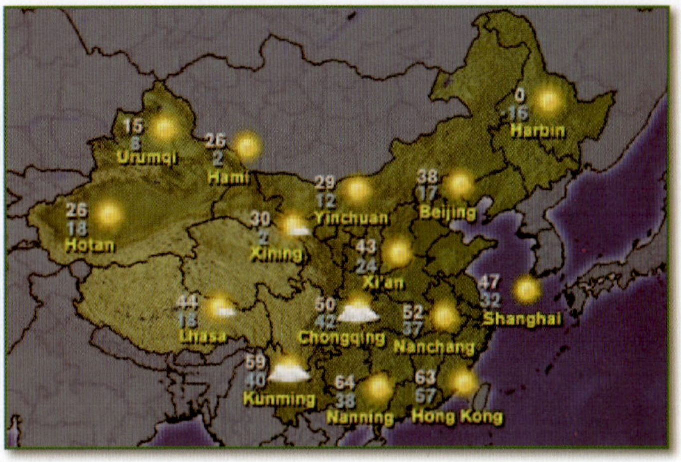

Study skills — Expand your knowledge

Having studied Chinese for a while, you are ready to look at other resources that can help you gain a broader knowledge of the language. Even if these resources are too hard for you now, you will still gain a lot from using them.

一 **Watch Chinese TV programmes online.**
Websites like www.youku.com have a large number of programmes that you can view. Often the programmes come with subtitles so you can see what is being said and look up words you don't know.

二 **Use online annotation tools to tackle more difficult texts.**
You can start to read blogs and news articles by pasting the text into an annotation tool that will look up each word automatically and give you an idea about the content. For example, www.mandarinspot.com/annotate/ provides a good tool.

三 **Make Chinese friends.**
There is no substitute for regularly meeting with a Chinese person to speak Chinese. If you don't yet have Chinese friends, now is the time to find them! You can link up with friends through pen-pal agencies online or by asking your Chinese teacher to put you in touch with someone. When you meet up, ask your friend to note down new words for you.

Section 2: On Holiday

VOCab

有名	yǒumíng	famous
海滩	hǎitān	beach
森林	sēnlín	forest
山	shān	mountain
寺庙	sìmiào	temple
花	huā	flower
风景	fēngjǐng	scenery
农村	nóngcūn	farming village
城市	chéngshì	city

Listen to the recording and match the sentence number with the corresponding picture in your notebook.

8.16 Pair activity — Tomorrow's plans

Practise this short dialogue, using the pictures as prompts.

Taking a journey

VOCAB

再	zài	again (in the future)
国家	guójiā	country; national
飞机	fēijī	aeroplane
快要	kuàiyào	just about to
订	dìng	to order; to book
票	piào	ticket
多长时间	duōcháng shíjiān	how long
小时	xiǎoshí	hour
司机	sījī	driver

Aeroplane

The word 飞机 is made up of two words. 飞 (fēi) means 'to fly' and 机 means machine. So 飞机 literally is 'flying machine'!

Again

再 can mean 'again'. For example, 再见 means goodbye, which literally means 'see you again'. It can also mean 'after a delay,' so 明天再说 means 'let's talk about it tomorrow.' You must always put 再 before the verb.

8.17 Listening activity — 再

Listen to these useful phrases and repeat after each one.

再来吧！	Come again!
请再说一遍！ (biàn)	Please repeat that.
明天再说！	Let's talk about it tomorrow.
明天再见！	See you tomorrow!

8.18 Listening activity — Visiting Mum

Listen to the dialogue and answer the questions based on what you hear. Write the answers in your notebook.

1) When is the woman going to see her mother?
2) Where does the mother live?
3) How will the woman travel?
4) Has she already bought the tickets?
5) How long will the journey be?

In pairs, practise the following dialogue, substituting different words each time.

国家 A	国家 B	多长时间
英国	中国	十个小时
美国	中国	十八个小时
中国	日本	两个小时
法国	韩国	九个小时

8.20 Pair activity — Travel plans

In pairs, practise this extended dialogue, substituting different words each time.

A: 你好！你今天怎么样？

B: 我很好。我下个月要去看我爷爷。

A: 他住在哪个国家？

B: 他住在日本。

A: 哦，你要坐飞机去吗？ (Ó; fēi)

B: 是，我快要订飞机票了。 (kuài dìng fēi piào)

A: 从英国到日本要多长时间？ (Cóng; dào)

B: 要十二个小时。

Person	Country	Transport	Travel time
我阿姨	中国	飞机 (fēi)	十个小时
我爸爸	美国	飞机 (fēi)	七个小时
我姐姐	法国	火车	三个小时
我弟弟	韩国	飞机	十一个小时

8.21 Listening activity — I slept for nine hours

Yesterday Wang Chun went to the hot springs (温泉 wēnquán) for a day out. Listen as she describes the day and match the time durations to the corresponding activities. Write the answers in your notebook.

A 30 minutes

B 15 minutes

C 9 hours

D 3 hours

E 20 minutes

About the language: 快要 (kuài)

快要 is put before the verb to say something is just about to happen. Usually 了 is put at the end of the sentence. This use of 了 does not imply a completed action.

快要 (verb) + 了

火车快要来了。(kuài)	The train is about to come.
我们快要吃饭了。(kuài)	We are about to eat.
姐姐快要走了。(kuài)	Older sister is about to leave.

In this structure, either of 快(kuài) or 要 could be left out of the sentence. So, two alternatives for the first sentence are: 火车快来了 (kuài) and 火车要来了。

About the language: Time duration

To say how long something lasts in Chinese, put the time duration after the verb.

(verb) + (time duration)

我要学习三个小时。	I will study for three hours.
你要等四天。	You must wait four days.

If the action has been completed, you must add 了 after the verb.

(verb) + 了 + (time duration)

我学习了三个小时。	I studied for three hours.
我等了四天。	I waited for four days.

If the verb takes an object, the object usually gets placed after the time duration.

我看了三个小时的书。	I read for three hours.
我游了两个小时泳。	I swam for two hours.

The exception to this rule is if the object is a person or place. In these cases the object gets put before the time duration.

我去中国两个星期。	I am going to China for two weeks.
我等了你三十分钟。	I've waited for you for thirty minutes.

Be careful to distinguish between when something happens (point in time) and how long something goes on for (time duration).

Remember: Point in time goes before the verb, and time duration goes after the verb.

Here are some sentences which include both types of time phrase:

我昨天看了四个小时的电视。	Yesterday I watched TV for four hours.
妈妈每天跑一个小时的步。	Every day Mum runs for an hour.

Finally, here's how to include half-hours in duration:

我等了你半个小时！	I've waited for you for half an hour!
他看了一个半小时的书。	He read his book for an hour and a half.
老师要跳两个半小时舞。	The teacher will dance for two and a half hours.

8.22 Writing activity

A Below are some activities and some time durations. Re-write each sentence, taking care to put the time duration in the right place. Note that as each sentence is referring to the future, you don't need to worry about the particle 了. Write your answers in your notebook.

1) 我要看书。(三个小时)
2) 我要坐车。(十分钟)
3) 我在森林。(一个小时)
   sēnlín
4) 我要去看我的老师。(半个小时)
5) 我明天要去市中心。(五个小时)

B Translate the following sentences into Chinese. Use characters whenever possible; otherwise, use pinyin.

1) Yesterday I read a book for 20 minutes.
2) I went to China for two years.
3) It is about to rain.
4) I am about to go to class.

Writing characters

南 nán
城 chéng
花 huā
山 shān
飞机 fēi jī
票 piào
再 zài
快 kuài
景 jǐng

With the new characters, you can also now write:

再见	zàijiàn	goodbye

West Lake, Hangzhou

Did you know?

China has a saying: 上有天堂(táng), 下有苏杭 (Sūháng) "Above there is heaven, and below there is Suzhou and Hangzhou." This describes the scenic beauty of these two famous cities near Shanghai. Hangzhou is famous for its green tea, 龙井茶 (Lóngjǐng chá) or Dragon Well tea. It is also famous for West Lake, which has been a tourist destination in China for many centuries.

8.23 Reading activity — Buying tickets

Two people are buying travel tickets. Read the following dialogues and answer the questions in your notebook.

A

A: 你好！我想订飞机票。
dìng fēi piào

B: 好，去哪儿？

A: 我要去中国西安。

B: 好。你几月几号去？

A: 我下个月二十号去。

B: 几月几号回来？

A: 二十八号。

B: 好。飞机票一千元一张。
fēi piào

A: 好。

1) Where is she going?
2) How is she travelling?
3) What are her travel dates?
4) How much is her ticket?

B

A: 你好！我想订火车票。
dìng piào

B: 好，到什么地方去？
dào difang

A: 我要去成都。

B: 哦，那儿的风景很好。几月几日去？
ó jǐng

A: 我四月八号去，四月十九号回来。
huí

B: 买几张票？
zhāng piào

A: 三张。

B: 好。火车票六百元一张，一共一千八百。
piào

A: 好，给你钱。

1) Where is he going?
2) How is he travelling?
3) What are his travel dates?
4) How much does one ticket cost?

Language in action — Chengyu

It is considered elegant style in Chinese to group characters into sets of four. Chinese has many special four-character phrases that are used in different situations to make apt and vivid comments. Often the phrases refer to a well-known ancient story or text. These phrases, called 成语 (chéngyǔ) in Chinese, are considered a sign of education, so if you learn a few of these phrases, you will definitely impress your Chinese friends! Here are four examples:

人山(shān)人海	people - mountain - people - sea	thousands of people in one place
五花(huā)八门	five - flowers - eight - gates	all kinds of things
对牛弹琴	towards - ox - play - zither	to cast pearls before swine
走马观(guān)花(huā)	gallop - horse - look at - flowers	to take a quick tour and merely scratch the surface

8.24 Sketch — Buying Tickets

In pairs, create a sketch in which a person buys tickets from a travel agent. Use the reading Buying Tickets on page 184 as an example. Include:

- The destinations （我要从……到……）
  cóng dào
- The method of transport （我要买……票）
  piào
- How many tickets are needed （我要……张票）
  piào
- Travel dates （我……月……日去，……月……日回来）
- The cost per ticket （……块一张）
  kuài

Step it up! If you want a challenge, consider spicing up your sketch by introducing problems. For example:

- Tickets are sold out （对不起，那天的票没有了！）
  piào
- Tickets are too expensive （票太贵了！）
  Piào
- There are no tickets for that route （没有从……到……的票）
  cóng dào piào

8.25 Reading activity — Email from Wang Chun

You've just received an email from Wang Chun about her travel plans. Read the email and answer the questions in your notebook. Take note of some of the chengyu introduced in Language in Action on page 184.

你好！

明天我要去中国南方。我先从台北到上海，然后从上海坐飞机到广州。广州是
cóng dào cóng fēi dào Guǎngzhōu Guǎngzhōu
中国的一个很大的城市。我要去市中心看一看。
chéng

我叔叔是商人，他常常去广州做生意。他说广州商店里的东西五花八门，在那
Guǎngzhōu Guǎngzhōu huā
儿买东西很好玩儿。因为我这次去只住两天，没有时间玩儿，所以只能走马观
cì
花。下次我要住一个星期，这样我能好好玩儿。
huā cì

我还没有订飞机票，今天就要买了。我在旅行社买票。因为人很多，所以要等
dìng fēi piào lǚ shè piào
很长时间！但是还好，我可以看书。

祝好，王春
Zhù Wáng Chūn

1) Which city will Wang Chun visit?
2) Why does her uncle go there?
3) What is fun to do there?
4) How long will Wang Chun stay?
5) What does Wang Chun say about the travel agency?

Glossary

做生意	zuò shēngyì	= to do business
这次	zhè cì	= this time
下次	xià cì	= next time
旅行社	lǚxíngshè	= travel agency
祝好	zhù hǎo	= good wishes
就	jiù	= indicates an action will happen soon

8.26 Writing activity — Your response to Wang Chun

Your email response to Wang Chun is drafted below. Copy the letter and fill in the blanks with characters.

王春，__ __！
Wáng Chūn nǐ hǎo!

__ __ __ __ __ 南__，__ __ __ __！ __ __ __ __。飞机票__ __ __？ __ __ __ __
Nǐ yào qù Zhōngguó fāng nà tài hǎo le Wǒ hěn gāoxìng Fēi piào guì bú guì Nǐ yǐjīng mǎi

票__ __？ __ __ 飞机__ __ __ __，__ __ 飞机 __ 较舒__。__ __ __ __ __ __？
piào le ma Suīrán fēi bǐ huǒchē guì kěshì fēi bǐjiào fu Nǐ hé shéi yìqǐ qù

__ __ __ __ 飞？ __ __ __ __ __拍 __ __ 照片 __ __ __，__ __？ __ __
Jǐ yuè jǐ rì fēi Qǐng nǐ zài nà-r hěn duō gěi wǒ kàn hǎo ma Wǒ bù

__ __ 广州 __ 风景 __ __ __。
zhīdào Guǎngzhōu de jǐng zěnmeyàng

__ __ __ __ 气 __ __，__ 冷__ 热。__ __ 公园 __ __ __ __花：__ __ 、__ __ 、
Zhōumò de tiān hěn hǎo bù lěng bú rè Wǒ qù kàn le hěn duō huā hóng de lán de

__ __ 、__ __ __ __ __，__ __ 漂亮！ __ __ __ __ __ __ __ __ __ 雨，__ __ __ __ __
bái de huáng de dōu yǒu fēicháng Yīnwèi xià ge xīngqī huì xià dà yǔ suǒyǐ wǒ zhè ge

__ __ __ __ __ 到 __ __ __ __ __。__ __ __ __ __ __ __ __ __ __ __ __。
xīngqī yào tiān tiān dào wàibian qù wán-r Míng tiān wǒ huì dǎ yí gè xiǎoshí de wǎngqiú

__ __ 平 __！
Yī lù píng ān

__ __ __ __

Glossary

一路平安！ yī lù píng'ān = Have a safe journey!

8.27 Writing activity — City life or country life?

Do you generally prefer big cities or rural areas? If you could live anywhere in the world, where would you choose? Pick a place and write a list of the pros and cons of living there. Think about:

- The climate (what is it like at various times throughout the year?)
- Access to transport (what transport options are there?)
- Access to shops (does this affect the cost of living?)
- Activities (what can you do for fun?)
- Job/educational opportunities (where will you most likely go to school? What would your job most likely be?)
- Housing options (could you live in your dream house, or are there only certain types of housing available?)
- Proximity to nature (how big is your environmental impact?)

Remember that characters are grouped in a dictionary by their 'radical'. A radical is the part of a character that usually contains a hint about its meaning. Here are some more common radicals that you can look out for:

艹 cǎo — Grass radical (called 草字头 in Chinese) - characters that relate to plants
花 = flower
茶 = tea
菜 = vegetable
蓝 = blue (blue dye is extracted from a plant)

雨 yǔ — Rain radical - characters that relate to the weather
雪 = snow
雾 = fog
雷 = thunder

⺮ zhú — Bamboo radical - characters relating to bamboo or things made from bamboo
笔 = pen
篮 = basket
筷 = chopstick

讠 yán — Speech radical - characters relating to language or speaking
语 = language
请 = please
谁 = who
说 = speak
话 = speech

Putting it together

8.28 Pair activity – Taiwan field trip!

You are planning a weekend trip in Taiwan (you are starting from within Taipei) and your budget is unlimited! The map below shows some of Taiwan's top tourist attractions. Research online about each of them and pick one you'd like to visit. Then outline the details of your trip, including reasons for your choices. Be sure to mention:

- Where you are going（我要去……） and why
- The best time of the year to visit, and why
- How you will get there and how long the travel will take（我要从……坐火车到……。坐火车要……个小时。）
  cóng dào
- The weather forecast for this weekend（下周末的天气会……）
  qì
- What you will do and see, and how long you will do each activity
- What you hope to eat, drink or buy (If you're buying a gift, who will receive the souvenir?)（我想买……）
- Where you will eat (Can you find a restaurant? A nearby park?)

Yangming Mountain
阳明山
Yáng Shān

Sun Moon Lake
日月潭
Tán

Alishan National Scenic Area
阿里山风景区
Shān jǐng qū

Penghu Islands
澎湖列岛
hú Lièdǎo

In Taipei:

- Sun Yat-sen Memorial Hall
  台北国父纪念馆
  Jìniàn
- Ximending
  西门町
  dīng
- The Palace Museum of Taipei
  台北故宫博物院
  Gùgōng Bó
- Taipei 101
  台北101

Taroko National Park
太鲁阁国家公园
lǔgé

Kenting National Park
垦丁公园
Kěndīng

Step it up! See if you can also include a chengyu mentioned in this chapter, or find out another suitable one from your teacher. Here are some other common chengyu used to describe scenery and weather.

名胜古迹 shèng gǔ jī	风和日丽 lì	车水马龙 lóng	高楼大厦 lóu shà
= famous sights and ancient places	= the wind is pleasant and the sun is bright	= cars flow like water and horses like dragons (busy traffic)	= tall buildings and large mansions

8.29 Reading activity — Yangming Mountain National Park

Read this article about Yangming Mountain National Park and answer the questions in your notebook.

阳明山

阳明山国家公园是一个
Yáng shān
非常有名的国家公园，公
园在台北市的北边。阳明
Yáng
山是死火山，风景非常
shān sǐ shān jǐng
美：有山，有水，有森
shān sēn
林，也有寺庙。每年三月
lín sìmiào
有很多花会开：最有名的
huā
是樱花、梅花和茶花。每
yīnghuā méihuā huā
个月会有100万人上山看
shān
花！
huā
从台北市到阳明山，可以
Cóng Yáng shān
坐公共汽车，也可以开
车，还可以骑自行车。坐
车去要一个多小时，骑

A smoking crater at Yangming Mountain

自行车要很长时间。可是
到了阳明山以后，山上有
dào Yáng shān shān
很多小路，所以骑车很方
fāng
便。
biàn
早上7点到10点，还有下
dào
午3点到7点，人比较多。
dào jiào
阳明山旅游中心上午9点
Yáng shān lǚ
到下午4点半开门。
dào

1) Where is Yangming Mountain located?
2) What kind of scenery can be found in the park?
3) When are flowers blooming?
4) How can you get to Yangming Mountain from Taipei?
5) What times of the day are 'peak' times?
6) When are the Welcome Centres open?

Did you know?

Food tourism

Travelling and eating local specialties go hand-in-hand, but Taiwan is particularly rich in this regard. In Taiwan, eating something delicious is always part of a day trip, and often becomes the entire reason for the trip. Local places with excellent food become renowned, and long queues form outside the door. For example, 鼎泰丰 Din Tai Fung (Dǐng Tài Fēng in pinyin) has become the famous place for dumplings, and 永和豆浆大王 Yǒng Hé Dòujiāng Dàwáng is the famous place for breakfast.

8.30 Writing activity — Describing the Scenery

Here are photos of some famous tourist destinations in Taiwan. Write three sentences about each photo to describe what you see. The first has been done as an example.

这是阳(Yáng)明山(shān)，有很多人在看花(huā)。天气(qì)很好，有太阳(yáng)。因为天气(qì)很热(rè)，所以人们都穿短裤。有的人也在拍照片。

一

二

三

四

Reading Challenge

说中文的人有谁？

金敏
你好！我叫金敏。我是韩国人。我住在首尔。我是商人，因为我和中国人做生意，所以我会说中文。我每个月会去北京卖韩国的电视机。我喜欢北京的饭馆。我明天要跟中国朋友一起吃晚饭。我觉得中国菜和韩国菜都很辣。

王天宝
你好！我叫王天宝。我是中国人，我家在上海。我会说中文。上海人也会说上海话。上海话的“我”是“阿拉”。很多北京人和香港人不会说上海话。

Joanne Smith
大家好！我叫Jo。我的中文老师也给了我一个中文名字，我的中文名字是周安。我是英国人。我爱学习中文，因为我喜欢写汉字。我爸爸在香港工作。他不会说中文。

于龙门
你好！我叫龙门，我是马来西亚人，也是福建人。我会说中文、日文、马来文和英文。我的家人都说中文。我是医生，我在医院工作。我的哥哥住在澳大利亚，他也是医生。

Anand Karunanithi
大家好！我叫 Anand。我是老师。我是新加坡人，也是印度人。我会说中文、泰米尔文和英文。我在家说泰米尔文。我买东西说中文，我在学校说英语。

李浩波
你好！我叫李浩波。我是台湾人。我家在台北。台北有很多山，也有海。我会说中文，我家人也说台语。台语的“你好”是“Li Ho”，不是“Ni Hao”！欢迎来台湾！

白晓梅
你好！我叫白晓梅。我不是中国人，我是美国人。我爸爸、妈妈是中国人，他们是四川人。我们在家说英文，所以我的中文不好。我在学校学习中文。

Glossary

首尔	Shǒu'ěr	= Seoul
泰米尔文	Tàimǐ'ěr wén	= Tamil language
台语	Táiyǔ	= Taiwanese
四川	Sìchuān	= Sichuan province
马来西亚	Mǎláixīyà	= Malaysia
福建	Fújiàn	= Fujian province
马来文	Mǎláiwén	= Malaysian language

Find the person/people who fit the following categories:

- Speaks a dialect of Chinese other than Mandarin (2 people)
- Speaks Japanese (1 person)
- Is ethnically Chinese or is of Chinese descent (4 people)
- Talks about learning Chinese (2 people)
- Speaks Chinese at home (3 people)

Language research

Using a dictionary or online tool, find 3 new words from the text and write them down. Find their pinyin, tones and stroke order.

Research online to find out where different dialects of Chinese are spoken in the world. What is the dialect with the most speakers? What is the dialect which is most widespread? Which dialects are most famous, and why do you think that is?

我会

Now you can…

…talk about the weather.

天气怎么样？	Tiānqì zěnme yàng?	What's the weather like?
今天刮风。	Jīntiān guā fēng.	It's windy today.
明天会下雨。	Míngtiān huì xià yǔ.	It will rain tomorrow.
北京明天会刮风。	Běijīng míngtiān huì guā fēng.	It will be windy in Beijing tomorrow.
天津明天会下雪。	Tiānjīn míngtiān huì xià xuě.	It will snow in Tianjin tomorrow.
天气太热了！有时候下雨，也常常多云。	Tiānqì tài rè le! Yǒu shíhòu xià yǔ, yě chángcháng duōyún.	The weather is so hot. It sometimes rains and it's often cloudy.
十二月非常冷，常常下雪。	Shí'èr yuè fēicháng lěng, chángcháng xià xuě.	December is very cold. It often snows.

…say where someone comes from.

力宇从什么地方来？	Lì Yǔ cóng shénme dìfang lái?	Where does Li Yu come from?
他从杭州来。	Tā cóng Hángzhōu lái.	He comes from Hangzhou.

…say where you are going on holiday.

我要去中国西安。	Wǒ yào qù Zhōngguó Xī'ān.	I'm going to Xi'an, China.
你去了什么地方？	Nǐ qù le shénme dìfang?	Where did you go?
我去了北京，然后从北京去了成都。	Wǒ qù le Běijīng, ránhòu cóng Běijīng qù le Chéngdū.	I went to Beijing and then I went from Beijing to Chengdu.
他从北京坐火车到西安。	Tā cóng Běijīng zuò huǒchē dào Xī'ān.	He went from Beijing to Xi'an by train.

我会

Now you can...

...talk about the scenery in different places.

这是一个很有名的农村。这里风景很好！	Zhè shì yígè hěn yǒumíng de nóngcūn. Zhèlǐ fēngjǐng hěn hǎo!	This is a very famous farming village. The scenery here is really great.
这是一座很有名的寺庙。	Zhè shì yí zuò hěn yǒumíng de sìmiào.	This is a very famous temple.
我明天要去森林。	Wǒ míngtiān yào qù sēnlín.	I will go to the forest tomorrow.

...say how long an activity lasts.

从英国坐飞机到韩国要多长时间？	Cóng Yīngguó zuò fēijī dào Hánguó yào duō cháng shíjiān?	How long does it take to fly from England to South Korea?
要十一个小时。	Yào shíyī gè xiǎoshí.	It takes eleven hours.
我在大门等了十五分钟，然后买票。	Wǒ zài dàmén děng le shíwǔ fēnzhōng, ránhòu mǎi piào.	I waited for 15 minutes at the gate, and then bought tickets.

...say something is about to happen.

我快要订飞机票了。	Wǒ kuàiyào dìng fēijī piào le.	I will reserve flight tickets soon.
火车快来了。	Huǒchē kuài lái le.	The train will arrive soon.

...write the following characters:

从 到 飞 机 冷 热 雨 雪 云 地 方 再 气 票
南 城 风 花 山 阳 快 景

Grammar Glossary

Unit 1

Structure	Example		Page
跟……一起	我跟我朋友一起去公园。	I go to the park with my friend.	11
去 + place + verb	妈妈去商店买衣服。	Mum goes to the shop to buy clothes.	11
"Play" in Chinese	打篮球、踢足球、弹吉他、玩儿电脑	play basketball, play football, play the guitar, play on the computer	16
会	她会说中文。	I can speak Chinese.	19
可以	你不可以上网。	You are not allowed to go online.	19
能	他明天不能来。	He can't come tomorrow.	19
还	爸爸会说中文，还会说日文。	Dad can speak Chinese, he can also speak Japanese.	20

Unit 2

Structure	Example		Page
在 + place + verb	她在家吃早饭。	I eat breakfast at home.	33
A 在 B 的 position	超市在银行的左边。	The supermarket is on the left of the bank.	33
见 "to meet"	我们三点见吧！	Let's meet at 3 o'clock.	36
subject + 很多	学校的电脑很多。	There are a lot of school computers.	41
坐 + transport + activity	姐姐坐火车去西安。	Big sister takes the train to Xi'an.	41

Unit 3

Structure	Example		Page
Dates in Chinese	2016年9月1日	1st September 2016	51
"It" is often dropped in Chinese	你买了吗？	Did you buy it?	51
Measure words	我有一条鱼。	I have one fish.	53
Subject + frequency + verb	哥哥常常打篮球。	Big brother often plays basketball.	53
将来 "in the future"	我将来想当科学家。	I'd like to be a scientist in the future.	59
Subject + object + verb + 得 + adverb	你饭做得很好。	You cook very well.	61
Words that replace 很	这本书有一点贵。	This book is a bit expensive.	61

Grammar Glossary

Unit 4

Structure	Example	Example in translation	Page
还是	你要吃米饭还是面条？	Do you want to eat rice or noodles?	76
adjective + 的	我买那个大的。	I'm buying that big one.	76
都 + verb	茶和咖啡我都喝。	I drink both tea and coffee.	76
是……的……	我是九点做的。	I did it at 9 o'clock.	78
large numbers	这个城市人口3百万人。	The population of this city is 3 million.	82
给 + indirect object + verb	我给奶奶打电话了。	I gave my grandmother a call.	85
太……了	这个菜太辣了！	This dish is too spicey!	85

Unit 5

relative clause 的 noun	这是我昨天买的书。	This is the book I bought yesterday.	99
noun + 比 + noun + adjective	我比你高。	I am taller than you.	99
noun + 没有 + noun + adjective	我的头发没有你长。	My hair isn't as long as yours.	100
每 + meaure word + noun + 都 + verb	每个人都能帮助别人。	Everyone can help other people.	107
真	真好吃！	Delicious! (Really good to eat!)	109
虽然……，可是……	虽然很贵，可是我要买。	Although it's expensive, I want to buy it.	109

Unit 6

Structure	Example	Example in translation	Page
用 + indirect object + verb	我用手机上网。	I browse online with my phone.	124
Polite commands	请看看吧。	Please look.	127
请	明天我请你吃晚饭。	I invite you to dinner tomorrow.	131
了 for completed actions	妹妹买了一个新包。	Little Sister bought a new bag.	135
没有 for negative past sentences	我没有吃早饭。	I didn't eat breakfast.	135

Grammar Glossary

Unit 7

跟……见面	她星期三跟我见面。	She's seeing me on Wednesday.	146
上…… 下…… "next" and "previous"	我下个星期去北京。	I'll go to Beijing next week.	147
Telling the time	现在十点一刻。	Now it is 10:15.	150
以前、以后	上课前请关手机。	Before class starts please turn off your phone.	150
因为……，所以……	因为她很老，所以她不能来。	She is unable to come because she is old.	157
正在……呢	我正在吃饭呢。		157

Unit 8

Structure	Example	Example in translation	Page
会 "will"	明天会下雨。	Tomorrow will rain.	173
要 "will"	我要回家看电视。	I'm going home to watch television.	173
从……到……	我从9点到4点上课。	I have class from 9 until 4.	173
再 "after a delay"	我明天再给你打电话。	I'll give you another call tomorrow.	179
快要……了	她快要走了。	She will go soon.	181
verb + time duration	她每天看一个小时电视。	She watches an hour of television every day.	182

Measure Word Glossary

把 bǎ	for things you grasp	
二胡	èrhú	Chinese violin
筷子	kuàizi	chopsticks
椅子	yǐzi	chair
吉他	jítā	guitar
杯 bēi	for cups	
茶	chá	tea
咖啡	kāfēi	coffee
牛奶	niúnǎi	cow's milk
本 běn	for bound volumes	
本子	běnzi	exercise book
课本	kèběn	textbook
书	shū	book

笔 bǐ	for money	
钱	qián	money
部 bù	for things with sections	
电影	diànyǐng	movie; film
场 chǎng	for events	
演唱会	yǎnchànghuì	(singing) concert
游戏	yóuxì	game
顿 dùn	for meals	
晚饭	wǎnfàn	dinner
午饭	wǔfàn	lunch
早饭	zǎofàn	breakfast

朵 duǒ	for flowers	
花	huā	flower
茉莉花	mòlihuā	Jasmine flower
幅 fú	for scrolls	
画	huà	picture
管 guǎn	for pipes	
笛子	dízi	bamboo flute
架 jià	for things with frames	
飞机	fēijī	aeroplane
钢琴	gāngqín	piano
家 jiā	for businesses	
餐厅	cāntīng	dining hall; restaurant
超市	chāoshì	supermarket
饭店	fàndiàn	restaurant; hotel
饭馆	fànguǎn	restaurant
工厂	gōngchǎng	factory
公司	gōngsī	company
银行	yínháng	bank
邮局	yóujú	post office
商店	shāngdiàn	a shop
图书馆	túshūguǎn	library
件 jiàn	for clothing and articles	
衬衫	chènshān	shirt
汉服	hànfú	Chinese traditional clothing
坎肩	kǎnjiān	waistcoat
毛衣	máoyī	wool jumper
事儿	shìr	a matter
衣服	yīfu	Clothes

间 jiān	for rooms	
教室	jiàoshì	classroom
节 jié	for things that link in sections	
画	huà	picture
课	kè	lesson
颗 kē	for pellet-like things	
巧克力	qiǎokèlì	chocolate
块 kuài	for pieces of things	
蛋糕	dàngāo	cake
面包	miànbāo	bread
辆 liàng	for vehicles	
巴士	bāshì	bus
公共汽车	gōnggòngqìchē	public bus
公交车	gōngjiāochē	bus
计程车	jìchéngchē	taxi (Taiwan)
汽车	qìchē	car
自行车	zìxíngchē	bicycle
列 liè	for things that go in a line	
火车	huǒchē	train
名 míng	for certain professions	
宇航员	yǔhángyuán	astronaut
运动员	yùndòngyuán	athlete
匹 pǐ	for horses	
马	mǎ	horse
片 piàn	for areas	
海滩	hǎitān	beach
森林	sēnlín	forest

扇 shàn	for doors	
门	mén	gate; door
双 shuāng	for pairs	
袜子	wàzi	socks
鞋	xié	shoes
眼睛	yǎnjing	eye
所 suǒ	for institutions	
大学	dàxué	university
小学	xiǎoxué	primary school
学校	xuéxiào	school
医院	yīyuàn	hospital
中学	zhōngxué	secondary school
台 tái	for electronic items	
电脑	diànnǎo	computer
电视	diànshì	television
手机	shǒujī	mobile phone
条 tiáo	for strips	
裤子	kùzi	trousers
路	lù	road
旗袍	qípáo	Cheongsam (Chinese dress)
裙子	qúnzi	skirt
鲨鱼	shāyú	shark
鱼	yú	fish
位 wèi	for esteemed people	
老师	lǎoshī	teacher
医生	yīshēng	doctor
作家	zuòjiā	author
项 xiàng	for activities	
活动	huódòng	exercise; activity

张 zhāng	for flat surfaces	
报纸	bàozhǐ	newspaper
照片	zhàopiàn	photograph
纸	zhǐ	paper
桌子	zhuōzi	table
嘴	zuǐ	mouth
支 zhī	for sticks	
笔	bǐ	pen
铅笔	qiānbǐ	pencil
只 zhī	for animals, boats, and one of a pair	
船	chuán	boat
狗	gǒu	dog
猴子	hóuzi	monkey
鸡	jī	chicken
猫	māo	cat
鸟	niǎo	bird
兔子	tùzi	rabbit
座 zuò	for large places	
城市	chéngshì	city
山	shān	mountain

Glossary

A		
啊	ā	oh!
阿姨	āyí	aunt; term of address for woman of similar age to one's parents
埃及	Āijí	Egypt
哎呀	āiyā	oh no!
爱好	àihào	interest; hobby
安静	ānjìng	quiet, peaceful
澳门	Àomén	Macao
B		
吧	ba	particle indicating a suggestion
八	bā	eight
巴黎	Bālí	Paris
巴士	bāshì	bus
爸爸	bàba	dad; father
白	bái	white
百	bǎi	hundred
班	bān	class (of students)
半	bàn	half
帮忙	bāngmáng	to help
包	bāo	bag; to wrap
包子	bāozi	steamed bun
抱歉	bàoqiàn	to apologize
报社	bàoshè	newspaper office
报纸	bàozhǐ	newspaper
杯	bēi	glass; cup
北	běi	north
北京	Běijīng	Beijing
北京烤鸭	Běijīngkǎoyā	Peking Duck
本	běn	origin; root; measure word for books
本子	běnzi	notebook; exercise book
比	bǐ	to compare; than
比较	bǐjiào	relatively
比萨	bǐsà	pizza
笔	bǐ	pen
遍	biàn	one time through from start to finish
便利店	biànlìdiàn	convenience shop
表演	biǎoyǎn	to perform; to act

Character	Pinyin	English
兵马俑	bīngmǎyǒng	Terracotta Army
冰淇淋	bīngqílín	ice cream
博物馆	bówùguǎn	museum
不	bù	not; no
不懂事	bù dǒngshì	immature
不客气	bùkèqi	you're welcome
不一样	bù yíyàng	different
部	bù	part; section; measure word for films
		C
才	cái	particle indicating 'later than expected'
菜	cài	dish; vegetable; cuisine
参加	cānjiā	to join (a club, activity)
餐厅	cāntīng	dining hall; restaurant
曹操	Cáo Cāo	Cao Cao, character in Romance of the Three Kingdoms
草	cǎo	grass
层	céng	floor; level
茶	chá	tea
茶艺	cháyì	the art of tea
茶馆	cháguǎn	tea house
茶花	cháhuā	camellia
尝	cháng	to taste
长	cháng	long
常常	chángcháng	frequently
长城	Chángchéng	the Great Wall
长江	Cháng Jiāng	Yangtze river
唱歌	chàng gē	to sing a song
超市	chāoshì	supermarket; abbreviated form of 超级市场
车水马龙	chēshuǐ-mǎlóng	Busy traffic (idiom)
陈	Chén	Chen (Surname)
衬衫	chènshān	shirt
成都	Chéngdū	Chengdu
城市	chéngshì	city
吃	chī	to eat
重庆	Chóngqìng	Chongqing (city in China)
宠物	chǒngwù	pet
出	chū	to go out
出门	chūmén	leave the house; exit
出租车	chūzūchē	taxi

Character	Pinyin	English
穿	chuān	to wear; to put on; to pass through
船	chuán	boat
春	chūn	spring
次	cì	time (这次 = this time)
聪明	cōngming	intelligent
从	cóng	from
	D	
打	dǎ	to beat; to play (ball game); to call (phone)
打车	dǎ chē	to take a taxi
打折	dǎzhé	to discount
大	dà	big
大鼓	dàgǔ	Chinese drum
大连	Dàlián	Dalian (city in China)
大使馆	dàshǐguǎn	embassy
大学	dàxué	university
大雁塔	Dàyàntǎ	Great Goose Pagoda in Xi'an
大闸蟹	dà zhá xiè	Shanghai steamed crab
带	dài	to bring
戴	dài	to put on or wear (accessories)
蛋糕	dàngāo	cake
但是	dànshì	but
单元	dānyuán	unit
当	dāng	to be (a job)
到	dào	to; until
得	de	particle used after a verb to indicate degree, manner, or effect
的	de	particle indicating attribution
灯光	dēngguāng	light
等	děng	to wait; et cetera
的士	dīshì	taxi
笛子	dízi	bamboo flute
第	dì	(used for ordinal numbers)
弟弟	dìdi	younger brother
地方	dìfang	place
地铁	dìtiě	subway; metro
点菜	diǎn cài	to order dishes (in a restaurant)
点心	diǎnxin	snack; dim sum
电池	diànchí	battery

Character	Pinyin	English
电话	diànhuà	telephone
电脑	diànnǎo	computer
电视	diànshì	television
电影	diànyǐng	movie; film
订票	dìng piào	to book tickets
东	dōng	east
东方明珠塔	Dōngfāng Míngzhū Tǎ	Oriental Pearl Tower
东京	Dōngjīng	Tokyo
东西	dōngxi	thing
冬天	dōngtiān	winter
动物园	dòngwùyuán	zoo
都	dōu	all; both
豆腐	dòufu	tofu / bean curd
豆浆	dòujiāng	soy milk
度	dù	degree
短	duǎn	short
短裤	duǎnkù	shorts
对	duì	correct; opposite
对不起	duìbuqǐ	I'm sorry
对面	duìmiàn	across (the street); face to face
对牛弹琴	duìniú-tánqín	to play the zither to an ox (idiom)
多	duō	many; much; often
多少	duōshǎo	how many; how much
多云	duōyún	cloudy
		E
俄文	Éwén	Russian language
蚵仔煎	ézǐjiān	oyster omelette
饿	è	hungry
嗯	èn	Yup; uh-huh
儿子	érzi	son
二	èr	two
二胡	èrhú	Chinese violin
		F
法国	Fǎguó	France
法文	Fǎwén	French language
饭店	fàndiàn	restaurant; hotel
饭馆	fànguǎn	restaurant
方便	fāngbiàn	convenient

Character	Pinyin	English
放	fàng	to place; to set off (kite, fireworks)
放假	fàngjià	to go on holiday
放学	fàngxué	to finish school for the day
非常	fēicháng	extremely
飞机	fēijī	aeroplane
飞机场	fēijīchǎng	airport
分	fēn	to divide; minute
风和日丽	fēnghé-rìlì	The wind is pleasant and the sun is bright (idiom)
风景	fēngjǐng	scenery
风筝	fēngzhēng	kite
佛教	Fójiào	Buddhism
福	fú	good fortune
福建	Fújiàn	Fujian province
服务员	fúwùyuán	waiter
服装店	fúzhuāng diàn	clothes shop
父母	fùmǔ	parents
父亲	fùqīn	father
		G
该你了	gāi nǐ le	it's your turn
改天	gǎi tiān	to change the date
感谢	gǎnxiè	heartfelt thanks
钢琴	gāngqín	piano
高	gāo	high; tall
高楼大厦	gāolóu-dàshà	Tall buildings (idiom)
高山流水	gāoshān-liúshuǐ	Tall mountains and flowing water (idiom)
高兴	gāoxìng	happy
搞笑	gǎoxiào	funny; hilarious
哥哥	gēge	older brother
个	gè	measure word for people or things
给	gěi	to; for; to give
跟	gēn	and; with
工厂	gōngchǎng	factory
工程师	gōngchéngshī	engineer
工人	gōngrén	worker
工作	gōngzuò	to work; job
公共汽车	gōnggòngqìchē	public bus
公交车	gōngjiāochē	bus

Character	Pinyin	English
公司	gōngsī	company
公园	gōngyuán	public park
宫保鸡丁	gōngbǎojīdīng	Kung Pao Chicken
功夫	gōngfu	Kung Fu
狗	gǒu	dog
购物	gòu wù	to go shopping
姑姑	gūgu	aunt; father's sister
古筝	gǔzhēng	Chinese zither
故宫	gùgōng	Forbidden City
故事	gùshi	story
刮风	guāfēng	to be windy
关门	guānmén	closed; to close a door
关羽	Guān Yǔ	Guan Yu, character in Romance of the Three Kingdoms
广场	guǎngchǎng	square
广东话	Guǎngdōnghuà	Cantonese language
广州	Guǎngzhōu	Guangzhou
贵	guì	expensive
国家	guójiā	country
果汁	guǒzhī	fruit juice
		H
哈尔滨	Hā'ěrbīn	Harbin (city in China)
蛤蟆	háma	toad
还	hái	still; also; yet
还是	háishi	or (used in questions
孩子	háizi	child
海滩	hǎitān	beach
韩国	Hánguó	South Korea
汉服	hànfú	Chinese traditional clothing
汉语	Hànyǔ	Chinese language
杭州	Hángzhōu	Hangzhou
好	hǎo	good; well; easy to
好吃	hǎochī	tasty
好喝	hǎohē	tasty (for drinks)
好看	hǎokàn	good-looking; good (for a movie, book)
好了	hǎo le	that's enough
好听	hǎotīng	sounds good
好玩	hǎowán	fun

Character	Pinyin	English
号	hào	ordinal number; day of a month
号码	hàomǎ	number
喝	hē	to drink
和	hé	and; together with
和尚	héshang	monk
黑	hēi	black
很	hěn	very
红	hóng	red
红烧	hóngshāo	simmer-fried (dish)
猴子	hóuzi	monkey
后面	hòumian	behind
花	huā	flower
花店	huādiàn	florist
华清池	Huáqīng chí	Huaqing Pool, a famous place in Xi'an
滑雪	huá xuě	to ski
话	huà	speech
画	huà	to draw; picture
画家	huàjiā	painter
欢迎	huānyíng	welcome
黄	huáng	yellow
黄浦江	Huángpǔ Jiāng	Huangpu river
皇帝	huángdì	emperor
回	huí	to return
回国	huíguó	to return to one's home country
会	huì	can; will
活动	huódòng	exercise; activity
火车	huǒchē	train
火锅	huǒguō	hotpot
火山	huǒshān	volcano
护士	hùshi	nurse
		J
鸡	jī	chicken
鸡蛋	jīdàn	egg
鸡肉	jīròu	chicken (meat)
吉他	jítā	guitar
几	jǐ	how many; several
计程车	jìchéngchē	taxi (Taiwan)

Character	Pinyin	English
家	jiā	home; family
家常菜	jiāchángcài	home cooking
家庭	jiātíng	family; household
加拿大	Jiānádà	Canada
件	jiàn	measure word for events and clothes
建	jiàn	to build
建筑	jiànzhù	building
毽子	jiànzi	Chinese shuttlecock game
见面	jiànmiàn	to meet
将来	jiānglái	in the future
饺子	jiǎozi	dumpling
叫	jiào	to shout; to call
教室	jiàoshì	classroom
节	jié	measure word for class periods
节日	jiérì	holiday
姐姐	jiějie	older sister
介绍	jièshào	to introduce
今年	jīnnián	this year
今天	jīntiān	today
经理	jīnglǐ	manager
九	jiǔ	nine
旧	jiù	old; worn out
菊花茶	júhuāchá	chrysanthemum tea
剧场	jùchǎng	theatre
俱乐部	jùlèbù	club
觉得	juéde	to think; to feel
		K
咖啡	kāfēi	coffee
咖啡店	kāfēidiàn	coffee shop
开车	kāi chē	to drive
开门	kāimén	to open a door; open for business
开心	kāixīn	to feel happy
坎肩	kǎnjiān	waistcoat
看	kàn	to see; to look at; to watch
看书	kàn shū	to read
炕	kàng	Kang (Chinese traditional bed)
科学	kēxué	science

Character	Pinyin	English
渴	kě	thirsty
可爱	kě'ài	cute
可口可乐	Kěkǒukělè	Coca-Cola
可怕	kěpà	scary
可是	kěshì	but
可以	kěyǐ	can; may; not bad
刻	kè	quarter hour
课本	kèběn	textbook
口	kǒu	mouth
哭	kū	to cry
苦	kǔ	bitter
酷	kù	cool
裤子	kùzi	trousers
块	kuài	piece; colloquial measure word for money
快要	kuàiyào	about to
筷子	kuàizi	chopsticks
昆明	Kūnmíng	Kunming (city in China)
困	kùn	sleepy (tired)
		L
拉面	lāmiàn	pulled noodles
辣	là	hot (spicy)
来	lái	to come; to arrive
蓝	lán	blue
篮球	lánqiú	basketball
兰州	Lánzhōu	Lanzhou (city in China)
老	lǎo	old
老板	lǎobǎn	boss
老师	lǎoshī	teacher
了	le	completed action marker
雷	léi	thunder
累	lèi	tired
冷	lěng	cold
离……很远	lí ... hěn yuǎn	far from ...
李	lǐ	Li (Surname)
理发店	lǐfàdiàn	hairdresser
里面	lǐmiàn	inside
礼物	lǐwù	gift; present

Character	Pinyin	English
历史	lìshǐ	history
练习	liànxí	to practice; to train
两	liǎng	two (used when counting)
辆	liàng	measure word for vehicles
聊天	liáotiān	to chat
零	líng	zero
刘备	Liú Bèi	Liu Bei, character in Romance of the Three Kingdoms
六	liù	six
龙井茶	lóngjǐngchá	Longjing tea
路	lù	road
陆家嘴	Lùjiāzuǐ	Lujiazui business district in Shanghai
路口	lùkǒu	road intersection
绿	lǜ	green
旅行社	lǚxíngshè	travel agency
旅游	lǚyóu	to travel
伦敦	Lúndūn	London
		M
吗	ma	particle indicating a yes/no question
妈妈	māma	mama; mother
麻烦	máfan	to trouble
马	mǎ	horse
马来文	Mǎláiwén	Malay language
马来西亚	Mǎláixīyà	Malaysia
买	mǎi	to buy
埋单	máidān	to pay the bill in a restaurant
卖	mài	to sell
忙	máng	busy
猫	māo	cat
毛	máo	hair; feather; classifier for money
毛衣	máoyī	wool jumper
帽子	màozi	hat
没关系	méi guānxi	it doesn't matter
没有	méiyǒu	not have; not exist; not (used for past)
梅花	méihuā	plum blossom
每	měi	each; every
美国	Měiguó	USA
美丽	měilì	beautiful

Character	Pinyin	English
妹妹	mèimei	younger sister
们	men	plural marker for pronouns
门	mén	gate; door
门口	ménkǒu	entrance
棉袄	mián'ǎo	cotton padded jacket
面包	miànbāo	bread
面条	miàntiáo	noodles
米饭	mǐfàn	rice
明年	míngnián	next year
名胜古迹	míngshèng-gǔjì	tourist sights (idiom)
明天	míngtiān	tomorrow
名字	míngzi	name
茉莉花	mòlihuā	Jasmine flower
母亲	mǔqīn	mother
		N
哪	nǎ; něi	which
哪儿	nǎr	where
那	nà, nèi	that
那儿	nàr	there
奶奶	nǎinai	grandma (paternal grandmother)
南	nán	south
南京	Nánjīng	Nanjing
男	nán	male
难过	nánguò	sad
呢	ne	particle indicating the question: What about…?
能	néng	can; to be possible
你好	nǐhǎo	hello
年	nián	year
年轻	niánqīng	young
鸟	niǎo	bird
您好	nínhǎo	hello (polite)
牛奶	niúnǎi	cow's milk
牛肉	niúròu	beef
牛肉面	niúròumiàn	beef noodle soup
纽约	Niǔyuē	New York
农村	nóngcūn	farming village
努力	nǔlì	to strive; diligent

Character	Pinyin	English
女	nǚ	female
女儿	nǚ'ér	daughter
女士	nǚshì	Miss; Ms
		P
拍	pāi	to take (photo)
胖	pàng	fat
跑步	pǎobù	to run
朋友	péngyou	friend
琵琶	pípa	Chinese stringed instrument
便宜	piányi	cheap
漂亮	piàoliang	pretty; beautiful
乒乓球	pīngpāngqiú	table tennis; table tennis ball
平	píng	even (used for even scores in a game)
苹果	píngguǒ	apple
普洱茶	Pǔ'ěrchá	Pu'er tea
普通话	pǔtōnghuà	Mandarin Chinese
		Q
七	qī	seven
骑	qí	to ride (an animal or bike)
旗袍	qípáo	Cheongsam (Chinese dress)
起床	qǐchuáng	to get out of bed
汽车	qìchē	car
气温	qìwēn	air temperature
千	qiān	thousand
钱	qián	money
钱包	qiánbāo	wallet
铅笔	qiānbǐ	pencil
前面	qiánmiàn	ahead; in front
巧克力	qiǎokèlì	chocolate
茄子	qiézi	eggplant (said when taking photos)
秦始皇	Qín Shǐhuáng	First Emperor of Qin
青岛	Qīngdǎo	Qingdao (city in China)
请	qǐng	to ask; to invite; please
请进	qǐngjìn	please come in
请问	qǐngwèn	may I ask…
去	qù	to go
去年	qùnián	last year

Character	Pinyin	English
		R
裙子	qúnzi	skirt
热	rè	hot
热闹	rènao	lively
人	rén	person
人口	rénkǒu	population
人民	rénmín	people
人民币	rénmínbì	Chinese Yuan
人山人海	rénshān-rénhǎi	thousands of people in one place (idiom)
人物	rénwù	character (in fiction)
认识	rènshi	to know; to get to know
日	rì	sun; day; date
日本	Rìběn	Japan
日文	Rìwén	Japanese language
日月潭	Rìyuètán	Sun Moon Lake (scenic spot in Taiwan)
容易	róngyì	easy
		S
三	sān	three
三杯鸡	sānbēijī	three-cup chicken (a dish)
散步	sànbù	to take a walk
三国演义	Sānguó Yǎnyì	Romance of the Three Kingdoms, a famous Chinese novel
森林	sēnlín	forest
鲨鱼	shāyú	shark
山	shān	mountain
上	shàng	up; above; previous
商场	shāngchǎng	mall
商店	shāngdiàn	a shop
商人	shāngrén	businessperson
上班	shàngbān	to go to work
上车	shàng chē	to get on (transport)
上海	Shànghǎi	Shanghai
上课	shàng kè	to go to class; to start class
上面	shàngmian	on top of
上网	shàng wǎng	to go online
上午	shàngwǔ	morning; a.m.
上学	shàngxué	to go to school
烧烤	shāokǎo	barbecue
少	shǎo	few; rarely

Character	Pinyin	English
谁	shéi	who
深圳	Shēnzhèn	Shenzhen (city in China)
什么	shénme	what
什么时候	shénmeshíhou	when
省	shěng	province
生气	shēngqì	angry
生日	shēngrì	birthday
生意	shēngyì	business
十	shí	ten
食物	shíwù	food
时间	shíjiān	time
时尚	shíshàng	fashion
是	shì	to be
事儿	shìr	a matter (to attend to)
世界	shìjiè	the world
市场	shìchǎng	market
市中心	shìzhōngxīn	downtown
首尔	Shǒu'ěr	Seoul
手机	shǒujī	mobile phone
瘦	shòu	thin
寿司	shòusī	sushi
舒服	shūfu	comfortable
叔叔	shūshu	uncle; term of address for man of similar age to one's parents
书	shū	book
书店	shūdiàn	bookshop
书法	shūfǎ	calligraphy
书院门	Shūyuànmén	Shuyuanmen, a street in Xi'an
属	shǔ	to be born in the year of
暑假	shǔjià	summer holidays
数学	shùxué	mathematics
帅	shuài	handsome
双	shuāng	pair
水	shuǐ	water
睡觉	shuìjiào	to sleep
说	shuō	to speak; to say
司机	sījī	driver
死	sǐ	dead
四	sì	four

Character	Pinyin	English
四川	Sìchuān	Sichuan province
寺庙	sìmiào	temple
塑像	sùxiàng	statue
虽然	suīrán	although
岁	suì	years old
孙悟空	Sūn Wùkōng	Sun Wukong, the monkey king
唢呐	suǒnà	Chinese oboe
所以	suǒyǐ	therefore; so
		T
他	tā	he
她	tā	she
它	tā	it
台北	Táiběi	Taibei or Taipei
台湾	Táiwān	Taiwan
台语	Táiyǔ	Taiwanese
太	tài	too (much)
太极拳	tàijíquán	Taiji, a traditional form of physical exercise or relaxation
太空	tàikōng	outer space
太太	tàitai	married woman; Mrs.; wife
太阳	tàiyang	sun
泰米尔文	Tàimǐ'ěr wén	Tamil language
弹	tán	to play (a string instrument or piano)
谈	tán	to chat (about)
汤	tāng	soup
糖	táng	sugar
唐三藏	Tángsānzàng	Tang Sanzang, character in Journey to the West
踢	tī	to kick; to play (football)
T恤衫	tīxùshān	T-shirt
体育馆	tǐyùguǎn	gym
天	tiān	day; sky
天津	Tiānjīn	Tianjin
天气	tiānqì	weather
天天	tiāntiān	every day
甜	tián	sweet
条	tiáo	measure word for long thin objects
跳舞	tiào wǔ	to dance
铁观音	Tiěguānyīn	Tie Guanyin tea
听	tīng	to listen

Character	Pinyin	English
停车场	tíngchēchǎng	car park
头发	tóufa	hair
图书馆	túshūguǎn	library
兔子	tùzi	rabbit
腿	tuǐ	leg
拖鞋	tuōxié	slippers
		W
哇	wa	wow!
袜子	wàzi	socks
外面	wàimian	outside
外滩	Wàitān	the Shanghai Bund
碗	wǎn	bowl; cup
晚安	wǎn'ān	Good night
晚饭	wǎnfàn	dinner
晚会	wǎnhuì	evening party
晚上	wǎnshang	evening
玩儿	wánr	to play; to have fun
万	wàn	ten thousand
王	Wáng	Wang (Surname); king
网球	wǎngqiú	tennis
微信	Wēixìn	WeChat (popular app)
魏	Wèi	Wei (surname)
为什么	wèi shénme	why
午饭	wǔfàn	lunch
武汉	Wǔhàn	Wuhan (city in China)
五	wǔ	five
五花八门	wǔhuā-bāmén	all kinds of things (idiom)
雾	wù	fog
		X
西	xī	west
西安	Xī'ān	Xi'an
西班牙文	Xībānyáwén	Spanish language
西瓜	xīguā	watermelon
西游记	Xīyóu Jì	Journey to the West
喜欢	xǐhuan	to like
洗手	xǐ shǒu	to wash one's hands
戏剧	xìjù	drama
虾	xiā	shrimp; prawn

Character	Pinyin	English
下	xià	down; below; next; to play (chess)
下车	xià chē	to get off (transport)
下课	xià kè	to finish class
下面	xiàmian	under; below
夏天	xiàtiān	summer
下午	xiàwǔ	afternoon; p.m.
下雪	xià xuě	to snow
下雨	xià yǔ	to rain
先生	xiānsheng	Mr; husband
咸	xián	salty
现在	xiànzài	now; present
香港	Xiānggǎng	Hong Kong
想	xiǎng	to think; to want to; to miss
象棋	xiàngqí	chess
小	xiǎo	small
小时	xiǎoshí	hour
小说	xiǎoshuō	novel
小学	xiǎoxué	primary school
笑	xiào	to laugh
鞋	xié	shoes
写	xiě	to write
谢谢	xièxie	thank you
新	xīn	new
辛苦	xīnkǔ	tough work, trouble
新闻	xīnwén	news
星期	xīngqī	week
行	xíng	OK
姓	xìng	surname; to be surnamed
幸福	xìngfú	happiness
性格	xìnggé	personality; character
休息	xiūxi	to rest
学	xué	to learn
学生	xuésheng	student
学习	xuéxí	to study
学校	xuéxiào	school
学院	xuéyuàn	college
寻人启事	xún rén qǐshì	missing person (poster)

Character	Pinyin	English
		Y
颜色	yánsè	colour
盐水鸭	Yánshuǐ yā	salted duck (Nanjing dish)
演唱会	yǎnchànghuì	(singing) concert
眼睛	yǎnjing	eye
演员	yǎnyuán	actor or actress
杨	Yáng	Yang (surname)
阳明山	Yángmíng Shān	Yangming Mountain (national park in Taiwan)
羊肉	yángròu	mutton
羊肉泡馍	yángròu pàomó	mutton stew
药店	yàodiàn	pharmacy
要	yào	will; must; want
要紧	yàojǐn	to be a big deal
爷爷	yéye	paternal grandfather
也	yě	also; too
夜市	yèshì	night market
一	yī, yí, yì	one; a (article)
一点	yìdiǎn	a bit; a little
一共	yígòng	altogether
一路平安	yīlù-píng'ān	have a safe journey (idiom)
一起	yìqǐ	together
一些	yìxiē	some; a few
衣服	yīfu	clothes; article of clothing
医生	yīshēng	doctor
医院	yīyuàn	hospital
以后	yǐhòu	after
以前	yǐqián	before
已经	yǐjīng	already
椅子	yǐzi	chair
艺术	yìshù	art
因为	yīnwèi	because
音乐	yīnyuè	music
银行	yínháng	bank
饮料	yǐnliào	soft drink
印度	Yìndù	India
应该	yīnggāi	should; must
樱花	yīnghuā	cherry blossom

Character	Pinyin	English
英国	Yīngguó	UK
英文	Yīngwén	English language
英语	Yīngyǔ	English language
赢	yíng	to win
用	yòng	to use; using
邮局	yóujú	post office
游戏	yóuxì	game
游泳	yóuyǒng	to swim
有	yǒu	to have; there is; there are
有名	yǒumíng	famous
有时候	yǒushíhou	sometimes
有意思	yǒuyìsi	interesting; fun
右边	yòubian	right side
于	yú	in, at, to (preposition used in formal writing)
鱼	yú	fish
宇航员	yǔhángyuán	astronaut
羽毛球	yǔmáoqiú	badminton
玉石	yùshí	jade
豫园	Yùyuán	Yu Garden, a famous place in Shanghai
元	yuán	unit of money
月	yuè	moon; month
运动	yùndòng	sports
运动场	yùndòngchǎng	stadium
运动员	yùndòngyuán	athlete
运气	yùnqi	luck
		Z
再	zài	again
再见	zàijiàn	goodbye
在	zài	(located) at or in
早饭	zǎofàn	breakfast
早上	zǎoshang	early morning
怎么	zěnme	how
怎么样	zěnmeyàng	what is ... like?
展览	zhǎnlǎn	exhibition
站	zhàn	station; to stand
张	zhāng	measure word for flat objects; surname Zhang
张飞	Zhāng Fēi	Zhang Fei, character in Romance of the Three Kingdoms
长	zhǎng	to grow; to appear

Character	Pinyin	English
赵	Zhào	Zhao (surname)
照片	zhàopiàn	photograph
照相	zhào xiàng	to take a photo
找	zhǎo	to search for
这	zhè, zhèi	this
这儿	zhèr	here
真	zhēn	really
真丝	zhēnsī	silk
珍珠	zhēnzhū	pearl
珍珠奶茶	zhēnzhū nǎichá	bubble milk tea
正在	zhèngzài	in the middle of
只	zhī	measure word for birds and certain animals, one of a pair
知道	zhīdào	to know
只	zhǐ	only
纸	zhǐ	paper
钟	zhōng	clock; o'clock
中国	Zhōngguó	China
中华民国	Zhōnghuá Mínguó	Republic of China
中秋节	Zhōngqiūjié	the Mid-Autumn Festival
中文	Zhōngwén	Chinese
中午	zhōngwǔ	noon
中心	zhōngxīn	center
中学	zhōngxué	secondary school
中央	zhōngyāng	central
周末	zhōumò	weekend
珠江	Zhūjiāng	Pearl River
猪八戒	Zhū Bājiè	Zhu Bajie, character in Journey to the West
猪肉	zhūròu	pork
住	zhù	to live
祝	zhù	to wish (good wishes)
追求	zhuīqiú	to pursue
桌子	zhuōzi	table
自己	zìjǐ	oneself
自行车	zìxíngchē	bicycle
棕色	zōngsè	brown
总是	zǒngshì	always
走	zǒu	to walk; to leave
走路	zǒulù	to walk